POWER
AND PROGRESS

POWER
AND PROGRESS

ESSAYS ON SOCIOLOGICAL THEORY

Robert Bierstedt

McGRAW-HILL BOOK COMPANY
New York . St. Louis . San Francisco .
Düsseldorf . London . Sydney . Toronto .
Mexico . Panama . Johannesburg . Kuala
Lumpur . Montreal . New Delhi . São Paulo .
Singapore

First McGraw-Hill Paperback Edition, 1975

Library of Congress Cataloging in Publication Data

Bierstedt, Robert, 1913–
    Power and progress.

    Bibliography: p.
    CONTENTS: On sociologists: The logico-
meaningful method of P. A. Sorokin (1937) The
means-end schema in sociological theory (1938) The
operationalism of George A. Lundberg (1946) [etc.]
    1. Sociology—Addresses, essays, lectures.
I. Title.
HM24.B44   301'.01   74–12192
ISBN 0-07-005231-X

1 2 3 4 5 6 7 8 9   BP BP   7 9 8 7 6 5

This book was set in Caledonia by Cherry Hill Composition and printed and bound by Book Press. The designer
was Ellen Seham. The editors were Nancy Tressel, Laura
Givner, and Phyllis McCord. Milton Heiberg supervised
the production.

Contents

Preface

When my publishers invited me to send them a selection of
my essays, they suggested that interest in them would be
enhanced if I would describe the circumstances under which I
had undertaken to write them. This would require rather more
autobiographic matter than I should normally like to include. I
nevertheless succumbed to the suggestion and present in this
book, in spare detail, introductions to the separate sections, in
which I offer some account of the intellectual and personal situations that stimulated me to write as I did. I can only hope that
I have avoided the egocentricity of Herbert Spencer who, in his
autobiography, seized the opportunity to write favorable reviews
of his own books.

Because of these introductions this preface can be brief. The
essays collected here have to do with people and issues that have

concerned me over what is now a considerable span of time. I have been fortunately placed in that I have known personally—at Columbia, Harvard, The London School of Economics, and elsewhere—all the major figures in contemporary sociology. For all of them, in spite of differences that led to disputation, I have the highest regard.

The title of the book has given me trouble. "Power and Progress" is the best that I can do. It is not accurate. Although there is an essay on power, and one on progress, there is none on power and progress, and to this extent the label is misleading. It is misleading especially because I believe in the reality of power and reject the illusion of progress. Most authors of collected works try to find a theme that binds the works together. Most of them fail. For myself, there is no central thesis, and I plead guilty therefore to the fault of idiosyncrasy.

I am reprinting the essays for the most part in the form in which they originally appeared. In some instances I have exercised an editorial privilege and have removed infelicities of expression. I have similarly corrected errors of tense and case and have eliminated typographical and grammatical mistakes. It is a game, however, that one can never win. The elves who supervise punctuation and who decide whether "that" or "which" is the proper word are always asleep when their services are most needed.

I should, I suppose, say something here about sociology itself. I shall not do so on the ground that the essays can speak for themselves. I shall say only that society is a fit and dignified subject of inquiry and that it belongs, along with others of the liberal arts, to the realm of humane letters.

Robert Bierstedt

POWER
AND PROGRESS

PART 1

ON SOCIOLOGISTS

This first section contains essays on some sociologists I have known—all of them except Toynbee and, of course, the Social Darwinists, in person. Among them Sorokin was by far the most dramatic. I had read his *Contemporary Sociological Theories* as a Midwestern high school student and was both stimulated by his style and staggered by his erudition. It was my introduction to a discipline called sociology. In the fall semester of 1936, some years later, I met the author of this "meaningful" book when, after two years of graduate study in philosophy at Columbia, I was privileged to go to Harvard. At that time there were fewer than two dozen graduate students in residence, most of whom were later to become prominent in the profession. The faculty consisted of one professor, Sorokin; one visiting professor, W. I. Thomas; two associate professors, Carle C. Zimmerman and

James Ford; one assistant professor, Talcott Parsons; one instructor, E. P. Hutchinson; and an assortment of first-rate tutors including Robert K. Merton, who was also Sorokin's section man.

As a lecturer, Sorokin had no histrionic peer. A man of astonishing physical vigor, he would mount huge attacks against the blackboard, often breaking his chalk in the process. One of his classrooms had blackboards on three sides. At the end of the hour all three were normally covered with his hieroglyphics, and clouds of chalk dust hovered in the air. If he was dramatic he was also, often, melodramatic. For no American sociologist did he have a word of praise—always, in fact, the contrary. For that matter, the only sociologists who escaped his strictures, indeed his contempt, were Petrajitsky, his old teacher, and J. L. Moreno, in whom he found "one little spark." His response to George A. Lundberg was typical. He arrived in class one morning, waved one of Lundberg's recently published papers before us, and declaimed in words I remember exactly, "Here is a paper by my friend Lundberg on a subject about which, unfortunately, he knows nothing! It is a disease with him! He was not born for this kind of work!" On another occasion, after I happened to mention with approval the name of John Dewey, he summoned me to his office and said, "John Dewey, John Dewey, John Dewey! I read [present tense] a book by John Dewey. I read another book by John Dewey. I read a third book by John Dewey. Nothing in them!" As an incidental note, Sorokin's English was always a broken English, even after he had lived in this country for more than three decades. In public lectures he would either apologize, with an engaging grin, for his "Harvard accent" or confess that he had forgotten his Russian and had never learned English.

Sorokin's attitude toward the work of his students was similarly one of an almost ritual hostility. After tea in the afternoon—a pleasant custom—the seminar would convene, with Sorokin in the chair. During the first hour one of the students would present a paper. During the second hour Sorokin, in full panoply, would tear it apart, paragraph by paragraph—almost, as it then seemed, syllable by syllable—until at the end of the period, vituperation unexhausted, he would conclude, "And so you see, gentlemen, this paper, it is worth nothing!" We were hardy souls in those days, and most of us wore our scar tissue with pride.

I decided nevertheless, with the impudence of youth, that I would turn his tactics against him—indeed try to emulate them— and accordingly wrote, as a term paper for one of his lecture courses, the paper with which this book begins: "The Logico-Meaningful Method of P. A. Sorokin." He was not amused. Indeed, as I should have predicted, he subjected me to an excoriation most colorful. W. I. Thomas, who took a benevolent interest in the fracas, suggested that I send the paper to the *American Sociological Review* where, to my surprise, it was accepted for publication. I reprint Sorokin's "Rejoinder" here, also. I still enjoy the merry quip at the end where, in a footnote, he put me in my place.

Were I to write the article today, I would give it an entirely different tone. I continue to agree, however, with its substance. Sorokin failed to notice that he had applied his compound adjective "logico-meaningful" both to a method and to a kind of cultural integration and that he was begging the question when he used the former to find the latter. In any event, he was never able to instruct anyone else in the use of this method, and it has since disappeared from the sociological scene.

Talcott Parsons, in a gesture more generous than he knew, offered his help in arranging a tutorship for me for the following year, but prudence dictated that I return to Columbia, where I later took my degree with MacIver and where, in any case, I found the environment more congenial. As a postscript I should say that Sorokin bore no permanent grudge and that in succeeding years our relationship was a cordial one. During the year of his presidency of the American Sociological Association I was able to help him with his administrative chores, and during the final years and months of his life our correspondence was wrapped in a warm and genuine sentiment. I have often said, and will say again, that whatever one might think of his answers, Sorokin always asked the right questions. He knew what sociology is.

My relationship with Parsons was a different one, but one that came to a similarly critical conclusion with the publication of my paper "The Means-End Schema in Sociological Theory." During the Harvard year I attended all of Parsons' lecture courses, and during the second semester we had weekly tutorial sessions. He was busily engaged in seeing *The Structure of Social Action* through the press and was bursting with his "empirical" demonstration of the convergence of the theories of Pareto, Durkheim, and Weber in a voluntaristic theory of action. It was an enterprise that I was wholly unable to comprehend. My lack of understanding was due to obstinacy on my part, not to dogmatism on his. It was due to my refusal to learn his language, his universe of discourse, and our failure to communicate was appallingly complete.

In any event, having returned to Columbia with a fellowship in sociology and a small teaching appointment in philosophy, I read every word of *The Structure of Social Action* when it appeared and sent an unsolicited review of it to the *Saturday Review of Literature.* The editor was glad to have it and published it almost immediately. I praised the book as the most learned contribution to social science I had seen in a decade and complimented the author on his superior exposition of the theories of Durkheim and Weber. On the other hand, I complained about Parsons' abuse of the English language; questioned the thrust of his interpretation of Pareto (who, after all, wanted to build a new sociology on the model of celestial mechanics); suggested that the "convergence" he discerned in Pareto, Durkheim, and Weber was an artifact of his own anfractuous dialectic; and affirmed that the book contained a map, however carefully drawn, of the road that sociology could not take if it was to be an objective science.

Parsons' response was prompt. In a bitter letter he accused me of atrocious errors, of unconscionable misrepresentation both of his ideas and those of Pareto, of failure to indicate the many ways in which he appreciated the role of nonrational actions, and of general incompetence to comment upon "difficult theoretical works." None of this could be excused by the fact that I was writing for a lay readership. I had informed him that I was preparing a paper for the spring meeting of the Eastern Sociological Society, and he concluded with the hope that in a paper addressed to professional colleagues I would be able to do better than I had "in this deplorable instance."

That paper, "The Means-End Schema in Sociological Theory," is the second paper reprinted here. It gives me some discomfort now because, again, its tone is more strident than I should like. It is an orthodox positivistic response to Parsons' theory, an assertion of the necessity of dispensing with subjective concepts in sociological inquiry, and a defense of determinism against voluntarism. At the time it was written I had fallen under the influence of George A. Lundberg, then a visitor in the Columbia department, and had read with increasing excitement all his polemical papers. There was no further response from Parsons. Unlike Sorokin and Lundberg, he had no zeal for intellectual combat. I should add that, as in the case of Sorokin, our future relations were friendly ones and that I came to have a high regard for his skill as a system builder, though not for the system itself.

Years later I began to understand why, at Harvard, there was so conspicuous an absence of resonance between us. The first reason was my own callow arrogance. A second reason, however, has some significance for the sociology of knowledge: Our discourse lacked a common grammar, and we had no one to serve as interpreter. Parsons had been trained in economics and knew that *Homo economicus* was confronted with the constant need to choose between two or more alternative courses of action—to buy or to sell, to spend or to save, and so on through an infinity of decisions. Here was a mind at work making choices that were as rational as possible. Of course, Parsons was aware, as Pareto was, of the nonrational factors that enter into even the sparest of economic decisions. But it was Parsons' hope that his means-end schema could take account of factors of both kinds and thus construct for sociology a system that would at once emulate the elegance and transcend the limitations of classical economics.

My own training at the time, in contrast to Parsons', belonged to epistemology and psychology, and I knew no economics at all. With F. J. E. Woodbridge—a truly great teacher—as my mentor at Columbia, I had studied the philosophers of the British empirical tradition—Bacon, Hobbes, Locke, Berkeley, Hartley, Hume, and Mill—but especially Locke whose *Essay concerning Human Understanding* we analyzed sentence by sentence in seminar. Belligerence, though not hostility, informed Woodbridge's pedagogical method; he would demand to know why Locke used this word rather than that one in a particular passage and would castigate us as stupid if we could not think of an answer. In Locke, of course, the mind at birth was a *tabula rasa*, a blank sheet of paper on which sensations imprinted their messages. We would have to contend, of course, with Immanuel Kant's answer to Hume, his transcendental deduction of the categories, but, Kant notwithstanding, in the empirical tradition the mind was a receiver of sensations, not a maker of decisions. This was part of the platen of thought that I brought to my discussions with Parsons.

This epistemological stance was fortified by William James, to whom we paid close attention also in another of Woodbridge's seminars. If the year 1890 meant for Parsons the publication of Alfred Marshall's *Principles of Economics*, the culmination of a classical tradition in economic thought, it marked for me the publication of James' *Principles of Psychology*, the herald of a new era in the history of mental philosophy. It was James, it seemed to me, who presided over the demise of a "faculty psychology"—a psychology in which the mind is an active entity possessed of three faculties: the intellect, the emotions, and the will—and who (in the more recent language of Thomas Kuhn) created a new set of paradigms which transformed the philosophy of mind into a science of behavior. For Parsons thus to entertain an antiquated conception of mind, as he so definitely did in *The Structure of Social Action*, was a retrogressive step and one that could only retard the development of sociology. For Parsons to embrace a faculty psychology rather than a scientific psychology in the fourth decade of the twentieth century seemed to me to be an exercise of an impermissible—almost medieval—privilege. Indeed, I came to the conclusion that Parsons' means-end schema did not belong to sociology at all but was instead a supererogatory social psychology.

I write at this length in order to suggest that my failure to learn from Parsons, although attributable to a personal fault, was also due in part at least to an incompatibility in universes of discourse. I take some comfort from the belief (if for no other reason than the paucity of American names in the Parsonian pantheon) that my language was the more orthodox one in the American sociology of the day. The issue itself—voluntarism versus behaviorism—has ceased to trouble me, as it has apparently ceased to trouble Parsons. My interests turned later to the structural components of the social order, to which individual behavior (or "action") was, in a genuinely Durkheimean sense, irrelevant. And the means-end schema also gradually faded from Parsons' concerns as he wrote his succeeding volumes.

My doctoral dissertation at Columbia, delayed by World War II, was devoted to the theory of operationalism, a theory of definition recommended by many as a panacea for the solution of the conceptual confusions with which sociology was afflicted. As proposed by the Harvard physicist Percy W. Bridgman, the theory generated a vast literature in the psychological, sociological, and philosophical journals—all of it controversial. In sociology, George A. Lundberg embraced it with enthusiasm and preached mighty sermons in its favor. Robert M. MacIver, a man for whose philosophical sophistication I had come to have increasing respect, greeted it first with scepticism and then with outright rejection. Thus, caught in the crossfire between Lundberg and MacIver (see especially their passage at arms in *Sociologus*, Volume 9, September 1933), it seemed appropriate to subject the doctrine to a close and critical examination of my own.

My suspicions were first aroused by Lundberg himself. He had given me the manuscript of the first two chapters of his *Foundations of Sociology* and asked me for my opinion. Needless to say, I was prepared to praise them. Here I expected to find a clear and forthright exposition of the methodological principles on which a positivistic sociology could be based. It was refreshing, in fact, to find so curt a dismissal of the Neo-Kantian distinction between *verstehen* and *erklären*. It was refreshing too to see a man try to give substance to the dream of Comte; to insist that all science, whether social or physical, was a single enterprise; and to maintain that sociology too could dispense with metaphysical questions of the kind that appealed only to "children, philosophers, and other semantically deranged persons." Lundberg was no mean polemicist, and here he was in full flower.

And yet, and yet, doubts began to gather and then to grow. Some of Lundberg's propositions contradicted the lessons taught by Cohen and Nagel in their *Introduction to Logic and Scientific Method,* which I used as a textbook in my own courses in logic. Lundberg's epistemology seemed simplistic, his methodology naive, and both gave too many hostages to his critics. On the logic of measurement he turned aside even the remonstrances of John Dewey, a man for whom he had an infinite admiration, in an exchange of letters that he shared with me. I began to suspect that Lundberg's radical empiricism, like that of Bridgman, had solipsistic consequences and would, if taken seriously, destroy the objectivity of sociological knowledge.

It became clear to me, in short, that Lundberg's operationalism erased the distinctions between nominal and real definitions on the one hand and between cardinal and ordinal measurement on the other, and that the erasures were in fact required by the theory. In my dissertation, therefore, I discussed the problem of language in sociology, the logic of concepts, the logic of definitions, the operationalism of Bridgman, the operationalism of Lundberg, the logic of measurement, and the operational "calculus" of Stuart Carter Dodd, and concluded with a chapter which summarized the reasons for rejecting the theory. After Lundberg read the dissertation, we had a battle royal on a rainy afternoon in Seattle, and he registered vehement objection to all of it. He was a veteran of many battles of this kind, however, with such antagonists as Sorokin, MacIver, Znaniecki, Blumer, Furfey, and entire armies of sociologists whom he considered traducers of the scientific method. He enjoyed the heat of controversy and, as he once wrote to Howard Odum, he regarded polemics as the "legitimate amusement" of an academic career. In any case, his friendship never faltered.

I did not seek to publish the dissertation in book form, and such an effort would doubtless have been unsuccessful. Later on, in response to an invitation from Llewellyn Gross, I revised the chapter on the logic of definitions for publication in his *Symposium on Sociological Theory*, a piece that appears in another section of this collection. Here I print for the first time two of the chapters of the dissertation, extensively revised and combined, under the title "The Operationalism of George A. Lundberg." If he were still with us he would surely re-enter the fray, to our mutual delectation.

The essay entitled "Toynbee and Sociology" requires little description or explanation. Although I can claim a footnote objecting to a paper of mine in one of his many volumes, I have not had the privilege of meeting him. I rank him, however, along with Spengler and Sorokin, as a man who has made a brilliant assault on the ark of history, the ark where Clio so closely guards her secrets. It occurred to me that in *A Study of History* Toynbee was not writing history but asking instead questions of a Comtean kind. His enterprise, in short, was sociological in a rather pure sense and not historical at all. For this reason I was startled to come across the paragraph in Volume IX, quoted at the beginning of the article, in which he denigrates not only sociology but logic, psychology, anthropology, and political science as well. Perhaps it would be profitable to examine at close range the relationships between sociology and history, and this is what I tried to do. I would only caution the reader that my contrasts are exaggerated and that they apply to logical distinctions between two different directions of inquiry, not to the actual practices of those who call themselves historians or sociologists.

The brief piece of Alfred Schutz—merely an essay-review—is another that requires little comment. I include it here because I raise in it a question that applies not only to a phenomenological approach but to "ethnomethodological" and symbolic interactionist approaches as well. It seems to me that if society is sought in the realm of the subjective, or of the intersubjective, or even of the symbolic, we shall be unable to find it, unable to discern its structure, unable to treat it, as Durkheim did, as a reality *sui generis*. "The paramount reality of commonsense life," as Schutz's editor expresses it, is one thing; the paramount reality of society quite another. The point is made in the essay but it requires, of course, an extended discussion.

The paper that concludes this section, "The Social Darwinists," is the other previously unpublished paper in this collection. It was not intended to be unpublished. Indeed, I wrote it at the invitation of a friend, a philosopher, for a volume of essays he was to edit. When I sent the manuscript to him, however, a long and unsatisfactory correspondence ensued, and finally I received, not from him but from his publisher, an elegant rejection slip. I say "elegant" because it was written with grace and care. Several of the essays originally scheduled for inclusion, although of impeccable scholarship, had unfortunately to be returned to their authors because they did not quite fit the scheme the editor had in mind. Mine was among them.

It may genuinely be the case that the article is deficient in quality. It may be that my reading of Social Darwinism is a mistaken one and that my interpretation has gone awry. It is self-serving to say so, but I entertain the suspicion that a different reason may possibly be involved. When the editor received the manuscript he responded with something akin to dismay. In the conventional interpretation, Social Darwinism had been "invented" by Herbert Spencer, and it was a doctrine with which Darwin himself had nothing to do. Although he had used such concepts as "the survival of the fittest" and "the struggle for existence"—as chapter titles no less—he was innocent of the implications that others, including sociologists, were to draw from them. To the editor, though not to me, my article seemed to suggest the contrary. The margins of the manuscript contain such queries and challenges as "Did Darwin ever agree to this?"; "Not true of Darwin"; and "Reference?" I was easily able to supply the references, and for the rest the article nowhere indicts Darwin for views he did not hold. But I could not entirely relieve him of notions associated with Social Darwinism, especially as expressed in *The Descent of Man,* and the article indicates what these notions were.

The roster of names in the history of ideas contains both heroes and villains. The diligent Darwin clearly belongs to the former category, stubborn Spencer to the latter. It is right that we praise Darwin for his accomplishments; we are no longer supposed to praise Spencer for his. But the views of the two men are too closely interlinked to make a total separation possible. Darwin too was to some degree a Social Darwinist. This view of the matter may, as my editor thought, be unfair to him. But I do not repent. I am content to leave the verdict to the reader.

I

The Logico-Meaningful
Method of P. A. Sorokin

[1937]

One cannot without trepidation undertake to comment upon the
new social philosophy which has emerged from the ruins of a
noisily disintegrating and over-ripe sensate culture. The sheer
magnitude of *Social and Cultural Dynamics,* together with the
prodigious research Professor Sorokin displays in analyzing all
the compartments of culture over a period of twenty-five centuries
without overlooking any part of our contemporary civilization,
demands that a critic proceed warily. It is unfortunate in one
respect that these pontifical tomes cannot be considered in their
entirety, for such a possibility would relieve the impression that
a few weak points have been singled out for attack. Since, however, the category of space presses so urgently upon the denizens
of sensate cultures, these remarks must be limited to a matter of
more strictly sociological interest, namely, the "logico-meaningful

method" which the author presents in his introductory chapter. Although a number of fallacies and inconsistencies require the employment of the forensic shillalah in opposition to this so-called method and the approach it represents, it is important to emphasize that subsequent statements are intended in no way to impugn or to evaluate Professor Sorokin's *magnum opus* either as a philosophy of history or as a social philosophy in general. The purview of this paper is stringently confined to an examination of the author's contribution to the methodology of sociology.

After a cursory discussion and definition of "culture" Professor Sorokin classifies the interrelations of the elements and traits of culture into four basic types, (1) spatial or mechanical adjacency, (2) association due to an external factor, (3) functional or causal integration, and (4) internal or logico-meaningful unity. Spatial or mechanical adjacency represents the lowest and loosest form of culture integration. Traits, attributes, customs, mores, institutions, rites, ceremonies, and artifacts related only spatially can hardly, in fact, be considered as integrated at all. Rather they may be regarded as a simple congeries of cultural elements "in a given area of social and physical space, with spatial or mechanical concurrence as the only bond of union."[1] The second type, "indirect unification through a common external factor" stands a step higher on the continuum of integration, but remains only a very low and loose form of association. The third type of relationship, the causal or functional, implies a combination of cultural elements held together by bonds inherent in their nature and becomes, accordingly, a relatively high form of integration. The relationship is a tangible one, and the parts cling together in such a way that none of them can vary independently without damaging the unity of the system as a whole. In Sorokin's own words, "Any cultural synthesis is to be regarded as functional when, on the one hand, the elimination of one of its important

---

[1] *Social and Cultural Dynamics*, American Book Company, 1937, vol. I, *Fluctuation of Forms of Art*, p. 10. All subsequent references are to this volume unless otherwise noted.

elements perceptibly influences the rest of the synthesis in its functions (and usually in its structure); and when, on the other hand, the separate element, being transposed to a quite different combination, either cannot exist in it or has to undergo a profound modification to become a part of it. Such is the symptomatic barometer of internal integration."[2] The more or less subtle differences between these first three forms of integration, the nature of the continuum which they represent, and the merits or demerits of the classification in general may be disregarded in favor of the greater significance of the fourth type of association.

Logico-meaningful integration is the supreme form of association of the elements of culture; beside it all other forms, including the causal-functional, merely adumbrate an integration. It is the type of integration exemplified by the lines of a great poem, the pages of the *Critique of Pure Reason,* the fragments of a statue, or the measures of a symphony. "If we know the proper patterns of meaning and value," says Sorokin "we can put these pages or parts together into a significant unity in which each page or fragment takes its proper place, acquires a meaning, and in which all together give the supremely integrated effect that was intended."[3] All the parts of these cultural manifestations are woven into a "seamless garment" whose unification is "far closer than that of mere functional association."[4] The minor premise and conclusion of a syllogism follow logico-meaningfully from the major premise—not causally or functionally. "To say that the chapters of Kant's *Critique,* or the head and the torso of the Venus of Milo, or the beginning and the end of the first movement of Beethoven's *Third Symphony,* or the foundation, flying buttresses, towers and sculptures of the Cathedral of Chartres, or the first and the second parts of the *Iliad*—to say that the connection between these is functional or causal is to say something almost

---

[2] P. 15.
[3] P. 19.
[4] *Ibid.*

absurd and, at the same time, to omit the higher nature of their unity."[5]

With these statements, however, Sorokin merely succeeds in bowling over a number of straw men. No one has ever asserted that the transcendental aesthetic of Kant's *Critique* causes the transcendental dialectic; that the head of the Venus of Milo causes the torso; that the beginning of a Beethoven symphony causes the end; or that the foundations of the Cathedral of Chartres cause the flying buttresses. It would be just as "absurd" —to use Sorokin's word—to say that a part of anything causes another part, or that the parts cause a whole. Rather, the parts *comprise* a whole, a sort of relationship wholly distinct from the category of causation, and also from the sensate-ideational categories of the logico-meaningful method. Sorokin's assertions at this point are unquestionably valid, and therefore unnecessary, for no one has yet denied them. When he believes that the logico-meaningful method excels the causal-functional on these grounds, however, he misrepresents the function and use of the latter.

When Sorokin begins his investigation of any congeries of culture traits he expects first of all to apply the canons of inductive and deductive logic to them to determine whether or not, and to what extent, they are logically related. Then, sprinkling in a bit of "meaning" he hopes to discover the presence or absence of integration. Since he admits the cumbersomeness of the concept "logico-meaningful" its use could easily be condoned if it did not, at the same time, exhibit a serious misconception regarding the nature of logic. There is no logical relationship between objects or phenomena; logic, as the formal science of the structure of thought, applies to the words we use to describe them. Not cultures, but only what we say about them can be *logically* integrated. Nor are culture traits logically related. Logic is an instrument of discourse and applies not to things in themselves but to what is said about them. Logical judgments find their

---

[5] *Ibid.*

proper locus in propositions; not in events or objects. The separate pages and parts of Sorokin's symphonies and sonnets and statues are no more logically related than they are causally related. To discuss logically-related culture traits or phenomena is to mix universes of discourse in the first instance, and in the second is to apply logic to a sphere where it has no place. Objects and traits either exist or they do not exist; they are not true or false or logically integrated. Only propositions and judgments are susceptible of truth claims, falsity claims, and logically related claims.

Although Sorokin states that what "must be used are the *logical* laws of identity, contradiction, and consistency,"[6] he fails to illustrate how they can be applied to culture traits. Possibly the illustration was omitted because it is difficult to furnish one. On the other hand, the fallacy can be illustrated. Consider any two traits or objects from an integrated culture such as, for example, the armor and the lance of a medieval knight.[7] Are the armor and the lance identical? Are they contradictory? Are they consistent? Consistent with what? Again, is a table fork more logically related to and therefore more consistent with a spoon than a pitchfork? Objects can not be identical, contradictory or consistent in themselves; only the statements we make about them in relating them to another principle or proposition can be consistent. It may be remarked in passing that consistency, although a desideratum of logical discourse, is not a law of logic in the sense that the principles of identity, contradiction, and excluded middle are laws. Thus, although Sorokin invokes logic to lend cogency to his method, it is impossible to concede that the "logico-meaningful method" has anything to do with logic. In addition, the selection of the word "meaningful" can only be regretted. The philosopher who first gives us an adequate explanation of meaning will not

---

[6] P. 20; also pp. 63–4.

[7] When two such disparate traits as the Discobolus of Myron and the Greek city state are considered—to take one of an infinity of examples—the inapplicability of logical laws is too patent to require mention.

have to construct an epistemological architectonic to gain a grade of twelve from Sorokin.[8]

The following statements demonstrate that the logico-meaningful method is more closely akin to mysticism than to logic: "Many . . . superlative unities cannot be described in analytical verbal terms; they are just *felt* as such";[9] "Some associations are *sensed* as the supreme unities";[10] "Some chains of reasoning are '*felt*' as logical";[11] and, "Not being completely describable in terms of language," the supreme unity of the creations of Bach, Mozart, Beethoven, Shakespeare, Phidias, Dürer, Raphael, or Rembrandt "is *felt* by competent persons as certainly as if they could be analyzed with mathematical or logical exactness."[12] Such expressions not only repudiate logic but recall the mystics of "ideational" cultures upon whom were bestowed gifts for explaining to their less fortunate contemporaries the mysteries of human life and destiny, the knowledge of which they had themselves secured through divine afflatus or, possibly, through logico-meaningful methods. That uninhibited "feeling" produces profound aesthetic pleasures need not be denied even by a "sensate" mentality. How an incursion into aesthetics or anagoge can help to integrate the highly complex traits of both literate and non-literate cultures, however, escapes the comprehension of a "sensate" critic. Furthermore, if a "felt" unity implies one that is self-evident, the caution of Bertrand Russell may be observed: "If self-evidence is alleged as a ground of belief, that implies that doubt has crept in, and that our self-evident proposition has not always resisted the assaults of scepticism "[13] Sorokin has, of course, wholly succumbed

---

[8] For Sorokin's "grades" see "Appendices" to vol. II, *Fluctuation of Systems of Truth, Ethics and Law*. He has ranked every philosopher from 600 B.C. to 1930 A.D. on a scale of 1–12 according to eminence and influence.

[9] P. 20. Italics mine in these phrases.

[10] P. 20, note. But not in "sensate" cultures!

[11] *Ibid.*

[12] Pp. 20–21.

[13] *The Analysis of Mind*, London, 1922, p. 263.

to phenomenological dialectics and has slipped innocently over the distinction between methods and objectives. As George A. Lundberg says, "The error lies in overlooking that insight and understanding are the ends at which all methods aim, rather than methods in themselves."[14]

What does Sorokin expect from his logico-meaningful analysis of the traits of a particular culture? He says:

> If we discover that this culture does contain the appropriate body of traits and variables, by one stroke we obtain several important cognitive results: (1) a highly intimate and certain understanding of many of the important aspects of the culture; (2) an insight into the nature and workings of most of its significant components; (3) a knowledge of the spectrum of its dominant mentality; (4) a comprehensive grasp of the very complex network of relationships between many of its traits which otherwise would escape us; and (5) an answer to the question as to whether or not, and to what extent and in what parts, the culture is indeed logically integrated.[15]

Because of the normative word "appropriate" which has been used here it becomes evident that the conclusions which Sorokin expects are tautological. To say that if we find that a culture contains the appropriate body of traits and variables we know that it is logically integrated is equivalent to saying that if we find that a culture is logically integrated we know that it is logically integrated. These "expectations" suggest further that the investigator is to be allowed to choose such traits from a heterogeneous collection which will "appropriately" fit a preconceived idea of a dominant mentality—a procedure entirely inadmissible. On the whole, these "results" of the logico-meaningful method leave the impression that Sorokin either is attempting to put the proverbial

---

[14] "Quantitative Methods in Social Psychology," *Amer. Sociol. Rev.*, 1, February 1936, 41. See the article in its entirety for a trenchant and irrefragable assault upon the "insights" of the sociological metaphysicians.
[15] P. 34–5.

cart before the equally proverbial horse, or that he supports a method which can end only in tautologies. These remarks pertain to his negative statement of the same idea, namely, that we can know a number of facts about a culture in case the expected variables and traits are not found.[16] "Expected" refers to those traits which will fit into a logically integrated unity. The assertion, therefore, that if the expected traits do not appear the culture is not logically integrated, is a mere restatement of everything comprehended by the word "expected."

Sorokin treats his readers to more mysticism when he answers his own methodological questions;[17] for instance, "How can a unifying principle be discovered?" This question, probably the most integral of the group, is surprisingly branded as "almost superfluous." "The principle may be suggested," he says, "by observation, statistical study, meditation, logical analysis, even by dreaming and by what is called mere 'chance,' or 'intuition.' " With observation and statistical analysis we unequivocally agree. Logical analysis, too, may be admitted if care be exercised to escape the misconceptions Sorokin harbors with regard to logic. A principle suggested by meditation, dreaming, chance, or intuition, however, would be worth nothing unless qualified, tested, and approved by objective scientific techniques—the very "sensate" methods that Sorokin pretends to scorn. Previous to such qualification the principle can be only the most tenuous hypothesis. Sorokin is unlikely to deny this, for doing so would leave him in the unusual position of advocating a dream sociology, with specters of key principles floating around in a bewitchingly logico-meaningful night air.

The point to be emphasized is that in spite of quarts of vitriol poured on scientific methods,[18] they must be utilized in every instance of logico-meaningul integration to save the key principle from being a stale and empty hypothesis. The guarantee that it is

---

[17] Pp. 35–6.
[16] P. 35.
[18] See especially vol. II, pp. 11 *et seq.*

an adequate principle must come from an impartial test by different observers, it is true, but an impartial test would exclude meditation, chance, dreams, and intuition. Sorokin comes very close to the contemned "sensate" traits in his answer to a question to which he ascribes importance: "How can it be ascertained that a given principle of logical integration is valid?"[19] "The answer is that the criteria of validity are virtually the same as for any scientific law"; the principle must "by nature be logical" and it must furthermore stand successfully the test of relevant facts. If a principle must successfully stand this test it may be pointed out merely that some method will have to be used for testing, and that the criteria of impartiality and objectivity will peremptorily remove the logico-meaningful "method" from consideration.

Professor Sorokin frequently utilizes the creations and systems of the great musicians, philosophers, poets, and painters as examples of logico-meaningful unities so supreme and sublime that they elude mathematical and logical analysis and, accordingly, causal-functional modes of integration. The following phrase is typical: "the specific logico-meaningful systems created by . . . such men as Phidias, Praxiteles, Aeschylus, Pindar, Sophocles, Polygnotus, Socrates, and later Plato."[20] In the first place, it is impossible to agree that the sculptures of Phidias and Praxiteles, the odes of Pindar, the paintings of Polygnotus, the plays of Aeschylus and Sophocles, and the dialogues of Plato (there is no extant work of Socrates) constitute logico-meaningful unities. Plato, for instance, gives students of the dialogues much trouble precisely because he did not create a "system." It would be enlightening if Professor Sorokin would explain—logico-meaningfully—the completely unrelated myth in the *Protagoras*. Sorokin himself falters with regard to the logico-meaningful unity of systems when he lists Kant, Fechner, Planck, Einstein, Duhem, Tschuprov, Brunschvicg, Heisenberg, and Bridgman both as de-

---

[19] P. 36.
[20] P. 29.

terminists and indeterminists.[21] We may venture the additional remark that a sociological theorist of many ages hence will experience difficulty in "feeling" or "intuiting" the logico-meaningful unity of *Contemporary Sociological Theories* and *Social and Cultural Dynamics* though they appeared in the same culture and are the work of one man. Even if the logico-meaningful unity of particular systems could be conceded, however, it is irrelevant. In order to proceed with sociological analysis we need to know whether the creations of all of the men at a particular time, taken together, provide a key principle for the culture to which they belong. The integration of a manifold of traits into a culture constitutes this different and more perplexing problem—a problem to the solution of which the constant reiteration of the logico-meaningful unity of single systems contributes nothing.

It is interesting to note Professor Sorokin's comparison of the logico-meaningful and the causal-functional methods. In a number of places he asserts that both are necessary for a study of socio-cultural phenomena, but the approbation which shines upon the former and the opprobrium which rains upon the latter serve to expose his methodological predilections. The major difference is that functional or causal integration is external and inferential and applies to the "inorganic, organic, and superorganic worlds."[22] Logico-meaningful integration, on the other hand, is intimate and internal, and finds its proper locus only where there is mind and meaning. When Sorokin draws this distinction he misses a point which not even antithetical doctrines of epistemology would deny; namely, that all knowledge is inferential. The problem lies in what has been called an "internalization of the external" and that is what happens in any knowing process, regardless of method and irrespective of the fact that the Kantian question,

---

[21] Volume II, "Appendix" to Chapter IX, pp. 699–700 and 703. Since there is no third category Sorokin ruptures the law of contradiction, one of the logical canons upon which he depends to escape the relativism of *Wissenssoziologie*. See especially vol. I, p. 64; vol. II, p. 208, note, and p. 312, note.
[22] P. 28.

"How can we know?", has not yet adequately been answered. Unless Sorokin is a subjective idealist and assumes that the ontology of all culture traits and cultures is of the nature of mind, it is quite apparent that even logico-meaningful integration must be external to the mind which knows it. That is, the integration must be *of* phenomena or else we are dealing with a highly subjective relationship which is integrated or not depending upon the pleasure of the person who perceives it. This, of course, is what the logico-meaningful method amounts to; it is of the essence of subjectivity. We learn also that "All the causal-functional connections in the field of the natural sciences . . . are free from additional logical bonds."[23] The mere fact that no relationship in the natural sciences exhibits the supremely integrated unity of "logic" and "meaning" throws us on guard with respect to the logico-meaningful integration of cultural relationships.

Most interesting of all, however, are the following statements:

> If variables A and B are not met with regularly, nor coexist, nor follow each other in immediate sequence, nor vary uniformly, such variables cannot be declared to be connected causally. . . . Considerably different is the situation in regard to logico-meaningful connection. Theoretically (and not infrequently in fact) this sort of association is comprehensible even when the interrelated fragments are met with at quite different periods, and in quite different places, and only once or a few times.[24]

For illustration Sorokin claims that if someone could demonstrate that the rate of divorce and the use of yellow leather shoes always fluctuate together, "we should have to agree that they were connected functionally, though we would not have the slightest understanding of why it is so";[25] and again, that this situation would represent an "exceptionless causal association."[26] Here of

---

[23] P. 27.
[24] Pp. 26–27.
[25] P. 25.
[26] P. 27.

course he confounds coexistence or covariation with causality. . . . There is no reason why the most strict functionalist would have to agree that the rate of divorce and the use of yellow leather shoes are causally or functionally related if they fluctuate together.[27]

Even more appalling, however, if Sorokin can find an "exceptionless causal association" in the covariation of yellow leather shoes and divorces, what kind of logico-meaningful connections will he perceive when he studies phenomena which are not met with regularly, which do not coexist, which do not follow one another in immediate sequence, which do not vary together uniformly, and which are "met with at quite different periods" and "in quite different places?" If a relationship can be discerned between such variables the culture they attempt to define could not possibly have even the lowest form of association, "spatial adjacency." Apparently the logico-meaningful method is so superior that it can find relationships where none exists. The statements of Sorokin in this connection, rather than demonstrating differences between the causal-functional and the logico-meaningful methods, simply throw a powerful spotlight upon the fallacies of the latter.

Probably the most serious methodological misconception in the entire exposition occurs in the assertion that "the investigation of each type of culture integration requires its own special procedure and brings about its characteristic results."[28] In other words, when the cultural synthesis is causal-functional we use the causal-functional method; when it is logico-meaningful, the logico-meaningful method is prescribed. Here Sorokin assumes that he knows what kind of integration a chance congeries of culture traits will possess before he investigates them. But we cannot know what kind of an integration the culture traits exhibit until

---

[27] Sorokin is merely inconsistent in his zeal to demonstrate the superiority of the logico-meaningful method. See p. 28 and the note to p. 36 where he recognizes the difference between causal and merely incidental association and effectively refutes himself.

[28] Pp. 30 et seq.

we apply a method to them and, once discovered, we no longer need to choose a "special procedure." This error cannot lightly be dismissed. We use a method in order to determine whether a particular group of culture traits are related at all. The relationship discovered may be (following Sorokin) mere spatial adjacency, relationship by an external factor, causal-functional, or logico-meaningful relationship. We do not in advance guess the kind of relationship into which the traits fall and then apply the method bearing the same label as the guess. On the contrary, a method justifies itself only when it enables us to discover both that some culture traits are related and that others are not; that in one case we have an integration and that in the other we do not. Sorokin's argument leads him into these shoals because he pins the word "logico-meaningful" both on a type of integration and on his method.

Admitting for a moment that the logico-meaningful "method" is a method, we discover that it does indeed differ very significantly from the causal-functional, in a way, however, which Sorokin has not recognized. The logico-meaningful method consists in clapping a key principle on a culture caught at a moment of time, primarily at its point of highest integration. The causal-functional method, on the other hand, consists in the application of the category of causality to the problem of social change. Cause is a "function" of time; an effect follows a cause in a chronological sense; the cause-effect relationship can not occur in timelessness. Simply to articulate a key principle of a culture, however, represents a task of description of culture elements as they are integrated at a moment of time. The difference is that between description of status and explanation of change, between social statics and social dynamics. And all the keys, principles of integration, and *Leitmotiven* in the world will not begin to explain how a culture changes.

How then do cultures change according to Sorokin? Apparently we shall have to wait for the fourth volume for a full discussion of the "dynamics" in the title of the work. Certain clues may be detected, however, in the following statements:

Systems change according to the course of life which is prede-
termined for them by their very nature.[29]

The functions, change, and destiny of the system are determined
not only and not so much by the external circumstances (except in
the case of catastrophic accidents), but the nature of the system
itself, and by the relationship between its parts. An aeroplane can
fly, but a cow cannot; a gun can fire, but a spade cannot. Whatever
are the external circumstances, man cannot help passing from childhood to senility and sooner or later dying. Likewise, a cultural system has its own logic of functioning, change, and destiny, which is
a result not only (and regularly not so much) of the external conditions, but of its own nature.[30]

Its life course is set down in its essentials when the system is
born. This is one of the specific aspects of the larger principle which
may be called "immanent self-regulation and self-direction."[31]

Needless to say, this invocation of the Hegelian *"Geist"* and the
Spenglerian "Destiny Idea" sheds no light on the infinitely complex problems of social change. Why does a gun shoot? It is its
nature to. Why does an airplane fly? It is its nature to. Why does
a culture change? It is its nature to. All of which explains exactly
nothing. Rather it recalls a stanza of Isaac Watts:

> Let dogs delight to bark and bite,
>   For God hath made them so;
> Let bears and lions growl and fight,
>   For 'tis their nature too.[32]

In response to these dicta of Sorokin the remark suffices that to
talk about immanent causation, inner logic of change, immanent
self-regulation and self-direction, and other hypostases is merely

---

[29] P. 50.
[30] P. 51.
[31] *Ibid.*
[32] *Divine Songs*, xvi.

to name our ignorance of the factors involved, to postpone the time when we shall finally come to an understanding of these phenomena, and to delude ourselves that we have an answer when we have only a phrase. Taking these doctrines seriously will encourage the observation of sociological problems through a metaphysical mist.

Turning, finally, to the ubiquitous jig-saw puzzle with which Sorokin illustrates the logico-meaningful method, it seems that the separate pieces represent mere spatial adjacency before they are put together and the completed picture manifests a different, a logico-meaningful form of integration. We sit down before the puzzle, decide upon a logico-meaningful unity, and attempt to juxtapose the parts in a way that will correspond to such a unity. To quote Sorokin, "In attempting to solve the puzzle one may make several guesses, each of which is logically irreproachable, as to what the figure is going to be."[33] That, of course, is precisely what we do not do. Instead, with no definite picture in mind we begin to put the pieces together and finally a picture appears. In like manner scientific anthropologists and sociologists articulate the pattern or key principle of a culture from an inductive analysis of its traits. Further, what does Sorokin imply when he characterizes a guess as "logically irreproachable?" A guess is not logically anything; it bears, in its pristine state, no possible relation to logic. However, let us assume for a moment that any guesses we might hazard concerning the jig-saw puzzle and, by Sorokin's own analogy, the key principle of a culture, are logically irreproachable. What crumbs of significance are left over for the "logico-" in logico-meaningful integration? If we cannot reproach a principle on logical grounds it will harry our investigation until some "meaningful" factor arises to eliminate it. If we assume, on the other hand, that a key principle intuited by the logico-meaningful method, though logically irreproachable, may be either correct or incorrect, it follows inevitably that some other method will have to be invoked to decide.

---

[33] P. 37.

And so, we come to the regrettable conclusion that the "logico-meaningful method" is neither logical nor meaningful, nor indeed a method. Taken in any other than a Pickwickian sense it becomes a suspicious mixture of logic, meaning, sensation, science, mysticism, and intuition: "logic" and "meaning" because these words unaccountably found their way into its name; "sensation" because we are asked to sense the supreme unity of culture traits; "science" because of Sorokin's half-hearted though significant attempts to draw scientific analogies; "mysticism" because the supreme unity may be imparted on the swift wings of aesthetic inspiration; and "intuition" because Sorokin himself suggests that the key principle may be intuited, guessed, felt, or dreamed.

The "cultural premises" upon which this critique is based may be questioned by Professor Sorokin with some justification. They are admittedly cribbed, cabined, and confined by "sensate" mentality with all its positivism, "scientism," objectivism, and anti-intellectualism. An appreciation or criticism of the logico-meaningful method on the premises of an "ideational" culture transcends both the boundaries of this paper and the ken of the writer. If it is maintained, however, that in the pure "ideational" culture for which the author of *Social and Cultural Dynamics* yearns there would be no criticism at all,[34] we are content to answer that in such a culture there would also be no sociology.

Rejoinder

Pitirim A. Sorokin, Harvard University

It seems that Mr. Bierstedt's main objection to the logico-meaningful integration of culture and method, as stated in the foregoing pages is the following:

> There is no logical relationship between objects or phenomena; logic, as the formal science of the structure of thought, applies to

---

[34] See chapter on the fluctuation of literature, vol. I, where criticism is characterized as a trait of "sensate" cultures.

the *words* we use to describe them. Not cultures but only *what we say* about them can be logically integrated. Nor are culture traits logically related. . . . Logical judgments find their proper locus in *propositions*; not in events or objects . . . Objects and traits either exist or they do not exist . . . *Only propositions and judgments are susceptible of . . . logically related claims.* (Italics are mine, P. S.)

By his own statement, then, the critic admits the applicability of the category of logical relationship to words, propositions, and judgments. Very well. Now are not these items a part of culture and cultural phenomena? Are not such main compartments of culture as science, philosophy, religion, law, ethical teachings, literature, many forms of music (opera, oratorio, musical comedy, etc.), ceremonies, mores, and customs composed largely of words, propositions, and judgments, with their substitutes and derivatives? How much would remain of culture and its components if the words, propositions, and judgments, with their substitutes and derivatives, were removed? Apodictically, therefore, it is clear that culture and cultural phenomena are made up largely of words, propositions, judgments, their substitutes and derivatives, and, of course, of the ideas, images, and meanings externalized by them. If the logical category is, according to my critic, applicable to all of these, self-evidently it must pertain to at least a major part of culture.

Thus from the very premises of the reviewer there follows an unavoidable conclusion which completely substantiates my position and invalidates the claims of an adverse point of view. The conclusion pertains not only to oral words, propositions, and judgments, but also to their derivatives and substitutes. It extends over all forms of "language," such as written words and propositions, gestures, mathematical and other symbols, mimetic, ritual, and ceremonial forms. The enormous variety of signs, pictures, songs, customs and mores through which the meanings are expressed and conveyed to others cannot be excluded. When all of these varieties of "language," together with their substitutes and derivatives, are considered in their totality they will be found almost coextensive with culture and cultural phenomena. Since by the critic's admission the logical category is relevant to all of them, this means it is applicable practically to almost the whole universe of cultural phenomena.

It is unnecessary to proceed with further details, as the argument has reduced itself to the syllogistic form given below.

Major premise: The category of the logical relationship is applicable to all words, propositions, judgments, and to their substitutes and derivatives (signs, symbols, pictures, gestures, ceremonies, rituals, music, customs, etc.)

Minor premise: Culture and cultural phenomena consist largely of words, propositions, judgments, and their derivatives and substitutes.

Conclusion: Therefore, the category of logical relationship is applicable to the larger part of culture.

Even to Mr. Bierstedt, one is scarcely warranted in imputing the logical incapacity necessary to draw from these premises the conclusion: "Therefore the category of logical relationship is quite inapplicable to cultural phenomena."

To keep my remarks congruous with the general reasoning of the review I have deliberately pitched my rejoinder on a very elementary logical level, and have invalidated derivative effusion with mere syllogism. It would be a sheer waste of time either to dispose of the main argument in other ways or to show the logical and factual fallacies of his minor contentions, such as the alleged "tautological character" of the logico-meaningful method, its arbitrary subjectivity, the past and present of the intuitive current of thought, the role of intuition in scientific discovery and invention, the inferential character of all cognition, the nature of "causal" and "associational" relationships, immanent causation, etc.* It is enough to say that in all of these minor points he

---

* In the fourth volume of my *Dynamics* I expect to answer all the important and mature criticisms of my work.

displays neither a better logic, nor (in his statements of factual character) a sufficient knowledge of the relevant facts. Finally, I wish to say that the "sensate mentality" acknowledged by my reviewer was evidently of such a cast that it proved an insurmountable barrier to a careful reading and understanding of my volumes.

2

The Means-End Schema
in Sociological Theory*

[1938]

In an intellectual climate where philosophers clamor for the abso-
lutes of medieval metaphysics, where astronomers turn from the
stars to peer into their own souls, and where physicists compare
notes on the intimations of immortality, it should perhaps elicit
no surprise that many sociologists too have renounced the positivistic tradition and have attempted to converse in more intimate
terms about the nature of social man and his social action. These
sociologists seldom deny that the human individual is a biological
organism, but they contend that it is much more important to
consider him as an enduring self or mind, an evaluating creature

* The writer expresses his appreciation to Read Bain, George A. Lundberg,
and, paradoxically, Talcott Parsons for helpful suggestions.

who strives to satisfy his heart's desires and his ego's ambitions. The history of humanity to them is the story of the strife of ideals, of a perennial quest for attainable and unattainable ends, of efforts to discover or invent means to attain these ends, and of a participation in social action whose structure, accordingly, can best be read and interpreted in terms of means and ends. Those who revolt against the positivistic tradition believe that these concepts possess an inner meaning for sociology and that sociologists who neglect them altogether commit the fallacy of misplaced concreteness,[1] surrender the only task which justifies the independent existence of sociology, and shirk a responsibility which gives social significance to the study of social science. Consequently, they substitute voluntaristic theories of social action for the deterministic facts of physiological psychology, and supply conceptual schemata which reputedly help sociologists to understand social meanings, social values, and social relationships in a manner to which positivistic theories can only unsuccessfully aspire. Among these nonpositivistic conceptual schemes which now pervade the analytical recesses of sociological theory, probably none plays so prominent a role as the means-end schema, the conceptual core of a voluntaristic theory of action which, it is claimed, emerged from the positivistic tradition in the work of Pareto and Durkeim and from the idealistic traditon in the work of Max Weber. This paper is an attempt to examine the efficacy of this schema for a scientific investigation of human behavior.

It must be emphasized first, however, that no criticism of the use of means and ends is implied insofar as they relate to problems of social welfare. If the science of sociology attains sufficient growth to enable it to dictate purpose, policy, or program in the sphere of practical affairs, no one can question that its recommendations will be expressed in terms of means and ends. In these cases, the end usually will be given and it will be the func-

---

[1] For a discussion of this "fallacy" see A. N. Whitehead, *Science and the Modern World*, 73–75, 81–86; L. J. Henderson, *Pareto's General Sociology*, 118–119; and Talcott Parsons, *The Structure of Social Action*, 29, 589, 753.

tion of the sociologist to discover the most efficient means for attaining it. Questions such as the following, for example, belong in this category: Is isolation or collective security the better means for attaining the end of peace for the United States? What is the best means for attaining the end of rehabilitating juvenile delinquents? Is the capitalistic system the best means to achieve an equitable distribution of wealth? Is sterilization the best means of eliminating the biologically unfit? These examples, and many more without limit, indicate that insofar as sociologists minister to the needs of an American culture and insofar as their recommendations may help to alleviate its stresses and strains, means and ends will be utilized implicitly or explicitly, and rightly so.[2] At the same time, probably few sociologists would contend that the effective use of such words as "means" and "ends" in this sphere has much in common with a means-end schema constructed as a conceptual tool for the theoretical analysis of social behavior. The same consideration applies to problems of scientific policy. For example, no inconsistency would appear in the statement that the means-end schema is not the proper "means" to attain the "end" of scientific objectivity in sociology, the very proposition, in fact, which this paper attempts to demonstrate.

The postulates which underlie the means-end schema may be enumerated briefly. Most of its apologists insist, as rigidly as any positivist, that social science use all of the observational and mensurational techniques available. They claim that they respect the necessity for the objectification of social data and that their results are derived in such a way as to be consistent with the most stringent methodological criteria. They resist attempts to indict them as opponents of whatever objective instruments have been developed for the advancement of sociological research, whether these instruments be observation, measurement, statistics, symbolic logic, or anything else.

---

[2] For an excellent account of the role of the social sciences in contemporary American culture, see the Stafford Little Lectures, delivered at Princeton University, March 21–24, 1938, by Robert S. Lynd. The lectures will be published by the Princeton University Press.

They do, however, break away from the positivistic tradition when they contend that objective categories do not suffice for the analysis of social action and that additional subjective categories must be employed. The difference may be illustrated most conveniently, perhaps, by suggesting that to protagonists of the voluntaristic theory of action, man is a rational agent endowed with a mind which has the power to choose one of a number of alternative means to attain a given end of action. To a protagonist of a positivistic theory of action, on the other hand, man is a biological organism endowed with a nervous system which responds to the extra- and intra-organic stimuli which motivate the organism to behavior. The difference between voluntarism and positivism in these terms is the difference between a "science" of action which employs both objective and subjective categories and a science of behavior which restricts itself to objective categories. Voluntarists regard the inclusion of subjective categories as a prime requisite on the ground that the subjective aspects of action are so important that one neglects them only at the price of an unawakened methodological self-consciousness and of a pallid and anemic sociological theory. Positivists concede the importance of the subjective aspects of action but assert that insofar as they are legitimate objects of scientific investigation they must be studied objectively in terms of observable, verifiable behavior and without recourse to such subjective categories as "mind." Indeed, in the interests of objectivity, communicability, and all the other canons of scientific method, positivists contend that subjective categories must be rigorously excluded from the analysis of behavior.

The means-end schema comprises subjective categories in this sense. According to a recent systematic exposition of the voluntaristic theory,[3] human action must be regarded in some degree and under certain conditions as rational, and a rational act becomes, by definition, one in which the chosen means serves adequately to attain a given end. In other degrees and under other

---

[3] Talcott Parsons, *The Structure of Social Action.* See esp. chap. 2.

conditions, human action departs from this defined norm of rationality but in all cases the capacity for a rational choice of means is involved. Unit acts become the basic elements of analysis and they possess, as minimum characteristics (1) an end, (2) a situation to be analyzed in terms of means and conditions, and (3) a norm toward which the action is oriented. "Conditions" is the only objective category in this schema. The other three, end, means, and norm, are subjective by definition; that is, they refer to the point of view of the actor rather than to that of the observer, and they have meaning only on the postulate that a human individual has a mind, is a free agent, and can choose one of a number of alternative means to attain his end. "Means," of course, as sharply distinguished from "conditions," refers to the active agency of the actor. The actor, however, is to be considered not as an organism or as a spatio-temporal configuration, but as an "ego" or "self":

> A still further consequence follows from the 'subjectivity' of the categories of the theory of action. When a biologist or a behavioristic psychologist studies a human being it is as an organism, a spatially distinguishable separate unit in the world. The unit of reference which we are considering as the actor is not this organism but an 'ego' or 'self.' The principal importance of this consideration is that the body of the actor forms, for him, just as much part of the situation of action as does the 'external environment.' Among the conditions to which his action is subject are those relating to his own body, while among the most important of the means at his disposal are the 'powers' of his own body and, of course, his 'mind.' The analytical distinction between actor and situation quite definitely cannot be identified with the distinction in the biological sciences between organism and environment.[4]

An end is an intrinsically subjective concept and bears only a residual application to the actual result of a unit act. Indeed, as

---

[4] *Ibid.*, 46–47.

recently defined, it is, in the concrete sense, "the total anticipated future state of affairs, so far as it is relevant to the action frame of reference,"[5] and, in the analytical sense, "the *difference* between the anticipated future state of affairs and that which it could have been predicted would ensue from the initial situation *without the agency of the actor having intervened.*"[6] All of these definitions deserve notice because they throw the whole means-end schema unequivocally over to the subjective pole of action where it becomes correspondingly vulnerable. Various other characteristics should perhaps be discussed, such as, for example, the exclusion of the space category,[7] but these will suggest its general nature.

One of the first considerations to arouse the scepticism of a critic of the means-end schema is its excessively deductive character. From a few well assorted though questionable premises about human nature and the human mind, a general system builds itself by conceptual accretion into a voluntaristic theory of action. The system generates its own concepts which require further clarification; this clarification, in turn, generates more concepts, and so on, ending in a relatively autonomous congeries of deductive propositions whose nexus with the empirical world grows proportionately more vaporous. No one questions the impossibility of divorcing induction from deduction in sociological theory. At the same time, it may perhaps be permissible to queston the utility of long chains of deductive reasoning by the recall of certain historical illustrations. Hegel, for example, proved with incontrovertible logic that seven was the only possible number of planets—and published his "proof" one week before the discovery of the eighth. Johannes Müller proved in exemplary fashion the impossibility of measuring the speed of a nerve impulse shortly before Helmholtz measured it. At the turn of the century, Henri Poincaré proved with impeccable mathematics that aviation was

---

[5] *Ibid.*, 48.

[6] *Ibid.*, 49.

[7] See *ibid.*, 45, note, where Parsons states that relations in space are not relevant to systems of action "analytically considered."

theoretically impossible, that men could not and never would be able to fly through the air.

At what point, then, does deduction become suspect? Precisely at the point where the concepts which comprise the propositions of deductive analytical systems cease to have referents in the empirical world or when they are not universals for particulars with such referents. One can have nothing but applause and encouragement for the processes of analytical abstraction, especially when they lead to integrated and systematic sociological theory. A surfeit of analytical abstraction, however, becomes a form of logical prestidigitation which destroys the nexus between an abstract schema and empirical content and leads ultimately to hypostasis and word magic.

If the means-end schema has any one defect more serious than others, it would seem to be the absence of empirical referents for its concepts, referents which have some form of existence in the empirical world and which are susceptible of sensory observation and measurement. The positivistic tradition, from which contemporary science has never severed its connection (except when careful scientists become careless philosophers) requires as the very minimum criterion of a concept that it be reducible to referents which can directly be related to sense-experince or be reached by empirical operations. Ends and means by definition fail to satisfy this criterion. They are not sensory objects to which an investigator can respond. They do not express relations between objects which can be verified independently by other observers. They cannot become a part of the sense-experience of a sociologist engaged in the study of social action. They are not universals the particulars of which are capable of sense-experience. They are not data because they never can be stimuli to sense-experience, and, in spite of all indictments of the positivistic tradition, sense-experiences of nonsymbolic objects continue to be the data of science. It is true, of course, that an investigator can respond to the *words* "means" and "ends," just as he can respond to unicorns, angels, nonsense syllables, and round squares. It is also true that valid syllogisms can be constructed around such words. Without empirical referents, however, the words are merely symbols which play spurious roles in scientific intercourse. Although the manufacturers of these voluntaristic conceptual schemes protest that they "stand squarely on the platform of science," until they supply empirical referents for their concepts they have a "science" without concrete existential entities susceptible of the sense-experience which is the prime criterion of science.

Without laboring this point at greater detail, it may be suggested that translation of the concepts of the means-end schema into another conceptual scheme which does refer to an empirical content would facilitate its introduction into scientific discourse. If ends could be identified with psychological motivations or physiological drives or organic needs, they would at once become the proper objects of scientific study. No one, of course, and no science, has been able to perform this job satisfactorily up to the present time. The possibility of its performance, however, is extremely remote when an end is defined as "the *difference* between the anticipated future state of affairs and that which it could have been predicted would ensue from the initial situation *without the agency of the actor having intervened.*" Means, also, could have been construed synonymously with environmental and organic conditions, perhaps, but Parsons' exposition of the means-end schema blocks any such identification and contains instead a discussion of means in terms of the powers of the mind. It may be significant that both "powers" and "mind" appear in quotation marks. In fact, when the actor in a social situation is identified not with an individual human organism but with a nonempirical "ego" or "self" or "mind" which is not "a spatially distinguishable separate unit in the world," the reclamation of the means-end schema for scientific purposes grows exceedingly difficult.

All of these concepts and subjective categories could escape positivistic criticism if the proponents of the means-end schema would concede the desirability of translating them into objective categories consistent with the conceptual schemata of, for example, the biological sciences, or any others which retain the virtues of observability and verifiability. When, however, they define these concepts in such a way as to contradict the possibility of such consistency and when they state that "A knowledge of psychology is a knowledge of 'the mind' and not merely of be-havior,"[8] they effectively eliminate the means-end schema from consideration both as a useful instrument for sociological research and as a valid generalization for sociological theory.

Sociology as a natural science can have no commerce with an "ego" or "self" which is not identical with the living biological organism, or at least which is not a symbol derived from sense experience of such an organism. To construct such a nontemporal nonspatial, nonsensory "self" for the purposes of analytical ab-straction is to remove "its" social action from the sphere of science. When subjective categories refer to this kind of an actor, they cannot evade the charge of invalidity because of the insuperable difficulty, not to say empirical impossibility, of dealing objectively with phenomena as they appear from the point of view of an actor who is not an organism and who is not in space. The attempt to know the mind of such an actor and to delineate its powers is an epistemological venture, not a sociological one. The social action of an individual can be dissocated from his social behavior only on metaphysical grounds and at the price of playing dialectical dominoes with concepts which died a natural and not unwelcome death with the demise of faculty psychology.[9]

Two or three other difficulties inherent in the means-end schema may be mentioned without elaboration. First, the extravagant emphasis upon the question of the rationality of social action is not only scientifically irrelevant but it tends to obscure the fact that the more rationality is imputed to individuals, the more irra-tional the explanation of their behavior becomes. Second, the human penchant for *post factum* rationalization of the ends and means of action should give ample warning of the practical im-possibility of explaining a given unit act in terms of the means which the actor says he has employed for the attainment of ends

---

[8] *Ibid.*, 85.

[9] For a clear contrast between the socal system criticized here and one unex-ceptionably free from any subjective or idealistic taint compare, for instance, the work of Max Weber and his disciples with the work of George Herbert Mead, especially the latter's *Mind, Self, and Society,* and *The Philosophy of the Act.*

he says he had in "mind." What the actor says about his action is no better and is almost always less reliable than what the observer could have learned simply by watching the action.[10] Even where the rationalized motives to which individuals attribute their action become important problems for investigation, as they do in many fields of sociological research, it is difficult to defend the application of a voluntaristic means-end schema. Finally, in spite of a highly complex superstructure, the means-end schema actually represents an oversimplification, an appeal to a popular rather than to a scientific psychology. When an individual reports to a sociologist that he has chosen certain means for the attainment of a certain end, the sociologist most urgently needs to know the factors which would cause large numbers of individuals to aspire to this end in the first place and to choose this particular means of attaining it in the second. Without this knowledge, sociology represents little more than popular or commonsense description of phenomena which require scientific explanation. Sociology thus surrenders the opportunity of disclosing valid generalizations about human behavior.

For all of the foregoing reasons, the conclusion seems inevitable that the means-end schema violates most of the canons and repudiates most of the criteria of objective scientific methodology. Certainly the time has come to cut the apron strings which in such schemata still bind sociology to her philosophic majesty, *Mater Scientiarum,* and to replace these arid playgrounds of fancy with the fertile fields of fact. For sociologists to ignore the factual contributions of modern psychology and physiology and to attempt to analyze human behavior with antiquated conceptual instruments is to encourage the multiplication of conceptual schemes which, however logically impeccable, aesthetically irresistible, and methodologically inviting, give the lie to the unity of science and make impossible any objective study of social action.

---

[10] E. B. Holt discussed this problem long ago in his *Freudian Wish and Its Place in Ethics,* and came to a conclusion of which the above sentence may be regarded as a paraphrase.

3

The Operationalism of
George A. Lundberg

[1946]

*For since men may know the same thing in many ways, we
say that he who recognizes what a thing is by its being so and
so knows more fully than he who recognizes it by its not being
so and so, and in the former class itself one knows more fully
than another, and he knows most fully who knows what a thing
is, not he who knows its quantity or quality or what it can by
nature do or have done to it.*—Aristotle

I

In sociology the name of George A. Lundberg has been preemi-
nently associated with the theory of operationalism. As a redoubt-
able champion of the scientific method in the study of society,
he has tirelessly attacked all forms of verbal mysticism in sociological theory and has steadily insisted upon the use of scientific
techniques in sociological research. Like all scientists of "flag
rank" he has, in his eagerness to guarantee the scientific status
of sociology, inevitably become involved in issues that have a
general methodological rather than a special sociological character. Although other sociologists have also accepted the operation-

alist label, we shall confine our discussion here to his book entitled *Foundations of Sociology*[1] and severely criticize his operationalism because the epistemological excesses of that theory reduce rather than enhance the merit of his achievement.

In Mr. Lundberg's treatment one notices, first of all, that no question concerning operationalism in its more abstract ramifications is introduced. The theory is accepted almost as a postulate, in terms of Percy W. Bridgman's earlier expositions of it, and, after acceptance, is elevated to the status of sole criterion of the meaning of sociological concepts.[2] Mr. Lundberg goes so far, in fact, as to assert that the current confusion in sociological terminology is directly due to the absence of operational definitions and to insist that "the only way of defining anything objectively is in terms of the operations involved." He goes on to say that most of the terms in current sociological use "cannot be defined operationally because they are mere verbalisms derived from metaphysical postulates incapable of operational definition."[3]

In the same section of his work, Mr. Lundberg offers examples of such operationally defined concepts as "attitude" and "intelligence." "Thurstone records his observation of certain behavior. This behavior, explicitly defined operationally, he calls an attitude."[4] Thus it is impossible to disagree because words do not have "true" or "correct" meanings. The case is similar with regard to "intelligence." In order to obviate the charge of misinterpretation and perhaps also the charge of criticizing a position to which

---

[1] Macmillan, New York, 1939, part I, *passim.*
[2] Mr. Bridgman, of course, was the originator of the theory of operationalism, a theory that was characterized by John Dewey as "one of the three or four outstanding feats of intellectual history." For Bridgman, see especially *The Logic of Modern Physics*, Macmillan, New York, 1927; *The Nature of Physical Theory*, Princeton University Press, Princeton, 1936; and *The Intelligent Individual and Society*, Macmillan, New York, 1938.
[3] Lundberg, p. 58.
[4] *Ibid.*, p. 59. One problem, of course, lies in the "certain behavior." In order to know what Thurstone understands by his concept it would be helpful to know the criteria by which he records his observation of certain behavior and ignores certain other behavior.

Mr. Lundberg does not adhere, it will be wise to quote directly what he says about intelligence.

> Perhaps the best known illustration of futile quarreling over the meaning of words instead of arbitrarily agreeing on them (which is how they got their meaning in the first place) is the voluminous controversy over intelligence testing or more specifically whether what the tests tested really was intelligence. Indeed, it was regarded as a *reductio ad absurdum* some years ago to accuse the testers of defining intelligence as *that which* the tests tested—a theoretically entirely defensible definition. Logically, and particularly in the logic of natural science, this is perhaps the best definition that can be given.[5]

Thus, the definition of intelligence as that which the intelligence tests test, which seems to suffer from circularity, is held up as an ideal that conforms to logic in general and the logic of natural science in particular. To this definition we shall return after examining some further contentions of Professor Lundberg.

Among the insistent questions that these definitions arouse is why anyone would want to define concepts in this way. The answer lies in the fact that only in this way can we avoid the erroneous platitude that "in order to measure, we must first define, describe, or 'know' what we are measuring."[6] On the contrary, measurement is a way of defining, describing, and "knowing"; measurement is, in fact, the best possible method of definition. Let us attend to Mr. Lundberg again:

> If one confuses words with the things they signify and regards the process of definition as a mysterious intuitive revelation, instead of an ordered and selective way of responding to a situation, the idea of measuring anything without first defining it (in words supposed to possess some final essence), seems the height of absurdity. In

---

[5] *Ibid.*, pp. 59–60.
[6] *Ibid.*, p. 60.

the meantime, however, it happens that physical scientists have proceeded in just this manner. Since Einstein, at least, they have blatantly declared that space *is* that which is measured with a ruler; time *is* that which is measured by a clock; force *is* that which makes pointers move across dials, etc. For a couple of thousand years before Einstein, physicists too, were of the impression that they must first "define" these "entities" before measuring them. Let the history of science bear witness to the barrenness of the quest, and to the enslavement of intelligence for some two thousand years by the persistence of this thought-pattern. Today the *definition* of force and its *measurement* turn out to be the same *operation*. Contrast the liberation and the forward strides of physics through the acceptance of the latter doctrine, namely, that things ARE *that which* evokes a certain type of human response, represented by measurement symbols.[7]

The question of measurement will occupy us a little later. For the present it will be enough to notice the peculiar advantage that Mr. Lundberg ascribes to operationalism. It resides in this: that it immediately resolves all controversies concerning the meaning of concepts. No one who observes the principle needs to know what electricity *is*, but only that it is that which under certain circumstances kills people, makes trains go, illuminates lamps, agitates the pointer of a voltmeter, and so on. Similarly, in sociology, only the unsophisticated would desire to know what social status is.

We shall be content to say that it IS *that which* under certain circumstances makes people beg on streets, cringe before the local banker, behave arrogantly to the janitor, *that* status which is associated with certain kinds of houses, food, clothing, education, occupation; more specifically, we shall probably say that a person will be accorded status, *i.e.*, people will behave toward him *according*

---

[7] *Ibid.*

to their estimate of the probability that he will achieve the maximum goals of socio-economic striving.[8]

And so with all sociological concepts: all we need to do is to devise operations—especially, and perhaps solely, instruments of measurement—to determine beyond the possibility of a doubt the meaning of the concept, which will then be the same for all observers under similar conditions. In fact, the operational definition of sociological concepts is, in Mr. Lundberg's opinion, a necessary step in order to ensure the future development of sociology as a science.

II

We turn to the task of criticism with many misgivings. As much as anyone, Mr. Lundberg has insisted upon the cleansing of sociological concepts, of making them subject to the kind of validation that the scientific method demands. If we have the temerity to question his operationalism, it is not because of a lack of sympathy with his efforts to place the science of sociology on sound foundations, but rather because his theory detracts from the ends it is his desire to achieve. We shall try to show that operationalism militates against the effort to give to sociological knowledge that public character which would make it scientific.

The first charge to be brought against the theory concerns the fact that none of its proponents has suceeded in informing us clearly and unequivocally what an operation is. By an "operation" does Mr. Lundberg mean something that a phenomenon itself does or something that we do when we investigate it? When he tells us that electricity is that which makes trains go, he obviously has the first kind of operation in mind. When he defines intelligence as that which the intelligence tests test or social status as that which the Chapin scale tests, he has the second kind of operation in mind. On this issue, then, we are in the dark. It is a

---

[8] *Ibid.*, p. 62.

situation that would be strange in any event, but it becomes even stranger in view of the fact that operationalism claims to be a theory of scientific concepts. Perhaps operations should be given an operational definition.[9] All we have from Mr. Lundberg himself is a series of examples—in some, the first kind of operation is given prominence, and in others the second kind. Let us call the operations that apply to the object under investigation object-operations and the operations that apply to the person investigating the object investigator-operations and consider what can be said for them.

We may use as examples of object-operations the definition of electricity as that which makes trains go and the definition of social status as that which makes a man cringe before the local banker. Clearly these definitions represent attempts to define something not in terms of its essence, but in terms of its function. In one sense no one can quarrel with this procedure. The use of a functional genus, that is, a genus that is the name of a function, is a legitimate variety of an Aristotelian definition. In some cases —for example, concepts that name a function, such as "catalyst," and the names of tools and measuring instruments—no other definition may be required. On the other hand, to define electricity as that which makes trains go is to ignore the fact that this is also the definition of steam—the operational definition, that is— and that electricity and steam are two very different things. To be satisfied with this definition, moreover, would indicate a lack of interest in electricity, for there are many other things about electricity, in addition to the fact that it makes trains go, that are scientifically appropriate to investigate. Even more serious, as Ernest Nagel has suggested,[10] such a definition would be sterile from the standpoint of electromagnetic theory. However useful

---

[9] Hornell Hart has made what must be considered an unsuccessful attempt to do this in his "Operationalism Analyzed Operationally," *Philosophy of Science*, vol. 7, 1940, pp. 288–313. See also S. C. Dodd, "Operational Definitions Operationally Defined," *American Journal of Sociology*, vol. 48, 1943, pp. 482–489.

[10] In a personal communication.

such a definition of electricity might be, say, for the instruction of children, it is apparent that it can contribute nothing to the advancement of knowledge.

The same considerations apply to the definition of social status as that which makes a man cringe before the local banker. A man may cringe before the local banker for many reasons: he may, for example, have assaulted the banker's son, he may be carrying on an affair with the banker's wife, or he may be way behind in the repayment of a loan. Although of low social status by other criteria, a person may fail to cringe before a banker because he does not know him. Furthermore, it is not clear that social status does anything as such; it is, rather, a concept we employ in describing a situation. Most sociological concepts are of this type. It is obvious that electricity has a function, that it does things, that it "operates," but what is the function of society, of a group, of poverty, of crime, of consciousness of kind, of assimilation, or of a "sensate culture"? Even in cases where functions can be discerned, they do not tell the entire story. To elevate functional definitions to supreme scientific status is to ignore other characteristics of a phenomenon. With respect to object-operations we can only conclude that the function of a phenomenon—where it has a function—is in many cases only one characteristic of it and not always the most important one.

The operationalists, however, do not pay much attention to this kind of operation. They emphasize what we have called investigator-operations, that is, the operations in which a person indulges in investigating a given phenomenon—particularly the operations of measurement and quantification. Let us assume for the moment that the definition of intelligence as that which the intelligence tests test is the best definition that can be given, and consider some of the consequences of this position.

Suppose that Johnny Jones, age nine, is given two intelligence tests, one the old Army Alpha and the other the Stanford Revision of the Binet-Simon. In the first place we cannot, according to the operational point of view, be sure that these are intelligence tests. We might happen to pick up in addition an attitude test, a vocational aptitude test, and a test of manual dexterity. With all five in our hands, we have no way of knowing which of them to use to test intelligence. Operationally they may all be used to test intelligence, for, as MacIver has pointed out, all tests are equally good for testing that which they test,[11] and there is no operational barrier to calling this intelligence. Suppose we decide in some arbitrary fashion, however, that only the first two are intelligence tests and that we have duly administered them to Johnny. With an awesome and wonderful simplicity we immediately know not only what Johnny's intelligence is but also what intelligence is: it is the score gained by Johnny on each test. But suppose, as might happen, that he scores an IQ of 112 on one test and 121 on the other. The question to be asked about this result is whether Johnny's intelligence is that which is measured by the Army Alpha or the Binet-Simon. The two tests, being different, represent two different operations. In view of the requirement that operations must be uniquely specified, we are somewhat at a loss to say which intelligence test tests Johnny's intelligence. If both do, we should have to say—in terms of the operational theory—that our fortunate scholar has two intelligences. We should have to go further and agree that the number of his intelligences would increase in direct proportion to the number of different intelligence tests taken. Conversely, a person who has never taken an intelligence test could not, under the circumstances, be intelligent.

A second absurdity into which operationalism leads, one more general in its implications, was suggested by Charles E. Whitmore:

> It is not so many years since the construction of a reliable instrument for measuring the velocity of wind; but no one yet knows how hard the wind can blow, because at its height it blows the measuring instrument away. Are we to conclude either that the wind did not exist before its velocity could be measured, or that it ceased to exist as soon as it blew the anemometer away?[12]

---

[11] R. M. MacIver, *Social Causation*, Ginn, Boston, 1942, p. 157, note.
[12] "The Analogy of the Record," *Journal of Philosophy*, vol. 37, 1940, pp. 716–717.

According to Mr. Bridgman, of course, it would have been meaningless or "footless" to inquire into the velocity of the wind before an operation had been devised which could be used to measure it. Historically, however, and also psychologically, it is curiosity about just such meaningless and footless questions which stimulates the invention of instruments and the planning of experiments. If all problems had to have operational meaning before they were investigated it is doubtful if science could ever have had a history. The scientific enterprise, in fact, may be viewed as a thoroughgoing attempt to devise operations and experiments to relieve the uncertainties occasioned by a prior recognition of a problem.[13]

A third absurdity to which the doctrine of operationalism leads concerns the ancient problem posed by Aristotle in his *Physics*: whether (to modernize the example) the road from Albany to New York City is the same road as the road from New York City to Albany. To a nonoperationalist the road is the Albany Post Road, U.S. Route 9, in spite of the fact that the operations for traversing the road are so far from being the same that they are contraries; that is, one proceeds to Albany over the road in a northerly direction and to New York in a southerly direction. If the operationalists are consistent, they would have to admit that since the operations are different it is not appropriate to use the same name or number for the road in both directions; that it would, in fact, be more in keeping with the tenets of exact science

---

[13] F. S. C. Northrop, in a book that appeared after these pages were written, has stated the matter as follows: "Again and again in the history of science deductively formulated theories such as Albert Einstein's theory of the finite universe have been constructed as answers to theoretical questions, and at the time of their construction no conceivable operation for testing them was at hand. With further theoretical investigation it often turns out to be possible to derive theorems which do permit the theory to be put to an experimental test. Were all concepts in a scientific theory solely operationally defined concepts, it would be difficult to understand how this could be the case. Then there could be no scientific theory without the operation for verifying it automatically being present." *The Logic of the Sciences and the Humanities*, Macmillan, New York, 1947, p. 130.

to refer to Albany Post Road, subscript 1, and Albany Post Road, subscript 2. The conceptual difficulties one would encounter in attempting to cross the road at any point between Albany and New York City become infinite in number. In short, to measure any line operationally, one must always measure it in the same direction. Otherwise it becomes two lines.

The theory of operationalism presents epistemological issues as well. A major problem, as with all radical empiricisms, resides in the fact that it is impossible to proceed from a knowledge of particulars directly to a knowledge of universals, and it is the latter alone that constitutes scientific knowledge. Although it is fashionable today to regard Aristotle as entirely superseded, it is nevertheless the fact that he noticed issues of which some of our contemporary operationalists seem unaware. It was Aristotle, for example, who first declared that "Scientific knowledge is not possible through the act of perception."[14] For our purposes we may modify this statement and assert that sense-experience, including perception, is a necessary though not a sufficient condition of scientific knowledge. To exhibit the force of this assertion it is only necessary to take an example of a scientific law, such as the formula for the velocity of freely falling bodies. One reason, although not the only one, why this knowledge cannot be attained by acts of perception alone, and correspondingly by operations on freely falling bodies, no matter how precise, is that there is no such thing in the universe as a freely falling body. No one has ever perceived one, and no one has ever performed an operation upon one. It is consequently impossible to arrive at a statement of the law by means of operations alone, and it is further impossible, in terms of operationalism, even to know the definition of a freely falling body. The concept of a freely falling body is, on operational grounds, "strictly meaningless."

It is impossible to arrive at scientific knowledge by means of operations for three reasons, two of which apply to radical empiricisms in general:

---

[14] *Posterior Analytics*, 87b27.

1. It is impossible to perceive universals.

2. It is impossible to observe all cases of a given phenomenon unless the universe is so limited that inductive conclusion becomes trivial.

3. It is impossible to ascribe meaning to general concepts or universals, since operations are all discrete, unique, incomparable, and particular (by Bridgman's requirements).

These consequences have been clearly perceived by some of Mr. Bridgman's critics.[15] They lead ineluctably to the conclusion that consistent application of the operational method would result not in a unified systematic theory but in an infinity of scientific concepts. In fact, the number of scientific concepts would equal the number of operations that individual scientists found themselves able to perform. Every time an astronomer used a different telescope he would, on the operational hypothesis, see a different universe.

Our next criticism of the operational theory has to do with the existential implications of the doctrine, which its adherents allow to creep into their pronouncements. Neither Mr. Bridgman in physics nor Mr. Lundberg in sociology has made it clear whether their definitions are nominal or real, whether intelligence actually is what the intelligence tests test, or whether the word "intelligence" means what the intelligence tests test. It is not possible to answer the question in terms of their direct statements, for these are ambiguous on this issue. Therefore, in what follows we shall consider the doctrine as a theory of existence and endeavor to determine what it implies.

Now it may be perfectly true that nothing that cannot be approached by concrete operations exists. In this sense, perhaps, as a theory of existence, or better as a test of existence, operation-

---

[15] For example, R. B. Lindsay, "A Critique of Operationalism in Physics," *Philosophy of Science*, vol. 4, 1937, pp. 457–458; Lindsay and Margenau, *Foundations of Physics*, Wiley, New York, 1936, pp. 411–412. See also R. H. Waters and L. A. Pennington, "Operationism in Psychology," *Psychological Review*, vol. 45, 1938, pp. 414–423.

alism has some degree of utility. But the proposition is unfortunately not convertible. To say that nothing exists that cannot be operationally approached does not guarantee the truth of the affirmative proposition that all things that can be operationally approached do exist. And here, indeed, we find another serious defect in operationalism. To use E. L. Thorndike's famous dictum that everything that exists exists in some amount and can therefore be measured, the danger is not that operationalists will fail to measure what does exist, but that their operational ardor will encourage them to "measure" things that do not exist. Thus, nothing would be easier than to define God, whose existence learned men have deemed it desirable logically to demonstrate, as "that which people worship," and the definition is surely as defensible as the one that intelligence is what the intelligence tests test. It is doubtful, however, that a respectable theologian would regard this definition as a new and improved argument for the existence of God. Similarly, it would not be difficult to find operational definitions of the Holy Ghost, unicorns, angels, dragons, hippogriffs, satyrs, and leprechauns.

One further example of this point may be found in Mr. Lundberg's use of the concept of phlogiston to illustrate one of the ways in which undue regard for words has postponed scientific advance. According to a theory of combustion proposed by Stahl and Becher in the seventeenth century, every combustible substance is a compound containing phlogiston as one of its elements. In every instance of combustion the phlogiston escapes and leaves the other element or elements behind. This theory had many fruitful results as a working hypothesis and remained current until overthrown by Lavoisier's discovery of oxygen. At that time, as suggested by Mr. Lundberg, many of the older chemists refused to accept the newer theory on the ground that without phlogiston something was being left out of consideration, i.e., an essential constituent was being ignored. As Mr. Lundberg says, the newer explanation did leave something out, "namely, a *word* to which the chemists of the day had become thoroughly habituated, and which was therefore as 'real' to them as the word 'wood' or whatever other words are used to symbolize the factors assumed to be present in a given fire."[16] Similarly, many sociologists feel that social phenomena cannot be explained or investigated except in terms of subjective, "mentalistic" concepts such as "mind."

Now, again applauding the sentiment that motivates Mr. Lundberg to object to the use of subjective categories and concepts, it is nonetheless a highly interesting fact that the operational criterion is not a sufficiently powerful instrument for removing them. Notice how simple it would be to define phlogiston operationally as that which makes fire burn, a definition as defensible as the definition of electricity as that which makes trains go. No fault can be found with either of these definitions on operational grounds; indeed, Mr. Lundberg considers the second a good example of such definitions. Whether they guarantee existence to the phenomenon in question, however, is a matter that the phlogiston theory answers. Had such an operational definition of phlogiston been accepted by Lavoisier and his successors, it is doubtful if chemical theory could have rid itself of this concept. Mr. Bridgman's claim that adherence to the operational point of view will forever obviate the necessity of revising our attitude toward nature thus turns out to be a defect rather than an advantage. Nothing seems easier, in fact, than to give an operational definition to any concept whatever. Such a definition, however, would not confer existence upon the referent of the concept nor would it guarantee that the concept so defined could play an efficacious role in scientific inquiry. Once again it is difficult to resist the temptation to quote the old-fashioned Stagirite who in spite of his lack of operational sophistication, realized that a definition is no guarantee whatever that the thing defined exists, much less a proof of its existence.[17]

The consequences for sociological theory are apparent. With the help of operationalism it would be possible to provide operational definitions of words like "will," "feeling," "ends," "motives,"

---

[16] Lundberg, *op. cit.*, pp. 10–11.
[17] See the *Posterior Analytics*, 92b18–26.

"values," "mind," and others that Mr. Lundberg would exclude entirely from the conceptual scheme of sociology. He specifically condemns these words. Yet anyone with an idle five minutes could easily construct operational definitions of all of them. What is worse, however, is that operationalism could in some cases validate not only a concept but an entire theory; for example, as Waters and Pennington suggest, on operational grounds the theory of extrasensory perception can be immediately accepted. Extrasensory perception *is* that which enables a subject to name a series of cards while blindfolded and with a higher than chance expectation of success.[18] Utilized in a similar manner in sociology, the operational theory would cease to be even a blunt conceptual instrument and become instead a dangerous weapon.

Our next criticism of the theory has to do with the criterion of selection between two or more operations of equal availability. In 1939 Mr. Lundberg conducted an experiment designed to compare ratings of socioeconomic status in a Vermont village made by the local banker, a local janitor, and the Chapin scale.[19] The experiment demonstrated that, within limits, the three ratings were in high agreement. Mr. Lundberg then proceeded to use this demonstration as an argument in favor of operational definitions in sociology. Actually, of course, his gratification with the conclusion depends upon anti-operational premises. He did not conclude that because three different operations were used to test socioeconomic status there were three socioeconomic "statuses," or three different phenomena, tested. On the contrary, he was gratified to note the high degree of conformity in the ratings to what he apparently assumed to be a single scale of socioeconomic status in the village.

Apart from this inconsistency, another question arises: What criterion enabled Mr. Lundberg to define socioeconomic status as that which is rated by the Chapin scale rather than that which

---

[18] Waters and Pennington, *op. cit.*, p. 421.
[19] "The Measurement of Socio-Economic Status," *American Sociological Review*, vol. 5, 1940, pp. 29–38.

is rated by the banker or the janitor? Operationally it would seem to be quite legitimate to define socioeconomic status as that which any given person rates. Since, to invoke Mr. MacIver's statement again, all tests are equally good for testing that which they test, there is no clear criterion for choosing the Chapin scale rather than the janitor. On operational grounds, for that matter, there could be no objection to defining socioeconomic status as that which Mr. Lundberg rates, and no other sociologist would ever have to bother with the question.

Two related discrepancies concerning sociological measuring devices become immediately apparent. In the revised edition of his *Social Research* Mr. Lundberg reproduces the third revision of the Chapin scale. It is clear that on operational grounds no sociologist would have any incentive for revising a test. The original draft would, by definition, test that which it tested. The problem of revising or improving an attitude test or scale—or any other kind—could not arise in a strictly operational science. Secondly, the problem of the validity of a test, to which Mr. Lundberg himself contributes an excellent discussion,[20] is meaningless in operational terms. The point can be briefly made: It is common practice in sociological and psychological measurement to distinguish between the reliability and the validity of a measuring device. Reliability refers to the internal consistency of a test or the degree to which results on repeated applications of it conform to one another. Validity, on the other hand, refers to the degree to which the test measures what it purports to measure. On operational grounds, however, it is obvious that a test cannot help but measure what it purports to measure. Whatever that is is given by the test itself, and no test, consequently, could possibly be invalid. All tests are equally valid, the first draft as well as the nth revision, because they all test that which they test. It is perhaps significant that Mr. Lundberg, in discussing the question of reliability and validity, the construction of sociometric scales, and related problems, forgets the operational point of

---

[20] *Social Research*, rev. ed., Longmans, London, 1942, pp. 201–202.

view altogether and discourses on intelligence as adjustment ability, on the possibility of erroneous scores, and on the fact that the discovery of simple and stable elements in social situations is the key to practical social measurement. All these observations may be accepted, but they are detrimental to the operational point of view. They may be accepted, in fact, because the foundation upon which they rest is an anti-operational premise.

Preceding criticism of the operational theory has been intentionally severe. The many negative aspects of the theory would include the following:

1. Operationalism has never been stated clearly nor used consistently, even by its most enthusiastic protagonists.

2. It lends itself to two interpretations, which are different in kind, of the concept of operation itself and to many more than two which are different in degree.

3. It leads to palpable absurdities.

4. It provides no method by which observation of or experimentation with particular phenomena can contribute to the formulation of scientific generalizations and laws.

5. It results in the multiplication of discrete concepts in such a manner that their number approaches infinity.

6. It provides no incentive for the construction of measuring instruments in sociology and none for their revision and standardization.

7. It provides no criterion for selecting one of several alternative operations for investigating a given phenomenon.

8. It renders redundant all questions concerning the validity of a test or other instrument of measurement.

For these reasons, the theory of operationalism removes from the scientific enterprise and from scientific knowledge the joint property of publicity and verifiability; it leads to subjectivism, privacy, and ultimately to solipsism; and, in consequence, it contributes to the degeneration of the scientific method. It is our conclusion, in short, that whatever the theory of operationalism has in it of novelty over and above a proper emphasis upon the experimental method is either fallacious or has deleterious consequences for the scientific enterprise.

III

It is an interesting paradox that those writers, like Mr. Lundberg, who have argued most vociferously for the adoption of mensurational techniques in the social sciences, have also subscribed to a doctrine which exercises its most pernicious effects precisely in the field of measurement. We shall here be concerned to show that the theory of operationalism leads in the field of measurement directly to contradictions—to contradictions, moreover, which occur in fact as well as in theory.

Let us begin by considering one of Mr. Lundberg's concerns, namely, whether attitudes can be measured. The answer to this question is usually either a dogmatic yes or an equally dogmatic no. Here, as elsewhere, a modicum of attention to the meaning of the word "measurement" and to the logic of measurement can resolve the issue completely. For if measurement means the use of cardinal numbers on extensive properties, then the answer is in the negative. If, on the other hand, it means the use of ordinal numbers on intensive properties, then the answer is in the affirmative. Antagonists on the issue characteristically employ their own conception of the word "measurement," characteristically misunderstand their opponents' conception of the word, and almost universally neglect to indicate that the word may refer to two related but distinct processes. We want therefore to examine the logical foundation of this distinction. Fortunately, as will be seen, the task can be accomplished in independence of any particular metaphysical or epistemological premises.

Turning then to the logic of measurement as such, we shall discuss the nature of numbers, the difference between intensive and extensive properties of the objects of measurement, and the distinction between fundamental and derived measurement. It seems hardly necessary to say that none of this logic is original. The formal conditions of measurement have been well known for some time although the knowledge has been confined for the most part to logicians and mathematical philosophers. Recently they have been described and explained insofar as they relate to psychological and educational measurement.[21] Norman R. Campbell suggests that natural scientists are as little conversant with the formal conditions of measurement as social scientists indubitably are in his remark that "probably more nonsense is talked about measurement than any other part of physics."[22]

Elementary mathematics recognizes three kinds of numbers, nominal numbers, ordinal numbers, and cardinal numbers.[23] Nominal numbers are numbers which serve the simple function of names. Thus, in any football game, the players will have numbers on their jerseys which help to identify them for the spectators. Similarly, convicts in penitentiaries and members of the armed forces are given numbers for the purpose of identification. The function of these numbers is quite familiar, and everyone recognizes that no meaning attaches to any mathematical manipulation that might be performed upon them. It would be an innocent gambler indeed who would compute the arithmetic means of the numbers worn by the opposing teams and place his bet on the team with the higher mean. Nominal numbers serve as names,

---

[21] See for example H. M. Johnson, "Pseudo-Mathematics in the Mental and Social Sciences," *American Journal of Psychology*, vol. 48, 1936, pp. 342–351, and "Index-Numerology and Measures of Impairment," *American Journal of Psychology*, vol. 56, 1943, pp. 551–558; Mark May, "Ten Tests of Measurement," *Educational Record*, April 1939, pp. 200–220; B. Othanel Smith, *Logical Aspects of Educational Measurement*, Columbia, New York, 1938.
[22] "Symposium: Measurement and Its Importance for Philosophy," *Action, Perception and Measurement*, Aristotelian Society, supplementary vol. XVII, Harrison and Sons, London, 1938, pp. 121–142. See also the same author's *Measurement and Calculation*, Longmans, London, 1929, and his chapter entitled "Measurement," in *What Is Science?* Methuen, London, 1921, pp. 109–134. See also A. D. Ritchie, *Scientific Method*, Kegan Paul, London, 1923, pp. 109–154.
[23] Our discussion follows closely the accounts given by Johnson, "Pseudo-Mathematics," *op. cit.*, and by Cohen and Nagel, *An Introduction to Logic and Scientific Method*, chap. XV.

their function is to identify, and they are amenable to no mathematical manipulation.

Ordinal numbers are serial numbers; they denote a place or position in an array. When written out they are easy to recognize as, for example, the first, second, third, twelfth, nineteenth, thirty-seventh, and so on. If a group of objects can be arranged in a series such that each is, with respect to some quality, greater than or less than any other, they can be arranged in a series, and ordinal numbers can be assigned to them. Note that the relations "greater than" and "less than" are transitive and asymmetrical. All relations that are both transitive and asymmetrical permit the arrangement of the objects they relate into an ordered series and the assignment of ordinal numbers to them. No relations that are not both transitive and asymmetrical permit such arrangement.

How then are the numbers assigned? Using a familiar example, let us say that we have before us a group of minerals and that we want to arrange them according to hardness. After first defining hardness in terms of the ability of one mineral to scratch another, we can perform a series of experiments, placing the mineral that scratches all the others at the left end of our series and the one that is scratched by all the others at the right end. By continuing our experiments we can arrange all the minerals in an order such that, with the exception of the two extremes, each scratches the one on the right and is scratched by the one on the left.[24] It is easy to talk about the hardest mineral in the group and also about the softest, but if the group contains very many members it will be inconvenient to talk about the eighteenth hardest or the fifty-sixth hardest. We consequently assign numbers such that the hardest mineral will have the largest number in the group and the softest mineral the smallest number. All the others will be ranked in between according to the ordinal number series.

Thus if we have ten minerals we can assign the number 10 to the hardest and the number 1 to the softest, and the numbers of

---

[24] Note that the minerals must not be arranged in a circle. Such an arrangement destroys the transitivity of the relationship at one point.

the others will follow in order. Note that we can also, if we prefer, assign the number 1 to the hardest and the number 10 to the softest. The selection of numbers for the extremes is completely arbitrary. Once assigned, however, the numbers for the intermediate minerals follow in accordance with a numerical scale. We usually choose the order of successive integers, but it is not necessary to use these numbers as they occur in counting. For example, a practical system of ordinal numbers in everyday use, the Dewey decimal system of library classification, includes decimals as well as the successive positive integers.

It is important to observe that the assignment of ordinal numbers to a series of objects arranged according to some relation is completely arbitrary, except with regard to order. Thus, it is incorrect to assert that one mineral is twice as hard as another, three times as hard, or any number of times as hard, or that in a given library a book numbered 306.12 has twice as much of something as a book numbered 153.06. In the latter example it is also incorrect to assume that the number of books numbered from 100 to 110 is equal to the number of books numbered from 300 to 310. The numbers have been assigned only with regard to order and have nothing to do with magnitude. The fact that we usually assign our ordinal numbers in conformity with the order of successive positive integers when we have a limited number of positions, as in attitude scales and intelligence tests, should not blind us to the fact that they are nonetheless nothing but ordinal numbers.

An illustration will exhibit the consequences of confusion on this point. If we have a scale of minerals arranged in order of hardness running from talc to diamond and numbered 1 to 10, with topaz and sapphire numbered 8 and 9 respectively, it would make no sense to say that diamond is ten times as hard as talc. We might find an eleventh mineral, carborundum, which scratches sapphire but which is scratched by diamond. We should then insert carborundum between diamond and sapphire and give it any number between 9 and 10 or change the number of diamond to 11 and call sapphire and carborundum the ninth and tenth respectively. Now the ability of one mineral to scratch another has not changed in the slightest particular, but the impropriety of saying that diamond is ten times as hard as talc has become apparent. It is similarly improper, of course, and for the same reason, to assert that one man is twice as intelligent as another or twice as radical. Ordinal scales do not permit a judgment concerning the number of times one object or person exceeds another in the possession of a given quality.

In summary, an asymmetrical transitive relation allows the assignment of any of an infinite series of ordinal numbers to the objects or qualities it relates in order to make determinate the positions of these objects and qualities with respect to one another. There is no objection to calling this procedure "measurement" if it be remembered that what we are doing is determining positions and not manipulating quantities.

A different kind of measurement, known as fundamental measurement, depends upon the fact that some qualities, such as length and weight, permit the manipulations that arithmeticians perform upon numbers. All qualities and only those which possess the characteristics of the cardinal number system can be measured fundamentally, and it is consequently necessary to discuss the nature of these characteristics. Cardinal numbers express the results of counting. The cardinal number of any collection denotes the number of objects in it—i.e., it answers the question "How many?" The resulting magnitudes can be manipulated in accordance with the principles of arithmetic. All the individuals in such a collection are interchangeable; consequently, they have no places or positions with respect to one another. Nor is it necessary to inquire into their names. The only qualification necessary to insist upon in counting them consists in ascertaining that they are discrete units. This qualification is illustrated by the fact that we can count the number of billiard balls on a billiard table, the number of students registered at a college, and the number of chairs in a room, but we cannot count the number of drops in a glass of water. If we could define drops as discrete units in terms of weight or volume, then they too could be counted.

In order to exhibit the nature of cardinal numbers, let us consider a piece of rope. It is possible to cut a piece of rope into a number of smaller pieces such that one piece will be equal in length to another; other pieces two, three, or four times the first; and still other pieces only half as long as the first. It is possible to join two pieces of equal length together and get a piece twice as long as either. We do not need a ruler in order to perform these operations. In other words, these relationships are independent of any particular scale, English, metric, or other. The rope is, in a sense, its own scale. The cutting of it can illustrate all the properties of the cardinal number system. These properties are the necessary conditions of fundamental measurement. All properties, characteristics, and qualities which correspond in a one-to-one relationship with these characteristics of the cardinal number system can be measured fundamentally. All such characteristics, properties, and qualities are called extensive properties. Others can be measured derivatively in terms of scales derived from the cardinal characteristics of extensive properties and are called, in contrast, intensive properties. Thus temperature, a nonadditive or intensive property, can be measured derivatively with ordinal numbers in terms of the length, in cardinal numbers, of a column of mercury in a tube.

The use of any particular scale, whether of derived or fundamental measurement, is wholly a matter of convention, but—and this is the vital consideration—scales of fundamental measurement exhibit relationships supported by the rules of addition, specifically (1) the commutative law of addition, (2) the group property of numbers, (3) the axiom of equals, and (4) the associative law of addition.[25] Intensive qualities differ from extensive qualities by virtue of the fact that the latter exhibit the additive property of numbers and the former do not. The only possible way of discovering whether qualities have this property is to

---

[25] These rules are expressed as follows:
1. If $a+b=c$ then $b+a=c$. This condition guarantees the interchangeability of units.
2. If $a=a'$ then $a+b>a'$.
3. If $a=a'$ and $b=b'$ then $a+b=a'+b'$.
4. $(a+b)+c=a+(b+c)$.

subject them to physical addition. Thus, it is possible to add lengths and weights and impossible to add temperatures, densities, radical attitudes, and social insights.

The use of the expression "physical addition" has been questioned, by Mr. Lundberg for example, on the ground that we never add lengths and weights but only magnitudes of length and magnitudes of weight. In one sense, of course, this objection has merit; in the sense that writers on these subjects frequently resort to elliptical statements and talk about adding lengths, for example, when they are adding magnitudes of length or units of length, i.e., mathematical units. To say that magnitudes are the only things that can be added, however, is incorrect. For it is a proper and indeed a usual mode of expression to talk about adding goldfish to a pond that already contains some, adding a border to a drape, or adding a number of books to a library. It is this kind of addition to which the word "physical" refers in the expression above. In this sense, however, we cannot add temperatures, densities, or attitudes. Thus, the critic is right who claims that only magnitudes may be added mathematically, but physically a pinch of salt may be added to any stew.

The word "addition," in short, is commonly used in two senses, one physical, the other mathematical. The important point is that in the case of extensive properties, such as length, we can add the pieces of rope together *and* we can add the magnitudes or units of length derived. In the case of intensive properties, such as temperature, we can add only the scalar numbers, and this is an operation which, as Cohen and Nagel observe, is "strictly meaningless." In fundamental measurement both qualities or properties and magnitudes or units conform to the rules of addition. In derived measurement the scalar numbers fail to pass the test.

It may be suggested, incidentally, that the rules of addition depend upon no particular metaphysical or epistemological presuppositions. A man experimenting with a piece of rope will arrive at the same conclusions whether he regards it as an agglutinative aggregate of "hard, massy, solid, impenetrable particles" existing independently in the real world, as a congeries of his own sensations, as a convocation of atoms, as an idea in his mind, or even as a pointer reading. In view of this situation it is perhaps strange that some proponents of the theory of operationalism have been constrained to deny the relevance to measurement of the rules of addition and, correspondingly, to deny the distinction between extensive and intensive properties.

IV

The manner in which George A. Lundberg has been led to this denial may be illustrated by his discussion of measurement in *Foundations of Sociology*, a discussion which follows to some extent the thesis of an earlier paper.[26] Arguing, first of all, that the problem of definition is inseparable from the problem of measurement, he proceeds to affirm that "social measurements can and do fulfill the same logical requirements as measurements in the other sciences."[27] His discussion, however, repudiates altogether the logical requirements of measurement. He regards the distinction between fundamental and derived measurement both as an implied refutation of the theory of operationalism, which it is, and as a subtle objection to sociological measurement, which it is not. In his own words, the fallacy involved in almost all objections to measurement in sociology "is that which finds certain things intrinsically measurable while others are regarded as measurable only in a secondary or less fundamental sense."[28] With this distinction he further associates the contention "that whereas weight, distance, time, or force are phenomena fundamentally and truly measurable, temperature, hardness, and density are measurable only in an ordinal or secondary sense, and that attitudes, aptitudes, ability, or intelligence are not measurable in either sense."[29]

---

[26] "The Thoughtways of Contemporary Sociology," *American Sociological Review*, vol. 1, 1936, pp. 703–723.
[27] *Foundations of Sociology, op. cit.*, p. 66.
[28] *Ibid.*
[29] *Ibid.*

Mr. Lundberg points out further that we never measure anything in all its aspects and that our selective responses to specific qualities as symbolized are the immediate data of science and consequently of measurement. We devise, in measuring, various means of ordering our successive responses in series, then standardize the process by constructing a scale which is applicable to all subsequent responses of the same kind and which operates in the same way regardless of the qualities to which we respond. In this sense, he continues, all units on any scale whatsoever are symbols of magnitude. Since magnitudes are themselves selective responses, units of magnitude are interchangeable and, apparently, additive, and they are in other ways amenable to mathematical manipulation. Only magnitudes can be added, however. It is nonsense to talk about adding bricks or pieces of string; we can add only pounds in the case of the former and inches in the case of the latter. As a matter of fact, "the familiarity of the operations with which we carry out some measurements has caused us to believe that others, less familiar and formal, involve other logical (or 'fundamental') principles. The same reasoning will hold for the alleged differences in 'direct' measurability of such phenomena as hardness and temperature as compared to weight."[30] And finally, walking way out on the operationalist limb:

> If, by the procedure described [the Thurstone technique], one person scores 5 and another 10, one may be called "twice" as radical as the other with precisely the same logic which declares that one stone is twice as heavy as another. The latter statement means that we have abstracted weight-quality out of a total complex of some kind and represented the abstraction by symbols of some kind, in this case, units-on-a-scale. In terms *of this scale*, one stone is twice as heavy as another and in no other "inherent," "fundamental" sense.[31]

The gist of the argument is now clear. Obviously the root of

---

[30] *Ibid.*, p. 68.
[31] *Ibid.*, p. 72. For the entire discussion see pp. 65–74 and notes to Chap. II.

the difficulty lies in Mr. Lundberg's denial of the validity of the distinction between fundamental and derived measurement and the corresponding distinction between extensive and intensive properties. The following assertions are quite explicit:

> The basic issue involved in this position is the philosophical dichotomy between intensive and extensive qualities. It may be said at the outset that if one chooses to postulate such a dichotomy as inherent in phenomena, the reasoning leading to the conclusion here under attack regarding the immeasurability, or different logical nature of measurement, in the cases of certain phenomena doubtless follows. But I reject this postulate.[32]

In what follows we shall show that this dichotomy proceeds not from a postulate but from a fact, a fact which robs the operational theory of cogency in the central area of its application. Note that it is possible to accept all of Mr. Lundberg's epistemological premises, including the one that the data of science are nothing but symbolized responses to whatever it is that causes them, and still exhibit the factual nature of the distinction between extensive and intensive properties.

A simple illustration will suffice. Let us agree to say that a piece of rope 100 feet long is twice as long as one 50 feet long and that, *in terms of our scalar units*, a metal bar at a temperature of 100° Fahrenheit is twice as hot as one at a temperature of 50° Fahrenheit. There is, however, an essential difference between these two assertions. The difference is that in the second case it is necessary to include the italicized phrase and in the first case it is not. In spite of an equivalent grammatical form, the two assertions do not mean the same thing. When we assert the first we mean that the first piece of rope is twice as long as the second—that its length is twice that of the second. When we assert the second we can only mean that the scalar number of the first temperature is twice that of the second. The latter assertion is

---

[32] *Ibid.*, p. 85, note 49.

furthermore clouded with confusion. It is wholly erroneous to say that one metal bar can be twice as hot as another. It is incorrect, though meaningful, to say that the temperature is twice as great. It is logically defensible to say only that the scalar number is twice as great.

Let us now perform a simple exercise. Change the temperature readings into the centigrade scale and the new readings will be 37.77° for the 100° Fahrenheit and 10° for the 50° Fahrenheit. Similarly, in the case of the rope, transform the lengths from the English scale to the metric scale and the 100 feet becomes 30.48 meters and the 50 feet becomes 15.24 meters. After this transformation the first temperature is no longer twice the second; the length of the first piece of rope, however, is still twice that of the second. This is the case in spite of the fact that, as Mr. Lundberg himself insists, "The units of the metric system have nothing in common with units of the English measure."[33] The accompanying table presents a summary view of these relationships.

Scale	Ratio	Scale	Ratio
		Length	
100 ft	2	30.48 m	2
50 ft	1	15.25 m	1
		Temperature	
100°F	2	37.77+°C	3.77+
50°F	1	10.00°C	1.00

This exercise demonstrates that one piece of rope can be twice as long as another piece of rope in terms of any scale whatever, or in terms of no scale. One metal bar, on the other hand, can be twice as hot as another only in terms of a particular scale, and even then, as we have said, it is improper to use the expression "twice as hot." It is the scalar number that is twice as great, not

---

[33] *Ibid.*, p. 87, note 58.

the temperature. In the case of the rope, both the scalar numbers and the length are twice as great. This is indeed a remarkable fact. It is a fact which obtains in independence of the scales that happen to be used. All scales will give equal ratios for lengths. No two scales will give equal ratios for temperatures. This fact proves beyond the possibility of doubt that there is a difference between the measurement of length and the measurement of temperature. The difference is a fact and not a postulate.

There is nothing mysterious about this difference. It raises no esoteric issues, either metaphysical or epistemological. If there are differences in the behavior of two phenomena, it is not only advantageous but also necessary to name them. And that is all we are doing when we say that some properties are extensive and others are intensive and that some measurement is fundamental and other measurement is derived. It is clear, therefore, that any theory of concepts, such as the theory of operationalism, which is content to define length as that which is measured by a ruler, temperature as that which is measured by a thermometer, and social status as that which is measured by the Chapin scale is guilty of ignoring a basic difference between two kinds of qualities and two kinds of measurement.

This fault is vital and stems directly from the theory of operationalism itself. For in the theory, operations are absolute in their determination both of the quality measured and the quality defined. The two operations merge, in fact, into one. Since the operation itself is the sole criterion, no inquiry may be made concerning the appropriateness of the operation in measuring the quality. Operationally, any measure is ipso facto appropriate. The operationalist does not ask himself whether this or the other quality is extensive or intensive. Indeed, he cannot, because the theory renders the question redundant. The only alternative—a straw grasped by Lundberg, and inconsistently grasped—is to attribute the difference to a lag in the technology of measurement and to assert that when mensurational techniques advance, more and more qualities will be brought into the extensive category. Unfortunately for the theory, the logic of measurement does not depend upon history.

It should be noted that the facts involved in the logic of measurement have been recognized by some of those who have made the most significant contributions to measurement in the psychological and sociological sciences. Alfred Binet, the original "intelligence tester," had this to say in 1898:

> I have not sought, in the above lines, to sketch a method of measuring, in the physical sense of the word, but only a method of classification for individuals. The procedures which I have indicated will, if perfected, come to classify a person before or after another person, or such another series of persons; but I do not believe that one may measure one of their intellectual aptitudes in the sense that one measures a length or a capacity.[34]

Similarly, E. L. Thorndike, writing in 1926, suggested that, although enormous improvements had been made since the time of Binet, it was still not known what the tests measured nor what the measures signified concerning intelligence. If the improvement up to 1926 was "enormous" there can be no question that techniques have been constantly developed since that time, not only in the field of intelligence testing but also in the ordinal measurement of attitudes, social status, public opinion, prestige, social distance, and many others. No refinement in technique, however, can compensate for errors in interpretation that are fostered by an extravagant theory of definition.

Two final misconceptions may be traced to the theory of operationalism. The first concerns the contention that it is fallacious to attempt to know what we are measuring before we measure it because measurement is in itself a method of definition. Mr. Lundberg supports this contention in the following words: "No platitude is more common in sociology than the remark that in

---

[34] "La Mèsure en Psychologie," *Révue Philosophique*, vol. 46, 1898, pp. 122–123. See also Edith Varon, "Alfred Binet's Concept of Intelligence," *Psychological Review*, vol. 43, 1936, pp. 32–58, where the above passage is translated.

order to measure, we must first define, describe, or 'know' what we are measuring. The statement usually passes as a self-evident fact which needs no examination. That measurement *is* a way of defining, describing, and 'knowing' seems to have been overlooked."[35] The author of this statement, however, overlooks something that he finds it necessary to stress in various passages, namely, that we do not measure things in all their aspects but only in one or some of them. Thus, we do not measure a man except elliptically. We measure his height, weight, blood pressure, metabolism, reaction time, intelligence, financial resources, social status, and specific attitudes—all partial aspects of a complex unit. No one of these measurements, nor all of them combined, can define a man nor tell us what it is to be a man. The Aristotelian account of man as a rational animal is at least a definition. An operational account of man as that which is measured by anthropometrical calipers fails to qualify.

A second and final misconception may be the most serious example of operational negligence. We commonly say that the size of an object is determined by a ruler. What does this statement mean? The answer that C. I. Lewis has given is so penetrating that we quote it verbatim:

> The size of Caesar's toga is relative to the yardstick. But if we say, "The number of square yards in the toga is determined by the yardstick," the statement is over-simple. *Given the toga, its size in yards is determined by the yardstick; given the yardstick, the number of yards in the toga is determined by the toga itself.* If the toga had not a determinate sizableness independent of the yardstick, or if the yardstick had no size independent of the toga, then there would be no such fact as the number of yards in the toga; the relation would be utterly indeterminate. This independent character of the toga, or of the yardstick, is what we should be likely to call its "absolute" size. This can only be described in terms of *some* measure, though the description will vary according to what

---

[35] *Foundations of Sociology, op. cit.*, p. 60.

this measure is. *The size of the toga in yards is relative to the yard-stick, but it is nevertheless an independent property of the toga,* a true report of which is given by its correct measurement in yards. Thus what is relative is also independent; if it had no "absolute" character, it would have no character in relative terms.[36]

This brilliant passage is a one-paragraph refutation of the theory of operationalism.

It has been said that all measurement is an act of comparison to which we introduce numbers only for the sake of precision. In order to compare two things, however, it is necessary to have two things. The operationalist has only one thing—his operation. Whatever his second thing is, it is provided entirely by his operation. It has no independent meaning and no independent existence. The act of comparison is thus impossible. This, in sum, is the metaphysical consequence of a circular definition.

The implications are clear. If intelligence were not an independent attribute of individuals, no intelligence test could ever measure it. If social status were not an independent property of individuals and of family units in the social structure, the Chapin scale would be powerless to classify them in rank order. If properties and attributes which it is of interest to the sociologist to investigate were not independent of the scale we use in measuring them, they could not be measured. And, since they are independent, they can be—and indeed must be—defined without regard to the instruments used in measuring them. This consideration gathers in a capsule the principal objections to the theory of operationalism. It also shows why, operational disclaimers to the contrary, it is necessary to know something about an object of measurement before we attempt to measure it.

It is clear, in conclusion, that the question of whether or not social status and other sociological variables can be measured depends upon the meaning that is ascribed to the word "measure-

---

[36] *Mind and the World Order*, Scribner, New York, 1929, pp. 168–169. Sentences not italicized in original.

ment." If measurement means the fundamental measurement of extensive properties, the answer is in the negative. If it means the ordinal classification of intensive properties, the answer is in the affirmative. In order to demonstrate the difference between these two kinds of measurement we had occasion to examine the logic of measurement, an examination that disclosed a fatal defect in the theory of operationalism. The purpose of the inquiry, in short, was to certify the difference in the face of Mr. Lundberg's denials. If this goal has been successfully pursued, it follows, as the night and day of Polonius, that a theory of definition that ignores the difference must to that degree be fallacious.

4

Toynbee and Sociology

[1959]

The eminent author of *A Study of History*, in Volume IX of that panoramic work, delivers himself of the following sentiments:

In all Western universities mid-way through the twentieth century of the Christian Era, officially established chairs of Logic, Psychology, Anthropology, Political Economy, and Sociology were to be seen 'parked' side by side with no less officially established chairs of History, without any apparent recognition of the academically awkward fact that, if the intellectual creeds of either the professors of History on the one side or the professors of the sciences of human affairs on the other side were to be taken at all seriously by the academic authorities, a decent regard for intellectual integrity would constrain them to rase from the parquet of their aula either one or the other of these two rows of professorial cathedrae. In other periods of Western history than an intellectually anarchic Late Modern and post-Modern Age, Western opinion would indeed have revolted against an intellectual inconsistency and a moral laxity of this cynical enormity; for the intellectual creeds respectively professed by the historians and by the mental and social scientists were irreconcilably contradictory; and, if either creed were ever to be canonized as a sacrosanct orthodoxy, the contrary creed would have to be anathematized in the same breath as a damnable heresy.[1]

Now the simultaneous existence in our halls of learning of history on the one hand and the sciences of human affairs on the other would hardly seem to warrant such colourful language. Something is obviously bothering Mr. Toynbee. It may not be presumptuous to suggest that our erudite author finds himself in an ambivalent position. His professional affiliation is clearly with the historians; his enterprise, on the contrary, belongs just as clearly to those who try to elicit sense and system from the infinite variety of human experience. His ten volumes, his 6,290 pages, his 3,150,000 words—all this, to be sure, is about history. But it is not itself history. It is not a history of the world, a history of civilization, or a history of twenty-one civilizations. It is not, in fact, a history of anything at all. It is, on the contrary, a search for sociological principles of a most general and universal kind. If we had to characterize this colossus of intellectual industry under a short label, therefore, we should have to call it a pure speculative sociology. The substantive question raised by these ten volumes is not whether *A Study of History* belongs to history or to sociology, but only whether it is good sociology or bad sociology.

In this essay, however, we address ourselves not to this substantive question but rather to the distinction that provoked Mr. Toynbee's outburst in the first place—the distinction, namely,

---

[1] Arnold J. Toynbee, *A Study of History,* Oxford University Press, London, New York, Toronto, 1954, Vol. IX, p. 189.

between history on the one side and the social sciences on the other. Since we cannot here deal with all of the sciences Toynbee mentions,[2] we shall confine our attention to the relationship between history and sociology. The curious notion that if one of these is a sacrosanct orthodoxy the other is of necessity a damnable heresy requires examination and, as we shall contend, rejection. The two disciplines are complementary rather than contradictory, both have a logical and methodological legitimacy, and each of them aids, guides, and supports the other. It is this complementarity that we wish to treat in the paragraphs that follow, and we shall do so in terms of a common variety of methodological categories.

The first of these categories stems from the southwestern school of Neo-Kantianism, and notably from the work of Dilthey and Rickert. According to the labels supplied by this school there are two kinds of sciences,[3] the nomothetic sciences on the one hand and the idiographic sciences on the other. A nomothetic science is one that aims at the construction of general laws which will describe and explain the phenomena that constitute its subject-matter. An idiographic science, on the other hand, is one in which the quest for general laws disappears and the focus instead is kept upon the individual datum, fact, instance, or event which is believed to merit investigation for its own sake. Nomothetic sciences, in short, are generalizing sciences, idiographic sciences are particularizing sciences. Sociology clearly belongs to the former class and history to the latter. The sociologist endeavors to arrive at the statement of general laws of social phenomena, the historian at the accurate and precise description of particular events. This is a genuine methodological distinction and one that characterizes a basic logical difference between two

---

[2] The inclusion of logic in this list of the sciences is somewhat puzzling. The rules of inference belong to an order of inquiry that is neither history nor science.

[3] The word 'sciences' is used here in the broad sense of the German *Wissenschaften,* meaning any disciplined inquiry, rather than in the narrower American sense in which science tends to mean physical science.

kinds of inquiry. Both kinds are legitimate and both are necessary, and neither is a heresy to the other's orthodoxy. Indeed, it is difficult to see the relevance in this connection of labels drawn from the vocabulary of theological disputation.

The observation that sociology is nomothetic, history idiographic, has numerous corollaries. History, as idiographic, is interested in the unique, the particular, the individual; sociology, as nomothetic, in the recurrent, the general, and the universal. The proposition that Caesar crossed the Rubicon in the year 49 B.C. is of much moment to the historian, as indeed it was to Mark Twain who found in that event the turning point in his life, the event that caused him to become a writer.[4] The historian needs to know whether this proposition is true or false, and all the circumstances surrounding it in both time and space. Every single event in time, every unique occurrence, every particular happening can similarly stimulate the inquisitive eye of the historian. He wants to describe it in all its unique individuality and then to relate it chronologically to its predecessors and successors. Only in so doing can he give us the record of the past. His task is that to which von Ranke gave immortal expression, to describe the past *wie es eigentlich gewesen ist.*

Something that happens only once, however, forms no part of the stuff and substance of sociology. In sociology we direct our investigations not to the unique but to the recurrent. The events that happen again and again in human societies come to be matters of sociological concern. In thus viewing them the sociologist has perforce to ignore their vagrant idiosyncrasies and to treat them as members of a class. It is classes of events about

---

[4] Toward the end of this engaging piece, 'The Turning-Point of My Life', Mark Twain concedes that he has not pushed his analysis far enough, that the turning-point is to be traced not to Caesar's crossing of the Rubicon but to certain events which occurred earlier in the Garden of Eden. Here, however, things might have been much different—especially if Martin Luther and Joan of Arc had been placed there instead of Adam and Eve. 'By neither sugary persuasion nor by hell fire could Satan have beguiled *them* to eat the apple.'

which he wishes to generalize, to discern, if possible, patterns of recurrence, and to find the functional relationship between one class and its congeners.

At the risk of considerable over-simplification one might summarize these observations in the following formulation. However idiosyncratic an individual historical event may be, it nevertheless has some resemblances to others. However much it may resemble others it nevertheless possesses its own unique individuality. Sociology emphasizes the resemblance, history the uniqueness. It is not too much to say that historiography is interested in the differences between similar events, sociology in the similarities among different events.

A second corollary is that sociology is abstract and history is concrete. Thus, to choose a few examples, sociology has little interest as such in the Alexandrine conquests, in the Gallic Wars of Caesar, in the Norman Conquest, in the Thirty Years' War, in the Wars of the Roses, in the War of the Polish Succession, nor in the World Wars of the present century. These wars belong to the historian. But sociology has a deep concern with war in general, and it is surely one of the aspirations of sociological enterprise some day to illuminate the nature and causes of war. There is, in short, a sociology of war, but particular wars have only a history. Similarly, sociology has no interest in the English Revolution of 1688, in the American Revolution of 1776, in the French Revolution of 1789, nor in the Russian Revolution of 1917. These again are subjects of historiographical inquiry to which the practitioner of the historian's craft hopes to give complete and exhaustive description. On this concrete level they do not attract the sociologist's attention. But they are all data for a sociology of revolution that, unfortunately still in the future, may disclose the causes of these commotions among men. Thus, when Crane Brinton uses these four revolutions as case studies in an effort to discern in them a common pattern, and publishes his findings under the apposite title *The Anatomy of Revolution*, his book is a contribution not to history but to sociology. His quest is sociological in character and has little or nothing to do with historiography. Whether a book belongs to history or to sociology depends, in short, not upon the professional label that its author wears but upon the goal and purpose of his inquiry. Every label, after all, is a kind of a libel, and has no relevance to the excellence of an enterprise.

Candor in fact encourages us to recognize that men who call themselves historians have made more contributions to sociology than sociologists have to historiography. We have just mentioned Crane Brinton, and earlier conferred upon Arnold J. Toynbee the title of speculative sociologist, an accolade he would doubtless greet with chagrin. We may in passing allude to two other examples in another sector of sociology. When Frank Tannenbaum, a professor of Latin American History, published his *Slave and Citizen* some years ago he had no intention of writing a history of slavery in either North or South America. His concern, on the contrary, was sociological. He wanted to know the factor or factors involved in the circumstance that slavery was abolished without violence in the Latin American countries and with violence in the United States. Using Mill's canons of induction he discovered that the differential variables in the two situations were the Roman Law and Roman Catholicism in one, Anglo-Saxon Law and English Protestantism in the other, the presence of a slave tradition in the former and its total absence in the other, and thus produced an important contribution to sociological research. Similarly, and more recently, C. Vann Woodward, in his *The Strange Career of Jim Crow*, had no direct interest in the history of Reconstruction but was intent upon correcting an historical misinterpretation in order to help to solve the sociological question concerning the functional relationship between the laws and the *mores*. His conclusion that the laws *can* change the *mores*, and did in fact change them to bring about initial segregation in the South, must again be called an important contribution to sociology. We may also refer in this connection to Max Weber, an economic historian who became a sociologist in fact when he began to question the economic interpretation of the rise of capitalism and directed his inquiries to the functional relationships that obtain in history between religious ideologies on the one hand and modes of production on the other.

As another example of the distinction we are discussing we may invoke a special kind of history known as biography. The history of a single life enters only remotely, if at all, into the purview of sociology. Whether the subject of the biography (or autobiography) made his mark in politics, war, art, science, philosophy, or religion, the details of his career belong to historiography. But achievement as such, as a recurrent and universal phenomenon in human societies, belongs to sociology, and any attempt to discover the functional relationship between eminent individuals on the one hand and the social process on the other is ultimately sociological. Similarly, no sociologist would write the history of a single family, neither the Adams family nor the Jukes family, but the family as such, in its general aspects and phases, is a universal social institution and thus a principal subject of sociological inquiry. And finally, no sociologist would write the history of a corporation. By the division of labour this is a subject for the historian. But a corporation is a recurrent and common form of social organization and social organization itself is a problem that falls squarely within the province of sociology. History thus again attends to the particular and the concrete, sociology to the general and the abstract. If the history of the past be conceived of as a giant and gaudy tapestry, history is interested in the single strands that make it up, sociology in the patterns it displays.

Sociology is thus analytical in its designs, and history descriptive, and these adjectives supply two more categories which characterize the distinction between them. The historian is interested in the event for its own sake; it is the *Ding an sich* to which historiographical inquiry leads. The sociologist on the contrary is interested not in a description of events but rather in an analysis of the relations classes of events have to one another. The historian emerges from his archives with the accurate fact; the sociologist takes the fact and analyses its significance, with others of its kind, in the thrust and counter-thrust of social forces. What does the story tell, when read between the lines, of the actions of men in groups and of the influences that one group exerts upon another? There is, of course, no such thing as a concrete sociological fact. All concrete facts are historical, and it requires the historian's technical skill to ferret them out and to make descriptive sense of them. The sociologist's *métier* is of a different order. What do these facts mean, what is their functional relationship to one another, and what do they disclose with reference to the structure of a society and the nature of its changes? For the sociologist, in short, the fact is the *terminus a quo*, for the historian it is the *terminus ad quem*.

We may also note that the category of time plays different roles in history and in sociology. In the former it is an essential category; in the latter it loses most of its significance. For it is history that traces the time-lines of the past in an endeavour to arrange in chronological sequence the events that have happened and are destined to happen no more. There are, of course, several kinds of history, depending upon the focus of the historian—military history, political history, economic history, the history of art, of religion, of science, of philosophy, and so on. To each of these time is relevant and the historian's quest, one that moves through time, is thus diachronic in nature. The inquiry of the sociologist, on the contrary, is synchronic. He is concerned with the functional relationships, time notwithstanding, of economic phenomena on the one hand and, for example, religious ideologies on the other; art and politics, warfare and literature, metaphysics and manners. The distinguishing differentia between a synchronic and a diachronic discipline is that in the former the category of time loses its centrality and in the latter it is an essential dimension. Universal propositions, when true, are timeless, and contain no existential implications; particular propositions on the contrary, since they carry an existential implication, have a locus in time and it is this locus to which one must perforce appeal in any determination of truth or falsity. It is for this reason that historical propositions have a date; sociological propositions, when genuine, do not.

We have not yet exhausted the methodological differences that our two kinds of inquiry exhibit. We may remark in addition that in the collection of its data history is selective, sociology (to borrow a term from Whitehead) is prehensive. That is, the fact that the historian ignores, or does not know, has exactly the same logical character as the fact that he records. For the sociologist on the contrary the fact itself is of no use until it becomes a member of a class of facts and then it belongs to a different level of abstraction. In this respect we confront one of the ambiguities in the meaning of 'history.' Is history everything that has happened or only everything that has been recorded? The second alternative would seem to be the preferable one. The craft of the historian cannot possibly encompass everything that has happened. In the first place, even if, by some prestidigitation, it were possible to record everything that has happened, the recording machines would run far behind the events themselves, and by this time would be numerous centuries in arrears. In the second place, not all events are worth recording. All of the most important happenings of yesterday are reported in today's New York *Times*, but not even this great newspaper can record any but the most insignificant fraction of the day's events. The fact that the journalist and the historian record some events and not others introduces a difficult problem. It is obvious that in this process some criterion of selection must be employed. The source and origin and validity of this criterion, and the fact that it too is susceptible to change with changing sociocultural circumstances, represent methodological and even epistemological issues of a complex character, issues that belong both to historiography and to the sociology of knowledge.

Many facts that might attract our interest, incidentally, are destined to remain forever unknown. Thus, no one knows the details of the life of Homer or even the city in which he was born, no one will ever know the breed of Alcibiades' dog, the colour of Alexander's horse, what the exact faults and merits of Themistocles were, just how the speeches of Pericles were delivered, whether Agesilaus was lame in his right leg or his left; and 'we may doubt whether Tiberius and Nero were the rascals that Tacitus said they were and whether the feeblemindedness of Claudius, the lasciviousness of Messalina, Caligula's passion for his horse, may not have beeen exaggerated.'[5] No one can estimate

---

[5] The expressions in quotation marks are taken from Gaetano Mosca, *The Ruling Class*, edited and revised by Arthur Livingston, McGraw-Hill Book Company, New York, 1939, pp. 44–5.

the effect of these unknown details upon the course of history, but it is clear that they exercise some effect upon the course of historiography. Unlike the positive sciences, history contains not only an *ignoramus* but also an ultimate *ignorabimus*.

The final methodological distinction to which we wish to invite attention concerns the direction of causal inquiry, which is different in the two disciplines. The historian seldom rests content with linear description; he seeks also the causes of the events he describes. He is interested, for example, in the causes of the decline and fall of the Roman Empire, the reasons for the rise of the Hanseatic League, the issues involved in the Protestant Reformation, the causes of the American Civil War, and so on. The sociologist, on the other hand, does not ordinarily anchor his inquiry to a phenomenon, an event, or a series of events of this kind. He begins, rather, with what might be called a class of causes, that is, a factor, which he heuristically regards as an independent variable in the social process, following which he endeavours to disclose the dependent variables in the same process. The independent variable—independent in an analytical and not an ontological sense—may be geographic, biological, demographic, political, economic, ideological, and so on. Any one of these may be taken as the independent variable in a given inquiry and the effort then becomes one f determining its dependent consequences. If multiple factors rather than single factors are employed the logical situation is the same.

The historian, therefore, as we have just suggested, is interested in the causes of the Civil War. The sociologist, on the contrary, is rather more inclined to wonder how much of this War, or any war, may be attributed to the operation of economic factors and how much, say, to ideological factors. Again we see the historian engaged in an exhibition and causal description of a unique series of events, the sociologist in a functional analysis of a class of events. The first endeavour issues, when successful, in a causal explanation of a single phenomenon, the second in a generalization, a principle, or a law under which many causal instances may be subsumed. Again at the risks of over-simplification we may say that the historian in general works from effects to causes, the sociologist from causes to effects.[6] We have to add at once, unfortunately, that neither of these endeavours has resulted in knowledge of universal validity or even in opinion of universal acceptance, and it is doubtless for this reason that the philosophy of history is today held in such low esteem and has so few practitioners.

We have now concluded our discussion of the logical and methodological differences between two closely related disciplines. We have said, in summary, that sociology is nomothetic, history idiographic; that sociology is interested in the recurrent, the general, and the universal, history in the unique, the individual, and the particular; that sociology is attracted by similarity, history by idiosyncrasy; that sociology is abstract, history, concrete; sociology analytic, history descriptive; sociology synchronic, history diachronic; sociology prehensive of its data, history selective; and finally that sociology seeks the functional relationships in social factors, history the causal explanations of linear series of events. Some of these categories may be more important than others, some say the same thing in different ways, and there are doubtless still others we have neglected to mention. But these at least will indicate significant methodological modes of distinction between two kinds of intellectual inquiry, both of which are concerned with human affairs.

We are induced to remark parenthetically at this point, and not without some perhaps unforgivable candour, that in at least one important respect historians would seem to be guilty of a dereliction of duty. History cannot be written at all without the use of concepts and categories that are ultimately sociological in character and yet historians as a professional group seem to eschew sociology with as much enthusiasm as a Viennese positivist eschews metaphysics. It is obvious, for example, that without the

---

[6] The degree to which causal explanation in history is always and inevitably only a *post hoc ergo propter hoc* is a question to which we should like merely to allude. It is possible that a linear series is not susceptible to causal analysis in a genuinely scientific sense.

category of time there would be no such thing as history and without the category of causation history would degenerate into mere chronology. And yet in the catalogue of historiographical literature we find few philosophically sophisticated analyses of either time or causation. A prominent member of the guild has recently remarked that 'Non-Marxist historians cannot tolerate doctrines of determinism'—implying, perhaps by inadvertence, that determinism is an emotional rather than a rational choice. Surely a doctrine of tychism, or pure chance, requires as much metaphysical justification as does determinism, and a satisfactory analysis of contingency would seem to involve rather more intellectual ingenuity than an analysis of causation. No rational account of either the world of nature or the world of history is possible without the category of causation and the difficult problem of social causation in particular is one to the solution of which historians and sociologists both might make important contributions. It might be instructive in addition if historians and sociologists would examine the sociological assumptions of historians. They are always present, even in that rare and precious work of history that is also a work of art. What makes history after all is not its fidelity to fact—though this, of course, is a necessary condition—but rather the resonance, the 'style,' and the sociological cogency of the historian's use and interpretation of the facts.

Before concluding this discussion we want to deflect an unfortunate inference that could be drawn from it. An incautious critic could infer from our categorical distinctions that of the two disciplines sociology is somehow superior, that history is shallow, sociology profound, history addicted to limited and easily attainable goals, sociology dedicated to sophisticated and adventurous ends. On this reading the historian is merely a drawer of water and a hewer of wood, a serf who supplies a necessary sustenance for the use and enjoyment of a higher intellectual caste. Two considerations refute so superficial an inference. In the first place historical data, that is, the facts of history, have an intrinsic importance that is surely not less than the still speculative and largely unsubstantiated generalizations which a general sociology might construct from them. We need to know the record of history for its own sake, as knowledge of its own kind, wholly apart from any lessons we might derive from it. It may be that we shall conclude with Heine that we learn from history only that we do not learn from history, and with Fénelon that 'L'histoire n'est qu'une fable convenue.' But the intrinsic significance remains, and is never to be demeaned.

In the second place, the books of the historians are always more than history. Every historian of eminence asks—and answers—sociological questions. The masterworks in the literature of historiography are not mere catalogues of facts, mere calendars and chronologies. The work of a Thucydides, a Tacitus, a Hume, a Gibbon, or a Macaulay—to mention no others—bears no more resemblance to a Ploetz's Universal Epitome than does the work of a De Tocqueville to a statistical table or of a Sumner to an abstract of the census. Every historian worth his salt, in short, is also to some degree a sociologist; he wants to know not only *wie es eigentlich gewesen ist,* but also *wie es eigentlich geworden ist,* not only how it was but also how it became. In order to answer his final questions the historian cannot escape an ultimate recourse to sociological concepts and sociological categories. Whether exposed in the details of his technique or concealed in the mystery of his art, sociological assumptions and sociological principles are always there.

It is equally obvious that sociology without history would be a weak and pallid thing indeed, a transparency of artificial correlations. Whatever one may think of the dream of Simmel that a purely formal sociology might serve as the geometry of social relations, it is clear that forms devoid of substance make a science devoid of significance. Sociology receives its data from various sources but from none so sure as history. Sociology, finally, must return to history for repeated confirmation of all of its theories. The assertion of Immanuel Kant, paraphrased perhaps too often, has still a large relevance to our present concern, for it remains the case that history without sociology is blind and sociology without history is empty.

If the relations we have discussed between history and sociology have any validity they imply that Mr. Toynbee, with whose remarks we began this paper, is afflicted with an unfortunate aberration. For it should be clear by now that history and sociology are not 'irreconcilably contradictory' but on the contrary and of necessity supplementary. Such expressions as 'intellectual inconsistency', 'moral laxity', 'cynical enormity', and 'damnable heresy' will have to be laid to a certain linguistic exuberance which sober reflection will fail to support. Any history that rises above sheer chronology requires the use of sociological premises and any sociology that rises above a statistical correlation requires the employment of historical continuities. 'Challenge and Response', 'Withdrawal and Return', 'Rally and Rout', the categories that Mr. Toynbee uses in his *maximum opus*, are sociological abstractions, not historical events, and a later historian of ideas will regard Mr. Toynbee himself as one of the most conspicuous of the sociologists of our 'Late Modern and post-Modern Age'.

5

The Common Sense
World of Alfred Schutz[*]

[1963]

The idealist and the materialist, the empiricist and the pragma-
tist, and even—or especially—the solipsist all have a relatively
short and direct approach to the commonplace world in which
we live. They begin with their own systems and deduce from
them whatever needs to be deduced in order to provide, establish, and guarantee the existence of such a world. The situation
is different, however, for those who start not with a theory but
with the world itself, the world of everyday action and intention,
and try to come to terms with it. To this latter group, of course,

---

[*] Schutz, Alfred, *Collected Papers: I. The Problem of Social Reality.* Edited
and introduced by Maurice Natanson with a preface by H. L. Van Breda.
The Hague: 1962. P. 361. Martinus Nijhoff. 28 guilders.

Alfred Schutz belonged, and it is a pleasure now to follow him through this posthumous collection of papers as he makes his distinctive contributions to philosophy and sociology. The pleasure would be immeasurably enhanced, of course, if Schutz were still with us, but, as most readers know, his death occurred in 1959.

One should pay a deserved tribute, first of all, to H. L. Van Breda, who offers a sensitive preface in which he writes a brief biography of this unusual sociologist. Therein, he points out the manner in which the methodological aspects of the science of man occupied Schutz's attention and the ways in which this attention was shaped and directed by the phenomenological philosophy of Husserl. As he says, "It was Husserl's theory of intentionality and his notions of intersubjectivity and of the *Lebenswelt* which were to guide Schutz's thought and to give it its specific character." The next tribute belongs to Maurice Natanson, who was Schutz's student at the New School for Social Research. Professor Schutz's writings are not—let us admit it— easy to grasp in their entirety. There is, of course, *Der sinnhafte Aufbau der sozialen Welt*, which Schutz published in Vienna in 1932 (second edition 1960). But many of Schutz's papers are fugitive papers in the sense of having been published in a variety of journals during his most productive periods. For this reason we can especially appreciate Professor Natanson's long introduction, in which he gives us a lucid and comprehensive account of Schutz's thought. He is able to describe the emphasis that Schutz gave to the category of meaning, as opposed to the category of existence, and to quote Schutz himself as saying that, "It is the meaning of our experiences and not the ontological structure of the objects which constitutes reality."

As his followers know, Schutz was a life-long opponent of naturalism in social thought and one who devoted a number of papers to a critique of naturalistic methods as they applied to the social world. The basic difficulty with these methods, according to him, is that they rely upon perception in a situation in which the basic *point de départ* must be action. Now Schutz, of course, did not stand alone in his preference for action over perception.

Florian Znaniecki and Talcott Parsons too, to say nothing of Max Weber, placed their sociological theory firmly in the context of action and resisted the efforts of the behaviorists to exclude the subjective—and especially the subjectivity of conscious choice—from sociological analysis. This, in essence, is what Znaniecki had in mind in emphasizing "the humanistic coefficient," which distinguishes the realm of the social sciences from that of the physical, and which continues to give relevance to the so-called Baden School of Windelband, Rickert, and Dilthey—a school to which all of these thinkers owe something of a debt. There is no evidence, however, that Schutz was influenced by Znaniecki in this respect, although he refers on occasion to Parsons and also to W. I. Thomas, whose "definition of the situation" attracted his favorable attention. The alembic from which Schutz drew his inspiration, was not Znaniecki or Weber, but Husserl, and the phenomenological reduction is never far from his concerns.

The defense of subjective categories in the acquisition of the "organized knowledge of social reality," which it is the responsibility of the social sciences to obtain, is no easy task. In particular, as Schutz insists, one has to guard against misconceptions such as those entertained by writers like Ernest Nagel and Carl Hempel. Certainly the subjective approach does not require the observer to identify himself with the actor, nor does it invoke the private value system of the observer himself. No one, least of all Weber, ever advocated a position from which these consequences would follow. The important thing is to avoid the identification of sensory experience with all experience—and it is this identification to which Schutz believes the objectivists must plead guilty. Of course, as Schutz may not have noticed, they might be willing to accept this degree of guilt and regard it as a small price to pay for verifiable propositions. Thus once more we have the familiar confrontation of empiricist and phenomenologist. This problem—actually a problem of general philosophical orientation and predilection—engages Schutz's dialectical talents again and again. He treats it with an especial subtlety in the second essay, "Concept and Theory Formation in the Social Sciences," which was originally prepared for the Conference On Methods in Philosophy and the Sciences and presented at its May meeting in 1953.

The middle portion of the collection is given over to a series of essays with the general title of "Phenomenology and the Social Sciences." In these papers Schutz treats the problem of intersubjectivity, especially as it appears in the work of Scheler, Husserl, Hegel, Heidegger, and Sartre. The difficulty faced by anyone adopting the phenomenological reduction is in guaranteeing the existence of the Other, or alter ego, and in escaping the snares of solipsism. The writers mentioned all appreciated this difficulty and tried to overcome it, each in his own way. That none of them was entirely successful is Schutz's point here, and he convinces at least one reader that this is indeed the case. In this connection he is able to show, however, that a number of Husserl's ideas can be applied to some central issues of social science.

The third and last section of the book carries the title, "Symbol, Reality, and Society," and here Schutz discourses on multiple realities, on the reality of the world of daily life, on the social structure of this daily world, on the world of working as a paramount reality, on the world of dreams and the world of scientific theory, on Goldstein's theory of language, on language and communication in general, and on relevance and typification. Bergson, James, and Husserl receive the major share of attention.

Schutz's work, as his followers and disciples well know, is marked by a number of highly suggestive distinctions. One of these is his distinction between sensible, reasonable, and rational conduct, a distinction that sheds a useful light upon the means-end schema. Another is a distinction between three different kinds of *verstehen*. Still another is an analysis of action from three different points of view—that of the actor, of the actor's partner, and of the observer. These and many more are accompanied by penetrating observations on the issues with which Schutz was principally concerned. Sometimes the distinctions receive a most felicitous expression, as when Schutz remarks, for example, that: "We have to distinguish between rational constructs of models of human actions on the one hand, and constructs of models of rational human actions on the other."

It would do the reputation of Schutz no service if we implied that his phenomenological approach to sociology is free of difficulties, or that he was always victorious in his jousts with the members of opposing, and particularly the positivistic schools, or even that he met with entire success in his enterprise. Indeed, the phenomenological reduction, difficult as it makes a solution to the problem of solipsism, has consequences of a similar and rather serious kind for sociology. It is one thing to argue against the positivistic approach in all of its variations, from behaviorism to operationalism and whatever other radical empiricisms may be involved. It is a comparable thing to defend the relevance and, indeed, the importance of the subjective in any effort to understand the actions of men and especially their interactions with their fellows. Some solution to the problem of intersubjectivity, in other words, is basic to any sociological analysis that assumes the responsibility of explaining the meaning of action. But there is one problem which presents to the phenomenologist a more formidable obstacle perhaps than any other, and that is that society itself, as an *objective* phenomenon, tends to disappear in the realm of the intersubjective. That is, society itself, insofar as it plays a part in these essays, comes to be a creation of mind in its intersubjectivity and something therefore that is wholly exhausted in the commonplace affairs of daily living.

There is no question of the utility, for certain purposes, of the phenomenological starting point, and Schutz has done as much as anyone to give it the philosophical validation that it would seem to require. But the distance travelled from this starting point is not very great if the destination is not in fact the explanation of daily life but rather the order, the structure, and the stability of society itself. This is a corollary, in a sense of the problem of solipsism; a corollary that operates on the sociological as well as on the epistemological level. For once society is seen as an emanation, as it were, of intersubjective processes, then it ceases to be a natural object that, with its culture, can shape the individual and guide, condition, and control his actions. Both the exteriority and the constraint, in Emile Durkheim's famous language, are missing—or at best receive only a most precarious support. Thus, the approach of Schutz can add something—indeed, a great deal—to our knowledge of social actions, social interactions, and social relations. It leaves something wanting, however, in the explanation of norms, institutions, and all of the other structural components of society.

This problem is too large, of course, and too complex for a short essay, and it may be inappropriate even to mention it in this place. Certainly the existence of the problem does not detract from the contributions which Schutz made to other problems—problems of experience, action, relevance, language, typification, and symbolism—which had a greater attraction for him and which stimulated his phenomenological invention and analytical power. The unassailable merit of these contributions makes one wait with impatience for the second and third volumes of collected papers which are promised for the future.

It is impossible to conclude without another word of praise for Maurice Natanson and his altogether admirable introduction. Quoting Bergson, who said that since philosophers have in fact only one point of contact with the real they can say only one thing in their lifetimes, he tells us that the one thing Schutz did—and an important thing it was—was to discover the signification and the meaning of the common sense world. "To see this world in its massive complexity, to, outline and explore its essential features and to trace out its manifold relationships were the composite parts of his central task, the realization of a philosophy of mundane reality, or, in more formal language, of a phenomenology of the natural attitude. The understanding of the paramount reality of common sense life is the clue to the understanding of the work of Alfred Schutz."

6

The Social Darwinists

[1969]

In his famous essay "The Influence of Darwin on Philosophy," John Dewey observed that change alone is only flux and lapse, and an insult to intelligence. Somehow men must find, in this otherwise flat and neutral phenomenon, a direction, a process, and possibly even a purpose. The idea of evolution, because it contributes direction and process at least, is thus as old as Empedocles and appears in almost every era of Western history. It assumed in the nineteenth century, however, a special force and significance under the label of Social Darwinism.

Social Darwinism essentially extends the Darwinian discovery of natural selection from nature to society, and might therefore be called "the great extrapolation." It is not a simple doctrine, but instead an entire colony of ideas, most of them receiving their initial thrust in the writings of Herbert Spencer. It includes, among other ideas, the notions that all social change exhibits differentiation, adaptation, and integration; that its direction is from the simple to the complex; that it occurs in regular and universal stages in the development of human societies; that society is an organism (or at least resembles one); that societies and individuals, like animal species and their members, are ineluctably engaged in a struggle for existence; and that in this struggle only the fittest survive. None of these ideas, of course, is original with Spencer. The notion of stages, for example, appears in the writings of Bossuet, Turgot, Condorcet, and Comte in France; in Herder in Germany; and in Adam Ferguson and James Mill in Scotland. The struggle for existence was noted perceptively by Mandeville and by philosophers from Heraclitus to Hume, and the organic analogy is as old as social thought itself.

Unfortunately, there is no straight line that one can follow from Spencer and Darwin forward because different writers emphasize different aspects of the doctrine. But the result is everywhere the same. Every social thinker, from roughly 1860 to 1920, had to respond, in one way or another, to Herbert Spencer. The essay that follows, therefore, will first treat the idea of Social Darwinism in Spencer and Darwin and some of their immediate disciples and then pursue three of its major themes: (1) the idea of stages of social development, (2) the struggle for existence, and (3) the organic analogy.

Early in his career Spencer was exposed to the sociology of Auguste Comte, the embryology of Karl Ernst von Baer, the geology of Charles Lyell, and the demography of Thomas Robert Malthus, all of which contained the germs of his own evolutionary philosophy. Malthus, incidentally, contributed more to biology than any sociologist since; it was, however, as has been said, a debt that Social Darwinism repaid with usury. In 1852, in an essay entitled "A Theory of Population," Spencer used the two expressions—"the struggle for existence" and "the survival of the fittest"—destined to become clarion symbols of a style of thought that was to dominate the later part of the nineteenth century and the early part of the twentieth. Few ideas have had such percussive consequences.

Spencer's *First Principles* appeared in 1862, ten years after his essay on population and three years after *The Origin of Species*. In this, the keystone of his system, he offered his definition of evolution: "Evolution is an integration of matter and concomitant dissipation of motion; during which the matter passes from an indefinite, incoherent homogeneity to a definite, coherent heterogeneity; and during which the retained motion undergoes a parallel transformation." It is easy to be facetious about this definition, its Latinate English and its sesquipedalian words. Spencer, however, took it quite as seriously as he took everything else. He insisted that everything in the universe moves inexorably and in response to immanent causes from a homogeneity that is unstable and amorphous to a heterogeneity that exhibits durability and structure.

For Spencer the idea of evolution had an explanatory power like no other, and all ten volumes of the *Synthetic Philosophy* are devoted to its application and elaboration—in biology, psychology, sociology, and ethics, but above all in sociology. In these books, and especially in the volumes on sociology, he emphasized that the world and its societies are part of a vast evolutionary process. Spencer does not, unfortunately, say what supplies the motive force for this engine of evolution. The knowledge that everything evolves from the simple to the complex, from the homogeneous to the heterogeneous, seems to suffice. Some things, like the first cause, for example, or the ultimate particle, belong to the realm of the unknowable, a realm in which—indeed by definition—all questions wait for an answer. Thus there was nothing in Spencer comparable to the principle of natural selection in Darwin, unless it was the struggle for existence itself. Whatever the key, however, Spencer had discovered to his own satisfaction, and to that of a legion of sociologists who succeeded him, the law that Comte had sought a generation earlier. It was a law that would explain not only the course of nature and the proliferation of species, but the history of human societies as well.

The law was in fact a universal formula. It explained the development of the cosmos, the solar system, the earth's crust and its geological transformations, the chemical changes of organic matter, the origin and development of species, the human organism, the movement of civilization as a whole and of every tribe and nation, social stratification and the division of labor, and the changes in every kind of thought and action, including language, architecture, painting, sculpture, poetry, and music. The law, for Spencer, was a veritable philosopher's stone, one that would transmute the base metal of opinion into the precious gold of knowledge.

The connotations now attached to Social Darwinism are fairly pejorative, and it would doubtless be unkind to affix the label to Darwin himself. Certainly he would have responded with dismay to some of the implications, racist and otherwise, that were to be drawn from his theory of natural selection. No one imagines that so gentle and diligent a man would have been an apologist for war or for a ruthless economic individualism. Nor did he think that the struggle for existence is the most important factor in the social progress of mankind. It is customary, in fact, to say that it was Spencer, a "metaphysician," who invented Social Darwinism and that Darwin himself was not a Social Darwinist. One may speculate that such labels as "Spencerism" or "Spencerianism" were awkward to the ear and that "Darwinism" possessed a certain euphony that was lacking in the more accurate alternatives. Nevertheless, it is difficult to see how the evolutionary ideas of Spencer would have flourished as they did without the scientific support they seemed to receive in *The Origin of Species* and especially in *The Descent of Man*. To say any less is to denigrate the role that the Darwinian doctrine played in the history of nineteenth-century thought. Although Darwin himself was innocent of responsibility for the extravagant use that others made of his conclusions, his influence in fact is a tribute to the power of an idea and to the manner in which an idea, independent of its author, assumes a life of its own.

Different in temperament and method from Spencer, Darwin happened to read Malthus "for amusement" in the year 1838. By that time he had already recognized that species are not immutable, a recognition so disturbing to him that he felt as if he were confessing to a murder. To the third edition of *The Origin of Species* (1861) he appended "An Historical Sketch" in which he traced "the progress of opinion" on the modification of species and in which he remarked on the skill and force with which Spencer had contrasted, in his paper of 1852, the theory of special creation and the theory of the gradual development of organic beings. He understood that such expressions as "natural selection," sometimes used synonymously with "the struggle for existence" and "the survival of the fittest" (all of which he used as chapter titles), were metaphorical, but no more metaphorical than "elective affinities" or "gravitational attraction." Somewhat ambivalently, after referring to Spencer as "our great philosopher" and after paying him the compliment mentioned above, he indicated that he found Spencer's work impressive but not convincing, suggested—in a note that must have been painful to the author of *The Principles of Sociology*—that Spencer used a deductive rather than an inductive method, and said in his autobiography that he was not conscious of having received any profit from Spencer's writings.

The Malthusian influence, however, is clear and ubiquitous. It appears especially in such observations as "that every single organic being may be said to be striving to the utmost to increase in numbers; that each lives by a struggle at some period of its life; that heavy destruction inevitably falls either on the young or old, during each generation or at recurrent intervals." And continuing, "Lighten any check, mitigate the destruction ever so little, and the number of the species will almost instantaneously increase to any amount" (1859).

That Darwin himself applied his doctrine to other than biological phenomena is abundantly clear in *The Descent of Man* (1871). In this book he discusses the natural selection that sometimes acts on the individual "through the preservation of variations which are beneficial to the community" and the natural selection that arises from the competition of tribe with savage tribe in their perennial warfare. He also deals at length with the development of the mental and moral faculties—curiosity, imitation, attention, meaning, imagination, reason, abstraction, language, the sense of beauty, religion, and the moral sense. The differences in these respects between man and the other animals are differences of degree and not of kind, and these too have "gradually evolved." Darwin is satisfied, in short, that in man, although other agencies are also at work, the higher faculties have arisen through natural selection and thus also belong to the evolutionary process.

The views of the Duke of Argyll and Archbishop Whately, widely current at the time and fortified by the Book of Genesis, that God created man as a civilized being and that savage peoples exhibit a descent or degradation from the original standard, could not withstand the evidence to the contrary supplied by Lubbock, Tylor, McLennan, and Darwin himself. In custom, belief, language, knowledge, morals, and religion, mankind has evolved from a barbarous to a civilized state.

> The evidence that all civilized nations are the descendants of barbarians, consists, on the one side, of clear traces of their former low condition in still-existing customs, beliefs, language, etc.; and on the other side, of proofs that savages are independently able to raise themselves a few steps in the scale of civilization, and have actually thus risen. (Darwin, 1871)

Finally, Darwin, although he does not deny the role of conscience in the moral sphere, nevertheless attributes the moral sense to the social instincts, with the suggestion that these instincts themselves have arisen through natural selection.

When it is recalled that there was no one in England at the time, except possibly Lyell and Huxley, who had the towering repute of either Spencer or Darwin, it can easily be seen that the influence of both of them together, alike in doctrine and direction, carried an intellectual potency of a rare degree. In an age still informed by a literal religion, theirs was a strong philosophy, strong enough to stand its ground against and even conquer Holy Writ, and thus to mark one more victory for science in the "history of the warfare of science with theology in

Christendom," to use the title of Andrew Dickson White's famous book (1896). It was not an easy victory. Echoes of it reverberated in the Scopes trial in 1925 and, as late as 1968, in a decision of the United States Supreme Court concerning the state of Arkansas. But when victory came it was complete. No one in the world of science and learning could any longer believe that the human species was a product of special creation. Few ideas at any time, except the "hypothesis" of Copernicus, have enjoyed such spectacular success.

In the United States the leading protagonist of the new doctrine was William Graham Sumner. Although Sumner was trained for a career in the Episcopal ministry, he soon directed his efforts to sociology and left his theological beliefs, as he said, in a desk drawer which he never thereafter reopened. Elected to a professorship at Yale in 1872, he gave in 1875 the first course in the United States, and possibly in the world, on sociology, a subject he later called the science of society.

According to Sumner's own account he was converted to evolution about 1875, both by a remarkable display of fossil horses exhibited by the American paleontologist Othniel C. Marsh in the Peabody Museum at Yale and by a rereading of Spencer's *Social Statics* and *First Principles*. During this same time Spencer's *Principles of Sociology* was appearing in installments, and Sumner organized a class to read them as they were published. In 1879 he clashed with Noah Porter, then president of Yale, who demanded that he abandon the use of Spencer's *Study of Sociology* as a textbook on the grounds that Spencer unfairly attacked everything tinged with theism and that it would bring "intellectual and moral harm" to the students who read it. Although the immediate issue was compromised, Sumner defended with spirit his right of choice and thereby won an important victory for academic freedom. On two other issues he annoyed the Yale establishment of his time—one of them was his stand against the protective tariff, and the other was his denunciation of the Spanish-American War.

Sumner objected to the protective tariff on the ground that it was a gross governmental intervention into what would otherwise be a natural evolutionary process. Like Spencer, who had a deep and abiding distrust of government, Sumner expressed laissez faire doctrines in their most extreme form. The evolution of society is an autonomous and spontaneous process, and any effort to interfere with it is utter folly because it is doomed to fail. In a famous essay he demanded to know "What Social Classes Owe Each Other," and his answer was a resounding "Nothing." In another essay, significantly entitled "The Absurd Effort to Make the World Over," he exhibited again his impatience with humanitarian sentiment and especially deplored the activities of those who would use the resources of government for purposes of social welfare. The trouble with all these schemes is that they ignore "the common man"—the man who works hard, does his duty, pays his taxes without complaint, and lives a frugal life. The struggle for existence is twofold. The first pits man against nature and the second pits men against other men. In these struggles only the fit survive. It is right that this should be the case. The only alternative is the survival of the unfit.

This was harsh doctrine, and it suggests that Sumner lacked the gift of *caritas*. But in his view it was also the law of the universe, and one that no human agency could change. The rising entrepreneurs of the business class in the United States were quick to agree that the growth of large-scale business enterprise was a clear example of the survival of the fittest, and thus they too joined the ranks of the Social Darwinists. Sumner's folkways themselves conformed to the universal law. The fittest of the folkways survive, that is to say, those that are best adapted to the needs they satisfy. In this respect, as in others, Sumner was consistent.

The first break in the rigidly deterministic pattern of Social Darwinism came with Lester Frank Ward. Ward, full of botany and Greek (symbiosis, karyokinesis, gynaecocracy), believed in the possibility of human achievement, the proper study of which was sociology. He saw two processes going on in society, one of them (genesis) spontaneous, and the other (telesis) involving conscious effort. One may "interfere" in order to "improve," and it is in telesis that man exerts some control over the evolutionary forces of society and helps to bring about such institutions as the state. The state, for example, is genetic in origin but telic in method, and its history exhibits four stages—the autarchic, the anarchic, the politarchic, and the pantarchic. Evolution itself is manifest in four spheres or stages—cosmogeny, biogeny, anthropogeny, and sociogeny. The system as a whole, firmly rooted in Darwinian doctrine and informed throughout by the concept of evolution, emphasizes nevertheless "the psychic factors of civilization" (the title of one of Ward's books) and offers a place for conscious control of the social process. Ward substitutes a dualism for the monism of Spencer and Sumner and the doctrine of laissez faire disappears. Indeed, Ward has been called "the philosophical architect of the welfare state," but this is a judgment that errs perhaps on the side of generosity. His sociology deviates from that of his two predecessors, but it depends nevertheless upon the language of Social Darwinism. In Ward's time there were few alternatives.

Sir Henry Sumner Maine, influenced by Savigny rather than by Darwin, published his *Ancient Law* in 1861, two years after *The Origin of Species*. In it he suggested that, like living creatures, legal ideas and institutions exhibit a coherent course of development and that social relations evolve from status to contract. Status and contract are two terms of a dichotomy that appears again and again in the literature of sociology, including the transition in Spencer from military to industrial societies, in Tönnies from *Gemeinschaft* to *Gesellschaft*, and in Durkheim (who was not, however, a Social Darwinist) from mechanical to organic solidarity.

The title of "unrepentant Darwinist" was reserved for Walter Bagehot, whose *Physics and Politics*, a series of essays first published in *The Fortnightly Review*, appeared in 1872. The book, which contains no physics and little politics, is dedicated almost entirely to the evolutionary point of view, as indicated for example by its subtitle: "Thoughts on the Application of the Principles of 'Natural Selection' and 'Inheritance' to Political Society." Bagehot had no doubt that civilized men were superior to "savages," that the difference between them was like that between tame and wild animals, that savages—like the lower classes in contemporary societies—had a "deficient sense of morals" because they practised communal marriage, and (correctly) that it is difficult to break the "cake" or "yoke" of custom. He quotes with approval Lubbock's observation that "savages unite the character of childhood with the passions and strength of men," emphasizes the predominant importance of natural selection in the early stages of human history, looks favorably upon war, thinks that civilization arose because it was a military advantage, lays it down as a law that in every age the strong prevail over the weak, and asserts that in almost every respect the strongest is also the best. "The child most fit to be a good Spartan is most likely to survive a Spartan childhood." And so also, although Bagehot does not mention it, the child of Victorian England. Spencer's slogan made it easy for those who survived to declare themselves the fittest.

If sociologists were eager to adopt the new doctrine, it was perhaps even more appropriate that the anthropologists did so. For it was Darwinism, as has been remarked, that gave anthropology its inspiration and almost its *raison d'être*. The quest for origins, the desire to know the sources of social institutions, motivated the early study of exotic peoples so far away from London. It was the American Lewis Henry Morgan, even more perhaps than the English E. B. Tylor, who gave to Spencer's developmental morphology an empirical support. In his *Ancient Society* (1877), a brilliant and original work, Morgan first refuted the "sociogeny" (to steal a word from Ward) of Archbishop Whately and then proceeded to exhibit the evolutionary process as one that moved from savagery to barbarism to civilization. The first two stages he subdivided again into lower, middle, and upper. It is in these stages, or "ethnical periods," that one finds the growth of intelligence and the institutions of government, the family, and property. The key to the process is invention, and thus each stage moves into the succeeding stage with such innovations as the use and control of fire; the bow and arrow; pottery making; the domestication of animals; the smelting of iron ore; and finally the phonetic alphabet, which ushers in the stage of civilization. Evolution, in Morgan's view, is not only technological. It has another side in which "germs of thought" accumulate in the human mind.

From Morgan through writers like Müller-Lyer, Kovalesky, A. G. Keller, and Hobhouse, the Social Darwinists, although recognizing for the most part differences in detail exhibited by different societies, sought to discover universal stages in the evolution of social institutions. Thus, technology exhibits such stages as the wood age, the stone age, the bronze age, and the iron age, the second of which is still a part of ordinary speech. The economic stages are gathering, hunting, pastoral, agricultural, and industrial. In religion the series runs from magic through animism and totemism to the reign of personal deities. Legally, the sequence runs from communal ownership to private property. Politically—although here there are more variations and doubts—a primitive headmanship marks the beginning and democracy the end of an evolutionary process. And marriage and the family, used most frequently perhaps as an illustration, was thought to have moved from sexual promiscuity through such stages as group marriage and polygamy to monogamy.

It was in the last of these, the evolution of marriage and the family, that Social Darwinism sustained its first empirical challenge. Westermarck was able to show that marriage arrangements were monogamous among peoples judged by other criteria to be quite primitive, and he cast doubt upon the theory of original promiscuity, no single instance of which could be found. Other writers disclosed that in some societies food gathering and hunting existed together, in a sexual division of labor, and that in some societies agriculture developed after hunting and without the intermediate pastoral stage. Still other peoples bypassed the bronze age in their technological evolution. The notion of the autonomous evolution of culture by means of independent invention suffered also from the contrary emphasis upon cultural diffusion in the work of Ratzel, Graebner, Koppers, Schmidt, Boas, G. Elliot Smith, W. J. Perry, and, interestingly enough, Tylor himself, who had maintained in the best Spencerian tradition that human institutions exhibit a succession that is essentially the same in all parts of the world. It may be worth an incidental note that efforts to trace standard stages in both social and cultural evolution gave rise to a discipline called historical sociology, which now has few practitioners.

A second aspect of Social Darwinism emphasized the struggle for existence among races and nations and provided an apologia both for war and for the imperial policies of the European states in the late nineteenth and early twentieth centuries. Ludwig Gumplowicz, for example, found the origin of the state in conquest and stressed the role of struggle, conflict, and war between human groups. Gustav Ratzenhofer, author of a milder conflict theory, believed nevertheless that struggle and war strengthen human societies whereas culture and commerce weaken them. Karl Pearson, although he expressed distaste for the horrors that resulted from universal hostility, insisted that without war the race would soon be populated by men of feeble type, sheltering themselves in caves. In the view of Ernest Renan, there is only one way in which civilization has advanced, and that is in the struggle of race with race and the survival of the superior.

The question was raised, however, whether the selection induced by war was positive or negative. Darwin at first inclined to the former view, maintaining that the incessant warfare among savage tribes was proof of the principle of natural selection in that only the strong survived to reproduce their kind. To this Alfred Russel Wallace, his generous critic, replied that the contrary was the case, that warfare eliminated the brave and strong and left the weak to reproduce—a position to which Darwin finally subscribed. The issue was unresolved in the writings of the Social Darwinists. Supporters of the negative view pointed to the fact that armies are constituted of the "finest flower" of a nation's youth, that soldiers are in the best of health because the physically and mentally defective are rejected for military service, and that they belong to the age group that could most effectively reproduce their kind. Unfortunately, they are the ones deprived of this latter possibility because for long periods they have no access to their wives and because they suffer disease, injury, and death. The civilians who remain behind—the mentally, morally, and physically deficient—escape the ravages of war and live to reproduce themselves. War thus exterminates the fit and preserves the unfit, with deleterious consequences for the race. Vaccaro especially made a point of this, suggesting that the conquerors in a war always do away with the strongest, most courageous, and most intelligent of the conquered, following the Roman rule *parcere subjectes et debellare superbos* (spare the submissive and demolish the proud). Thus war strengthens the traits of servility in those who survive. War not only preserves the unfit; it creates unfitness in that it increases the incidence of injury and disease, especially venereal disease, and thus serves as a primary instrument of negative selection.

The positive school argued, on the contrary, that these dire consequences do not ensue. Even in war, the strong, the brave, and the intelligent have resources that contribute to their survival and permit them to retain a reproductive advantage over the weak, the cowardly, and the dull. It is the person of this superior type who can more easily sustain the hardship and disease that are the inevitable accompaniments of war. Disease kills more soldiers than enemy action, and thus the strong maintain their advantage. Students of war, like C. P. Steinmetz for example, suggested that it is not war but peace that is negatively selective because peace maximizes the chances of weaklings and introduces vice and a loss of virility into a population. Furthermore, even if it be conceded that war negatively selects males for survival, it has the opposite effect upon females. As the number of males decreases in proportion to females, as a result of war's decimation, it intensifies the competition among the latter for mates and consequently only the fittest among *them* win the opportunity to reproduce. Finally, whatever may be said about individuals, war positively selects societies for survival. Nations struggle with one another for power, prestige, and imperial glory; the victor deserves to win, and the superior societies survive. Without war such selection among nations would not be possible. It is for this reason that Treitschke spoke of war as a "holy ordeal" and one that rightly determines the destinies of peoples.

With respect to social selection apart from war, there were

again both optimists and pessimists among the Social Darwinists. Otto Ammon, an optimist, believed that the selection of the fittest has favorable consequences and conduces to strong individuals. In a Malthusian world, the weak die of hunger and fail to reproduce, and thus nature has one method, so to speak, of correcting her mistakes. Two social institutions produce the same result. One of these is education and the other is the law. The former filters out the mentally dull, those who literally cannot make the grade, and the latter banishes the delinquent and criminal to a limbo, whether incarceration or not, in which opportunities for procreation are minimal. F. H. Giddings supported this view with the suggestion that the transformation of immorality into crime was one of the ways in which the socially unfit are eliminated, thus giving an advantage to the law-abiding. Ammon also viewed egalitarian doctrines with disfavor: a class society is to be encouraged because it helps to prevent an otherwise indiscriminate breeding that would lead to the degeneration of the race. With sentiments like Sumner's he argued that humanitarianism must be resisted because it can only lead to the survival of the unfit and then to the vengeance of nature itself when a nation, forced into war, finds itself left with only the weak to fight it.

Vacher de Lapouge, on the other hand, was a pessimist. In his view, social selection, unlike natural selection, has negative consequences and assures the survival of the unfit. If war destroys the brave and preserves the timid, so do politics, religion, morality, the law, economic systems, occupations, and urban living. In politics it is the demagogue, the cunning person, the manipulator, who win the prizes. In religion it is the leaders— most notably in Catholicism—who conform most closely to the ideal of continence and who therefore leave the fewest children. Law is a set of artificial codes which strong men violate. They are thereupon sent to jail, where they are unable to reproduce. Monogamy prevents even the superior man from reproducing more than once a year. In the economic sphere the speculators are hardly society's ideal, and yet it is they who succeed. In occupational selection the highest skills accompany the lowest fertility—contrast the factory laborer with the Oxford don. Finally, urban life contributes its doleful bit to the degenerative process. It is the adventurous and the enterprising who are attracted to the city, which then robs them of their vitality. On the other hand, those who are too inert to move, the farm and village dwellers, reproduce their kind. Social selection in short is negative to the degree that it interferes with the natural selection that would otherwise obtain. Once more the issue was unresolved, but the arguments on both sides were informed and motivated by evolutionary theory. Social Darwinism was so pervasive a creed that even its critics were members of the school.

A third aspect of Social Darwinism is the stimulus it gave to a renewed use of the organic analogy. For Spencer, societies, like organisms, begin as germs (i.e., minute masses), undergo continuous growth, exhibit "increase of structure," have parts that show differentiation of function, and finally constitute an aggregate that resembles in many ways an individual organism. Conversely, every organism of any size is also a society. Spencer pursues his analogy in detail and finds systems of organs in society, including the sustaining system, the distributing system, and the regulating system. He notes also the respects in which society is unlike an organism, but some writers neglected his qualifications. Bluntschli, for example, thought of the state as an organic being with a body (its constitution) and a soul (the national spirit) and convinced himself in addition that the state was masculine and the church feminine. Lilienfeld insisted that society actually is an organism and not merely like one, that it exhibits all the biological processes that are found in nature and possesses a cellular structure. Schäffle found five types of social tissue in the "organ-system" of the state—a skeletal, a nervous, a muscular, a nutritional, and a locomotional system. Fouillée, less extreme, enunciated a theory of society as a "contractual organism" which was both a natural and an artificial product. Worms, at first the most extravagant of these writers, conceived of society as a superorganism and wrote of its anatomy, physiology, pathology, and hygiene, but in a late edition of his book *Organism and Society* he moderated his views and began to question the merits of the analogy.

The organic analogy gradually disappeared from the literature of social science during the second and third decades of the twentieth century, and it would now be difficult to find a sociologist who takes it seriously. Expressions that have their source in the vocabulary of biology, however, are not always easy to avoid, as the works of Spengler (especially), Sorokin, and Toynbee testify. But ever since Durkheim, and in large part because of him, sociologists have insisted that society is a reality *sui generis* and cannot profitably be identified or compared with anything else. Indeed, it was a late Social Darwinist, Hobhouse, who said that to speak of society as if it were a physical organism was to indulge in "a piece of mysticism."

No one can date the demise of Social Darwinism. There was no funeral. The evolutionary view of society, once the majority view, has few contemporary protagonists, and none in the old Spencerian terms. If those who celebrated, in 1959, the centenary of the publication of *The Origin of Species* mentioned natural selection, or social selection, or the struggle for existence, or the survival of the fittest, it was as a tribute to Darwin and not as a reaffirmation of the evolutionary principle as an explanation of the history of human societies. Darwin and Spencer and all the members of their school provided one, and it was an explanation that gave satisfaction for the better part of a century. But Social Darwinism has now expired, and the story of society requires a new and different theory in terms of which its changes, its harmonies, and its vicissitudes can be read and understood.

PART 2

ON METHODOLOGICAL MATTERS

The essays in this section require less description and certainly less autobiography than those in Part 1. In these the contumacity that disfigured several of the earlier essays has, I trust, disappeared, and the shouting matches have given way to more sober study and reflection. This is not to say that they lack all polemical quality. On the contrary, each is addressed to an issue on which responsible scholars have held a variety of opinions.

The first essay, "The Limitations of Anthropological Methods in Sociology," was stimulated by the rise to prominence during World War II of anthropologists on the general cultural scene in the United States. Previously a relatively obscure tribe occupying a small and somewhat remote terrain in the groves of academe, anthropologists began to venture forth and to explore some of the lands long settled by earlier colonists. Once limited, by their own designs, to the study of nonliterate peoples, they began to hobnob with the literate and to talk about the Russians, the Japanese, and the Americans as they had previously talked about the Zuni, the Hopi, and the Kwakiutl. Indeed, mention of these last three recalls Ruth Benedict's justly famous *Patterns of Culture*, a book that everyone read and everyone welcomed as a new approach to the understanding of societies. Anthropologists began to explain total cultures in terms of "character structure" or "basic personality type." The key to the Russian character, for example, was discovered in the fact that Russian infants were placed in swaddling clothes, and the key to the American in father rejection, i.e., the native sons' rejection of their immigrant fathers. The toilet-training practices of various peoples were examined in detail and used as clues to national character. We were told indeed that because of the successful methods of the anthropologists we knew more about the Trobrianders than we did about ourselves. Anthropologists thus found themselves in demand as advisers to military intelligence agencies and sought after for high posts in both governmental and educational administration. The first director of the Russian Research Center at Harvard, for example, was a brilliant anthropologist whose linguistic abilities, though considerable, did not extend to the Russian language.

It seemed to me that many of these interpretations were meretricious and that, whatever advantages they might have in helping us to understand nonliterate societies, they were wanting in credibility when applied to the literate. Toilet training surely had much less to do with the American society in the twentieth century than, say, the history of constitutional law. In any event, it was reflections like these that induced me to question the use of anthropological methods for sociological purposes in the paper reprinted here. I reprint also the gentle rejoinder by the late Clyde Kluckhohn, a personal friend of mine for whose work I had, and still have, a large respect.

The paper entitled "A Critique of Empiricism in Sociology" is a negative response to an orthodoxy. In the sociology of the

1940s—and perhaps even more today—the methodological emphasis rested almost entirely upon empirical research. In few disciplines was there so embarrassing a hiatus between research and theory. Both Parsons and Merton had addressed important papers to the relations between the two. Their conclusions, however, left me vaguely unsatisfied. Even more unsatisfactory was the constant and almost tiresome stress upon empiricism in the purely theoretical and abstract writings of American sociologists, even among those, like Parsons and Dodd for example, so disparate that they hardly fit into the same discipline. In any event, it seemed to me that the virtues of empiricism were simply assumed; that an appreciation of the limitations and consequences of so one-sided an emphasis had not been exhibited; that empiricism, however appropriate when controlled, does not exhaust the resources of sociological method; and that the subject could profit from further examination.

This is not the place to expatiate upon the role of rationalism in sociological inquiry. It does seem to me, however, that many of the research studies required for advanced degrees in sociology in the United States are carried on for their own sake, as exercises in technique, and that most such studies lack all theoretical relevance. Sociological knowledge is thus noncumulative, quasi-scientific paradigms persist, and principles and laws are conspicuous by their absence. As I have said elsewhere, the intellectual significance of much of the research done in sociology varies inversely with the precision of the methods employed. Method takes precedence over substance, and research is driven into smaller and smaller corners where we learn what we have no desire or need to know. I do not contend, on the other hand, that rationalism can cure all our ills. I contend only that both rationalism and empiricism are susceptible to the excesses of enthusiasm and that, whatever the philosophers have said in their epistemological endeavors, sociological inquiry requires a judicious mixture of both.

The brief paper entitled "*Wertfreiheit* and American Sociology" is a distillation of views I have expressed in a number of other papers. It was commissioned by the Department of State, along with other articles on American sociology, in the interest of cultural exchange between the United States and Poland and published in *Przeglad Kulturalny* (The Cultural Review). I was later informed that a rebuttal appeared in *Pravda*, but I made no effort to find it.

The arguments for and against ethical, political, and ideological neutrality are so well known that no one would profit from a rehearsal of them here. One of the ironies in the history of the discipline, however, is that for several decades early in this century sociologists fought valiantly to free themselves from any taint of social reform and avoided identification with missionaries, preachers, politicians, and others engaged in moral uplift. Now, as the century wanes, the newer sociologists have joined those on the other side of the barricades and tell us that we have political responsibilities we may not neglect; that the world situation requires political action on the part of sociologists; and that there are two kinds of sociology: "Marxist" sociology and "academic" sociology. One wonders, parenthetically, if these sociologists would also argue that there is a Marxist botany and an academic botany or, to dredge up a disgraceful episode in the history of thought, a Stalinist genetics and a scientific genetics. However much one may respect the passions of the activists and salute their ambitions, it remains the case that advocacy is one thing, inquiry quite another, and no good— sociological or otherwise—can come from confusing them. If action requires commitment, as it surely does, scholarship on the contrary requires detachment. One importunes; the other operates *sub specie aeternitatis*.

The essay entitled "Nominal and Real Definitions in Sociological Theory" contains nothing original, except insofar as a distinction in logic is applied directly to sociology. My indebtedness to Cohen and Nagel and to Ralph Eaton for the distinction itself is apparent and sincerely acknowledged.

The essay was written at a time when American sociologists were indulging in intense criticism of the language of their own discipline. It was an era, in the thirties and forties, in which something called "general semantics" was in fashion. Count Alfred Korzybski had published his *Science and Sanity* and founded a movement—some would say a cult—dedicated to the dry cleaning of words. Let us eradicate all the Aristotelian assumptions hidden in our use of language, let us build "structural differentials" to keep us from hopping carelessly from one level of abstraction to another, and let us acknowledge that the purification of language can have therapeutic results in everything from physics to sociology and from psychiatry to dentistry. Writers like Stuart Chase and S. I. Hayakawa wrote immensely popular treatises on "the tyranny of words" (Chase's title), and no less a person than Bertrand Russell added a book to the list. Most of them took no cognizance of the fact that what they had to say had been considered with much more sophistication and expressed in much better prose by the philosophers of the British empirical tradition.

A problem of language nevertheless remains. Controversies arise and often persist because of linguistic ambiguities. Some of them, though not all of course, succumb to linguistic clarification. William James, for example, recounts somewhere the problem of the man, the squirrel, and the tree. A squirrel on a tree will keep the trunk between itself and the man who tries to watch it. Thus, the man may walk 360 degrees around the tree without seeing the squirrel because the squirrel is always 180 degrees away, behind the trunk of the tree. There is no doubt that the man goes around the tree and that the squirrel goes around the tree. The question is, does the man go around the squirrel? It is a question that could stimulate an angry debate. It is, however, easily resolved. The answer depends upon what we mean by "around." If we mean that the man occupies successive positions to the east, north, west, and south of the squirrel it is clear that he does go around the squirrel. If, on the contrary, we mean that the man occupies successive positions in front of, to the left of, behind, and to the right of the squirrel, then it is equally clear that he does not. Thus easily do we put the argument to rest.

In the same way we can answer such questions as whether the definition of sociological concepts ought to be clear and distinct before we begin our inquiry or whether they only can become so in the process of inquiry. Here again the answer depends on what we mean by "definition." As the essay indicates, if we are talking about nominal definitions the first answer is correct; if we are talking about real definitions the second is correct. Once more a controversy loses its heat and, in fact, disappears.

The last essay in this section carries an awkward title—"The Ethics of Cognitive Communication"—for which I have no responsibility. It was assigned to me by an editor. The editor and I were both members of a seminar which met from time to time in New York City to discuss issues of mutual interest and concern. Among the members were theologians, philosophers, psychiatrists, social scientists, physical scientists, and several representatives from the humanities. When it came my turn to lead the discussion, I raised the problem of the advantages and disadvantages accruing to the construction and use of technical vocabularies in various disciplines. These vocabularies are easily recognized in the physical sciences, less so in the social sciences. In the latter, words are taken from the lexicon of ordinary speech and assigned technical connotations. They thus carry a double burden—one connotation that is common and another that is technical—and one of the consequences is an ambiguity that can interfere with communication. The problem is the desirability of technical terminologies on the one hand and the abuses they invite on the other. One of my colleagues, the editor mentioned, asked me to reproduce my remarks in writing, and the result is the article in question. I should say that the fact that I found five arguments against technical vocabularies and only four in favor does not necessarily mean that my vote would finally go for the negative.

I have an additional sentiment with which to conclude these observations on my methodological essays. It has to do with an

Aristotelian mean. There are two mistakes that sociologists can commit with respect to methodology. (By methodology, of course, I refer to the logic of inquiry and not to methods of research.) The first mistake is never to be concerned with methodological issues, and the second is never to be concerned with anything else. Sociological theory presents serious methodological issues, some of them unique (e.g., the appropriate level of abstraction on which to operate), and neither innocence nor disdain can help our discipline along. Too much concern for methodological issues, on the other hand, can be equally unproductive because it leads ineluctably to epistemological questions to which two thousand years of philosophical speculation have been able to supply no wholly satisfactory answers. Some methodological problems, in short, have no solutions, and a profitless pursuit of them can therefore contribute neither to methodology nor to sociology. For sociologists two levels of sophistication are involved—the first a sensitivity to methodological problems and the second a recognition of their ultimate irresolvability. With respect to methodology, an Aristotelian mean resides somewhere between too little and too much.

7

The Limitations of
Anthropological
Methods in Sociology

[1948]

One of the more interesting of contemporary developments in the
social sciences is the increasingly intimate relationship between
sociology and anthropology. The influence of anthropological
methods, concepts, and even theories has become so powerful in
recent years that for many purposes and in many areas of investigation the two sciences have become indistinguishable. In a
number of academic departments the personnel is the same, and
in the universities where separate departments are maintained
research and teaching in social anthropology and sociology are
characterized by ever closer co-operation. This development has
reached a point, indeed, where it is assumed that an anthropologist can, without further preparation, teach introductory courses
in sociology, although, for some reason, the contrary assumption
is seldom made. In the meantime, anthropologists have, in recent
years, begun to invade the precincts of literate societies and have

begun, in addition, to talk even more broadly about American culture as a whole.

All these developments indicate that the historical and still somewhat common distinction between sociology and anthropology, which would have the former deal with peoples who read and write and the latter with those who do not, has come increasingly to be one without significance. In general, of course, this is a wholesome sign, as is any indication that the doors which often separate the sciences are beginning to open a little and to admit fruitful hypotheses, ideas, theories, methods, and techniques from one to another. It is even more encouraging in the case of anthropology and sociology, for the contributions they have to make to each other are beyond all reckoning. It may be recalled that only a systematic and thoroughgoing study of the nonliterate peoples in the far corners of the earth was able to rectify the naïve faith in the necessary evolution of social institutions which had characterized the social thought of the nineteenth century.

Indeed, anthropologists have made enormous contributions to contemporary thought in sociology, political science, law, and economics—contributions which have been of the highest import even when not entirely original or exclusively anthropological. They are so well known that they require no repetition. The notion of cultural relativity, for example, is indispensable in any objective inquiry into human societies.[1] The comparative study of societies could not have been accomplished at all without the detailed data collected by anthropologists among nonliterate peoples widely separated in space. It is only through a profound appreciation of contrasting cultures, of "perverse" and exotic customs, that the sociologist is able to achieve that extra-dimensionality without which he cannot hope to understand his own society. Goethe's remark, "Wer fremde Sprache nicht kennt,

---

[1] This notion was well known to many of the ancients, including, for example, Boethius, who remarked: "The customs and laws of diverse nations do so much differ the one from the other, that the same thing which some commend as laudable, others condemn as deserving punishment" (*De consolatione philosophiae* ["Loeb Classical Library"], II, 215).

weiss nichts von seiner eigenen," applies with equal force to societies. Such contrasts supply the data which enable the sociologist to transform the details of social relationship and of social organization into sociological principles. For this again the sociologist owes a not inconsiderable debt to the anthropologist. The debt became incommensurable when Robert and Helen Lynd asked anthropological questions of a contemporary American community and when other sociologists, too numerous to mention, followed them in the like design.

Therefore, if we now raise certain questions bearing upon possible limitations of these anthropological procedures and methods in sociological research, the questions are prompted neither by a lack of appreciation for anthropological contributions nor by a desire to minimize their importance. They relate rather to the opinion, to be fortified in what follows, that there are compelling reasons for supposing that it is still profitable and, indeed, necessary to maintain a distinction between the two sciences, to say that anthropological concepts and methods are one thing and sociological concepts and methods quite another. Because of the ever increasing pressures of the former upon the latter the problem is not without importance in defining the orientation of sociology and particularly in articulating its position with respect to anthropology.

The first limitation of anthropological methods in sociological research is that, designed as they were for an approach to nonliterate societies,[2] they cannot do full justice to societies that

---

[2] The expression, of course, is an ellipsis. Only people, not societies, are literate or illiterate. The term "nonliterate" is preferred by many anthropologists because it avoids a possible value-judgment contained in the term "illiterate." "Nonliterate," however, is a contradictory of "literate" rather than a contrary, and accordingly it embraces too much. The two terms together exhaust the universe itself and not merely a universe of discourse, for it is obvious that not only "savages" but also shoes and sealing-wax and sidewalks are nonliterate. "Illiterate" is thus the more logical term, and it need not have a pejorative connotation. "Preliterate," on the other hand, has a temporal prefix from which an invalid inference can easily be drawn. In spite o. .he logical fault in "nonliterate," however, we shall conform to current practices and continue to use it.

are literate. This is, in fact, their principal limitation. The term "nonliterate" has become so familiar as a label that the sociological significance of nonliteracy has been ignored, and with it the contrasting significance of literacy. No difference could be more fundamental than that between peoples who can read and write and those who cannot. It is a difference which exercises a profound effect upon all the attributes of the two kinds of societies, on all their functions and relations, and in their entire social organization. It is not for nothing that our foremost social thinkers have constructed dichotomies and invented labels to characterize not two different social phenomena but two different kinds of social phenomena—the *Gemeinschaft* and *Gesellschaft* of Tönnies, the community and society of MacIver, the status and contract of Maine, the mechanical and organic solidarity of Durkheim, the military and industrial society of Spencer, the ethnic and demotic societies of Giddings, the folk-culture and civilization of Redfield. While these famous labels do not all point in precisely the same direction, they nonetheless signalize types of differences that can be ignored only on pain of incomplete understanding. And the most important distinction of all is that between those societies which have the gift of literacy and those which do not. An approach which has in general confined itself to the nonliterate aspects of culture is likely to be unduly narrow and not altogether free from unintentional bias when applied to societies that are distinguished, above all, by their literacy.

It ought not to be forgotten, in fact, that a literate society has a literate culture and that its written traditions and recorded conventions, its theories of man and nature and society, determine in considerable measure its historical destiny. The contrast between literacy and nonliteracy is an extreme one, a contrast whose ramifications extend to every sphere of social life. Although a nonliterate society has a language, it has no alphabet; it has customs but no laws, legends but no literature, techniques but no science, art but no aesthetics, religion but no theology, a Weltanschauung but no philosophy. Thus, although anthropological methods are well adapted to the nonliterate, behavioral aspects of culture—those indicated by the first term in each of the above pairs—they are not at all adapted to those literate aspects indicated by the second. The utilization of anthropological methods encourages an undue emphasis upon the first and relative neglect of the second. Proper as these procedures are when applied to societies in which nothing corresponds to these second terms, they lose their exclusive propriety when applied to societies which, because of their literacy, we call "civilizations." The anthropologist or the sociologist who restricts himself to anthropological methods is likely to ignore the profound importance of these things when he studies contemporary literate societies. Indeed, just as anthropologists are notorious for their neglect of library research,[3] so sociologists, and particularly American sociologists, are notorious for their neglect of historical methods and materials. Any method which emphasizes the nonliterate aspects of culture at the expense of the literate invites a set of conclusions which, however sound and suggestive in themselves, are destined to miss the main streams of significance in a literate society.

By "anthropological methods" we mean all the techniques currently employed by anthropologists both in the field and in the study: the autobiography, the life-history, the case study, participant and nonparticipant observation, the use of informants, linguistic analysis, statistical manipulation of traits when possible, psychological and psychiatric testing, and others well illustrated in a number of recent studies of nonliterate peoples. It is not contended that these methods and techniques fail to supply correct answers, for, indeed, the contrary is the case. It is asserted instead that they are methods designed to answer questions whose significance is limited when the subject under investigation is a literate society. These questions almost always have a great deal of intrinsic interest, but they have much less relevance to the society as a whole than have certain other questions which can be answered only by other, more sociological methods.

---

[3] An admission by one of their number, to whom the criticism does not apply (see Clyde Kluckhohn, *The Personal Document in Anthropological Science* [Social Science Research Council Bull. 53 (1945)], p. 83).

The inefficacy of one of these methods in sociological research can be easily illustrated by a simple comparison. The anthropologist in the field usually employs one or several members of the society he is studying to act as an informant and often uses these people both as informants and as interpreters. The sociologist, on the other hand, is embarrassed by a plethora of informants—informants who have themselevs described and analyzed their culture in published works of an infinite variety, ranging from novels and poems and newspaper columns to historical, scientific, and popular studies. This latter phenomenon, universal in literate societies, does not occur in the nonliterate. The anthropologist must rely upon informants personally known to him because he has no alternative. "When he gets a little closer to town," however, as Everett C. Hughes once expressed the change,[4] and begins to meet people who are neither illiterate nor inarticulate, this method loses all its efficacy.

A second limitation of anthropological methods in sociology is that they necessarily focus upon a society at a particular time and that that particular time is always the present—the day, season, year, or even period of years during which the anthropologist does his field work. The methods work, when they do, only because the society, being nonliterate, has no history. If it has a history, these methods do not disclose it. They cannot grasp historicity. The societies themselves, to use one of C. F. Atkinson's words, are distinguished by their "historylessness." And this—this "historylessness"—is a differentiating characteristic that ranks next to nonliteracy in sociological importance. The first consequence of this condition is that the past, an understanding of which is indispensable in the study of literate societies, has no significance which can be discerned by anthropological methods. It is probably unnecessary to document, by illustration or example, the importance of the time dimension for even an elementary effort to explain the present circumstances and contemporaneous

---

4 In a review of *Suye Mura: A Japanese Village*, by John Embree (*American Journal of Sociology*, XLVI [1940], 253).

customs of literate societies. Civilized societies are continuous developments, their destiny accords with their history, and their most complex and intricate structures have been conceived from causes operating in both the near and the distant past. Such is the power and importance of a written tradition. Nothing like it can be discovered in the annals of nonliterate peoples, not because their past, too, may not have been important but because they have no annals. No man knows their history. The application of anthropological methods to literate societies, therefore, cannot help but encourage the illusion that it is possible to understand a culture without understanding its history.[5]

A corollary of "historylessness," a third limitation of anthropological methods, is that, like the category of time, the category of causality tends largely to be ignored. Explanations, when indulged in, are sought chiefly in the life-histories of individuals. Analyses of the society as a whole, as well as of its folkways, mores, and institutions, proceed in terms of psychological processes and concepts. The temperament and character of individuals are given more weight than are historical antecedents and events, some of which may have been of momentous consequence. Indeed, the problem of personality takes precedence over problems of institutional history. Some anthropologists do not regard this as a limitation but see it rather as an additional virtue or advantage of their methods. For example, Ruth Benedict has written: "In studies of Western nations one who is untrained in studies of comparative cultures overlooks whole areas of behavior. He takes so much for granted that he does not explore the range of trivial habits in daily living and all those accepted verdicts on homely matters, which, thrown large on the national screen, have more to do with that nation's future than treaties signed by diplomats."[6]

---

[5] Mr. Kermit Lansner, a graduate student of philosophy at Columbia University, has expressed it in this way: "In the case of nonliterate societies you can read only one page, the last; in the case of literate societies you have the whole book."

[6] *The Chrysanthemum and the Sword* (Boston: Houghton Mifflin Co., 1946), pp. 9–10.

The point at issue does not concern the importance of knowing "the range of trivial habits in daily living" in all societies, literate as well as nonliterate. It concerns rather the assumption that these habits exercise a determining influence upon a nation's future. This assumption is not only a gratuitous one but also, because it is becoming increasingly axiomatic among anthropologists, a dangerous one. No evidence is offered to support it. It would seem, on the contrary, as if most folkways and mores, including "trivial habits," operate as conservative and stabilizing elements in a society and that explanations of innovations and changes which bear upon the future would have to be sought elsewhere. It is more probable indeed, although this is likewise a proposition bereft of evidence, that a *knowledge* of foreign folkways and mores, such as is exhibited in books like Miss Benedict's, will be more influential in affecting a nation's future, and especially its public and foreign policies, than would the folkways and mores themselves. The cultural fact that Miss Benedict published this book might just possibly be a fact at variance with one of her own assertions.

Since foreign folkways are usually discovered, described, and explained in terms of the life-histories of individuals, the methods involved, as suggested above, introduce a covert psychological bias into the study of societies. To assume, for example, that toilet-training—a cultural device which currently fascinates a number of anthropologists—can explain the rise of Hitler, the waning of the British Empire, the conflict between Hindu and Moslem, an American presidential election, the power of a Petrillo, the growing tension between Russia and the United States, or any of the general type phenomena of which these are special cases, is to illustrate how ludicrous some of these approaches have become and to steer perilously close to nonsense.

A fourth principal difference between the two distinct kinds of societies, the nonliterate and the literate, is a purely demographic one. Size is a significant conditioning factor in any society. It helps to determine the number, kind, and intensity of the social relationships that obtain in it. The multiplicity of roles which each individual in a populous community plays, the numerous statuses he possesses, can hardly be compared to the number of roles and statuses which a nonliterate society, with its limited division of labor and with its little diversification of function, offers to its members. Once again it is unnecessary to illustrate this point in detail, for illustrations of it are infinite. It may be suggested, however, that kinship positions largely exhaust the status possibilities of the nonliterate. For the members of our modern, complex, civilized society, on the other hand, the statuses derived from family or kin membership as such seem fairly small in number and of no great consequence. Social mobility, both vertical and horizontal, within the large culture area of a modern society further reduces the significance of kin status and enhances the importance of roles and statuses that are beyond the ken of men who have not learned to read and write.

A corollary of size, of course, is cultural diversity and variety. As the number of social relationships increases, as social interaction is intensified by increase in size of population, so do the different kinds of relationships increase. The number of different occupations in a city the size of Chicago, for example, is again almost infinitely large in contrast to those available to the denizens of a thinly populated island in the sea. For that matter, there is no nonliterate phenomenon that is comparable in any way to a modern city. To assume that the methods which will garner knowledge about the Indians who live in the vicinity of a trading post in New Mexico will serve equally well when applied to the Americans who live in the vicinity of Times Square in New York is to indulge in a recklessness that is unusual in modern social science. Although the individuals in both situations may have a number of things in common and although some of these things may be quite basic, such as, for example, certain physiological and psychological and even cultural needs, it is only what they do not have in common which affects the different destinies of the two societies. The nonliterate may be conscious of the certainty of death, but of the certainty of taxes he knows nothing.

A fifth fundamental difference between a nonliterate and a literate society is that the former is almost always relatively isolated from other societies. This is by no means universally the case, for some contacts between two adjoining societies do occur and sometimes they come to be relatively common, even though seldom institutionalized. In general, however, such is not the case, and the anthropologist has been justified in attending to a culture as if it were, in fact, an isolated unit. In no case in the nonliterate world do we find it necessary to take account of constant interrelations between societies. In the literate world, on the contrary, recognition of all kinds of intersocietal contact and interaction, from the apparentation and affiliation of Toynbee to political, diplomatic, military, commercial, and cultural exchanges, is required for even an abecedarian understanding.

The sociological consequences of geographical isolation are considerable. In the absence of literate communication, geographical isolation means also cultural isolation. Both kinds of isolation, the one a corollary of the other, tend to intensify the cohesion, the unity, and the integration of the isolated society. Thus it is sometimes possible to speak of "patterns of culture" and of cultural integration in the case of the nonliterate situation; it is seldom, if ever, possible to do so in the same sense in the case of the literate. In the latter case, as was already recognized by Spencer, heterogeneity is the rule; formal organizations, institutions, and ideologies are themselves in conflict or at the very least engaged in the service of diverse and sometimes contrary goals; and individual deviation is at a maximum. The multiplicity and relativity of norms prevent universal conformity and consequently inhibit integration even when individual deviation is at a minimum. In any civilized society there is a plurality of systems of government, of economics, of religion, of ethics, and so on, placed in juxtaposition the one to the others and each striving for hegemony. Thus, without exaggerating the degree of integration of nonliterate societies, it is yet possible to see that the same degree of uniformity in literate societies is almost inconceivable. The same conclusion holds, inversely, with respect to stratification.

One of the principal reasons for the absence of homogeneity and integration in the case of a civilization is the rapidity and frequency of intercultural contacts between civilizations. These contacts occur in both space and time. They are both institutionalized and noninstitutionalized. A literate society is never isolated from its contemporaries. Indeed, its relations with its neighbors in space determine in large measure its own internal activities. The social and political history of the society which is the United States, for example, has been determined to an extreme degree by its relations with such other societies as the English, the French, the Mexican, the Spanish, the German, the Japanese, and the Russian. This phenomenon, though naturally not wholly absent in nonliterate societies, has there a significance that is minuscule in comparison. In other words, it is not necessary to study a nonliterate society in terms of its relations with others, even though such relations are sometimes present. In studying civilization, on the other hand, these relations may not be ignored. Recognition of this difference brings with it recognition of a correlative limitation of anthropological methods. These methods focus primarily upon a society itself, as it is bounded by geographical and cultural dimensions. For an investigation of the contacts between civilizations, contacts which have been constant in the history of literate societies, the sociologist must use other procedures. The importance of the enterprise, especially at this nervous stage of the world's history, is probably not less than that of understanding a society itself in terms of its internal relations and structures.

The remarks of the preceding paragraphs apply equally well and perhaps even more obviously when attention is shifted from spatial to temporal relations, for it is apparent that, whereas the nonliterate responds to only one environment—that which is contemporaneous with his own lifetime—the literate man responds to many—environments from all ages, including the Arabian and Phoenician, for example, for his numbers and letters—and is therefore never simply the creature of his own time and place and culture. He may, if he chooses, "live" in the ancient age of Athens or of Rome or in any of the remote recesses of history. He is consequently never restricted as to time, never "timebound" in the way that the nonliterate is.

Anthropology has done much to lay the ghost of ethnocentrism, the Baconian "idol of the tribe" which in an earlier period impaired the objectivity of social research. Anthropological methods at the present time, however, are giving rise to a complementary "idol," an idol which, for want of a better name, may be called "temporocentrism." "Temporocentrism" may be defined as the unexamined and largely unconscious acceptance of one's own century, one's own era, one's own lifetime, as the center of sociological significance, as the focus to which all other periods of historical time are related, and as the criterion by which they are judged. It is thus the temporal analogue of ethnocentrism. Now, although anthropology has performed a distinguished service in reducing the subjectivism necessarily associated with ethnocentrism, it has had a contrary influence with respect to temporocentrism. Anthropological methods, atemporal and unhistorical as they are, induce an implicit assumption that the days when the anthropologist happens to be in the field observing a particular society are typical days in the life of that society. This assumption may often be warranted when the society is a nonliterate one and when the processes of social change move with a slow and deliberate pace. Even if unwarranted, little can be done about it. The same assumption is never warranted, however, in the study of literate societies. The transference of anthropological methods over to the literate historical society, therefore, does serious injustice to the passage of time and ignores the changes that make the days, the years, and the decades differ from one another. The sociologist who limits himself to anthropological methods cannot escape the restrictions with respect to temporocentrism that these methods impose. He cannot escape the illusion which they foster that the present is more important than the past.[7]

---

[7] It is interesting to note, incidentally, that the Lynds, widely hailed for their application of anthropological methods to an American community, did not limit themselves to these methods. They utilized, of course, all the written records they could find. But it is of the utmost significance, in addition, that they found it desirable to write *two* Middletowns, not one, and that they were steadily and consistently conscious of the fact that the second Middletown was not the first Middletown, even though only a decade separated the investigations.

In the preceding pages we have emphasized a number of differences between two kinds of societies, the nonliterate and the literate, which restrict the efficacy of anthropological methods when applied to the latter. There are other differences, of course, and nothing would be easier than to expatiate upon them. For the present purpose, however, these five, with their corollaries, will suffice. We may summarize them as follows: (1) Some societies are literate; others are nonliterate. Constant use of these terms as labels has obscured the very great sociological significance of the distinction. Indeed, it is probable that the single most important distinguishing characteristic of any society is its literacy or its nonliteracy. (2) A literate society has a history; a nonliterate society has none. The time category may not be ignored in the study of a historical society; it has no relevance to historylessness. (3) Without time and history, questions of social causation suffer a diminished importance in the study of non-literate societies. The category of causation depends, after all, upon time; the category of social causation upon history. (4) Differences in size invariably produce other differences, which ramify in all the compartments of culture and all phases of social interaction. Finally, (5) nonliterate societies are relatively isolated geographically and culturally. Literate societies, on the other hand, are intersections of intercultural influences in both time and space. The former can be investigated largely in terms of themselves; the latter can be understood only by attending, in addition, to their relations with other societies. Anthropological methods, however adequate they may be for anthropological research into nonliterate societies, are consequently inadequate for full sociological inquiry into literate societies. When applied to the latter, they introduce unsuspected biases into the premises and hypotheses of research, encourage the development of dubious emphases, and result in the elaboration of insignificant and often trivial complexes of culture traits. In all cases they miss altogether the trends of most significance—historical, political, economic, legal, literary, scientific, and philosophical—in the life of a literate society.

These conclusions are nowhere exhibited to better advantage

than in the application of anthropological methods to American culture as a whole, a practice that has become increasingly popular during the past decade. An enthusiast for this practice has written:

> Developments in anthropological theory and practise in recent years make it possible to apply the methods used in studying primitive societies to an analysis of American culture. The American way of life . . . has remained, curiously enough, beyond the direct scrutiny of most social scientists, and the ironical fact is that more is actually understood about the culture of the Trobriand Islanders, for example, than of Americans.[8]

This is the kind of statement which tends to drive sociologists and historians to such dissipations as the excessive use of exclamation points. Anthropologists doubtless know more about the Trobrianders than they do about the Americans. A facetious critic might remark that if they continue to use anthropological methods in the study of American culture they will continue to know more about the Trobrianders; for these methods do not disclose the data which are most significant for the development and contemporary condition of American culture. For this latter inquiry historical and sociological methods must supplement the anthropological. The culture of the Americans, after all, is a historical, literate culture.

A stunning example of the inadequacy of anthropological methods in the study of American culture is the well-known and popular book by Margaret Mead.[9] This book is full of insights. It is also full of alarums, excitements, and exhortations. In manner and matter it is perhaps the most patriotic journalism ever to pose as a product of the scientific method.[10] The reader trained

---

[8] John Sirjamaki, "A Footnote to the Anthropological Approach to the Study of American Culture," *Social Forces*, XXV (1947), 253.

[9] *And Keep Your Powder Dry* (New York: Morrow, 1943).

[10] Miss Mead herself seems to be uncomfortably conscious of this (see *ibid.*, Introd., pp. 10–11).

in this method can hardly fail to notice that Miss Mead's asseverations are presented with more than a modicum of confidence and with less than a suspicion of corroboration. The most basic question in all scientific endeavor—What is the evidence?—receives no answer. There is little in the book, however "right" or "fitting" it may superficially seem, that enlists the assent of the critical scientific reader. Another example, an article to which these strictures similarly apply, was written by Geoffrey Gorer and published, more appropriately perhaps, in a weekly picture magazine.[11] One unanticipated result of these attempts to describe and to analyze American culture is to stimulate the growth of skepticism concerning the information that anthropologists have given us about nonliterate peoples. That American children learn not only how to use the bathroom but also how to read is a fact which seems to be of no interest to the anthropologist. In consequence, one has only to contrast these anthropological analyses of American culture with the sociological analysis of such a writer as F. S. C. Northrop, for example, to see the limitations of the former approach.

Some things—and some important things—anthropological methods may accomplish when applied to literate societies. They may, for instance, illuminate the "character structure" or "basic personality type" of literate people, as Mead has tried to do for the Americans and Benedict for the Japanese. They may also invite attention to customs, mores, and behavior patterns which obtain in the relatively more unlettered and passive members of a population and so disclose areas of conservatism and of resistance to change which it is useful for administrators and other manipulators of public policy to know. They may, in addition, correct or partially compensate for a comparable onesidedness in a historical approach which concerns itself sometimes too narrowly with the succession of political regimes or the sequence of singular events. The sociologist can unquestionably use anthropological methods to advantage in some areas of his research, just as he can use historical methods in other areas. Since both

---

[11] "American Character," *Life*, XXIII (August 18, 1947), 94–96.

approaches are susceptible to the excesses of enthusiasm, the sociologist has the unique privilege of combining them in a judicious way and of utilizing, in addition, methods that are distinctly sociological. Only by so doing can he discharge his equally unique responsibility as a student of literate societies.

Comment on "The Limitations of Anthropological Methods in Sociology"

Clyde Kluckhohn

Professor Bierstedt's points are well taken. I should, however, like to make the following comments:

Many anthropologists would assert that the primary difference between the anthropological and the sociological approach was the comparative—not that one is the study of nonliterate and the other the study of literate societies. As far back as Tylor, anthropologists have resisted the tendency to identify their discipline with a kind of "higher barbarology."

Within the anthropological profession there is substantial agreement as to the limitations of the synchronic character of many monographs. It is recognized that the processes that determine events are imbedded in time as well as in space (situation). This was a fundamental position of Boas, and this criticism has been made repeatedly by anthropologists who are radical functionalists. The two-dimensional, "photographic" quality of certain studies by Malinowski and his followers has been regarded as a defect by the majority of American anthropologists (cf. Chapple and Coon, *Principles of Anthropology*).

Almost all American anthropologists will read with astonishment the words, ". . . it is not necessary to study a nonliterate society in terms of its relations with others." Shades of Boas, Dixon, Nordenskiöld! Both the Americanist and the Viennese culture-historical schools have been extensively criticized both within the profession and without for excessive emphasis upon diffusion and this whole aspect of the historical process.

With the proposition that anthropologists, in general, have stressed the cultural dimension to the neglect of the social, I can only express hearty agreement.

The number of anthropologists who think that toilet-training can explain the rise of Hitler, the waning of the British Empire, etc., is negligible, if, indeed, there be one. Extravagances in this direction on the part of a few individuals have been probably more savagely attacked within the profession than outside it. Similarly, Professor Bierstedt ludicrously overestimates the use of biographical materials in explanations. The fact of the matter is that the life-history approach is still peripheral research.

The two disciplines, anthropology and sociology, clearly have much to give to each other. We have tended to be topheavy in detail, sociology perhaps in abstract theory. With the occasional arrogant member of my profession who tends to express the view that anthropology is a "better" sociology, I have no sympathy. This attitude is naïve and indicates serious ignorance of the literature and of the history of science.

In my opinion the extent to which anthropology and sociology, in spite of professed similarity in most major objectives, have remained somewhat separate intellectual currents is itself an interesting problem for the social scientist. On the whole, sociology has been distinguished for its interest in the pragmatic and ameliorative, though this is much more true of American than of European sociology. On the whole, anthropology, until quite recently, has been interested in "pure science" to such a degree that Robert Lynd has understandably characterized the vast mass of anthropological endeavor as "aloof and preoccupied." This may be related to the fact that sociology has developed more from interest in the masses, anthropology from interest in the classes.

If Professor Bierstedt is primarily warning sociologists against seduction by an anthropology suddenly fashionable, if he is protesting against the sweeping claims of anthropologists who have spent too much time in the field and too little in the library, if he is insisting upon the validity and indispensability of the peculiarly sociological contribution to a unified socal science, I applaud and do not dissent in principle.

HARVARD UNIVERSITY

8

A Critique of Empiricism
in Sociology*

[1949]

Scientists and scholars in other areas of inquiry have sometimes subjected sociologists to a kind of polite ridicule because of their pre-occupation with problems of method. Henri Poincaré, for example, the great mathematician and philosopher of science, once remarked that natural scientists always discuss their results while social scientists discuss their methods. Another Frenchman, Etienne Gilson, who stands with Maurice De Wulf in the very front rank of authorities on scholastic philosophy, has asserted with some vivacity that no inquiry that begins by wondering whether or not it is a science will ever be one.[1] Gilson's observa-

---

* Paper read before the annual meeting of the Illinois Academy of Science, Knox College, Galesburg, Illinois, May 5–7, 1949.
[1] In a seminar on Descartes and Malebranche, Harvard University, October 15, 1936.

tion, it is hardly necessary to say, was directed squarely at soci-ology. We are often warned in addition, and in a somewhat supererogatory fashion, that if Copernicus, Galileo, and Newton had spent much of their time considering methodological issues they could never have made their impressive contributions to the development of modern science in the sixteenth and seventeenth centuries. And, as a final *caveat*, we are reminded that Francis Bacon, who putatively laid the methodological foundations for the modern inductive, empirical sciences, never himself made a single significant contribution to any of the sciences and was per-haps the last of the great European intellectuals to refuse to accept the heliocentric hypothesis of Copernicus.

The implication of these observations, an implication that is almost universally supported by American sociologists, is that methodological discussion in sociology is singularly fruitless. The "hard-headed" and "tough-minded" empiricists among us insist that we have got to get into the field if we want to get on with the job. Methodological notes are indeed considered proper as introductions to empirical research, as in *The Polish Peasant*, or as part of the appendices to empirical research, as in *An Ameri-can Dilemma*, but almost nowhere else except possibly in presi-dential addresses to the American Sociological Society, where they are indulgently received as prerogatives of status. In addi-tion, methodology is often confused with sociological theory, and "theory" has come to have a somewhat pejorative connotation in current sociological discourse.[2] In this connection it is recognized, and correctly, that methodology is not itself a scientific discipline but rather a normative one, and that there is no *scientific* reason for using the scientific method.

---

[2] The following clear and concise statement by Calvin F. Schmid is useful for resolving the confusion: "Sociological theory is closely associated with methodology, but the two are not identical: first, many phases of methodol-ogy are not peculiarly sociological, but rather cut across all sciences, and, second, methodological questions that are distinctly sociological represent merely one aspect of sociological theory." "Some Remarks on Sociological Theory and Sociological Research," *Research Studies of the State College of Washington*, June, 1947, Vol. 15, p. 117.

Although there is no doubt that methodology is a normative discipline, one may nevertheless question the proposition that it therefore belongs exclusively to philosophy, or even to logic. In these fields the problems become so general or so abstract or so technical that they are of little use to the practising scientist. Even Lotze, a logician, was led to remark that the constant whetting of an axe is apt to become a bit tedious if it isn't proposed to cut anything with it. Certainly contemporary logicians, busy with esoteric symbols and paradoxes of double implication, have given sociologists much less help than the latter have a right to expect. The sociologist must therefore become, to some extent at least, his own methodologist.[3] And indeed, there are imposing reasons for believing that methodological discussion in sociology is not only not fruitless but vital and necessary in the present state of our discipline. One cannot forget that there are many approaches to the human scene, ranging from the philosophic to the journalistic, and that the only thing that distinguishes sociology from these other approaches is its method. There is therefore adequate justification for methodological concerns, especially in the middle of a century when we are confronted with social problems to the solution of which sociology has not as yet been able to make any very respectable contribution.

Fortunately, some of the methodological issues that have agitated the history of sociology have ceased to trouble us. Other

---

[3] There may possibly be an historical reason for the fact that sociologists have become immersed in methodological problems while those who contributed heavily to the early development of the natural sciences did not. Galileo and Newton wrote before Immanuel Kant asked his important questions concerning the possibility of human knowledge and, more specifically, the possibility of synthetic judgments *a priori*. Epistemology did not, of course, begin with Kant, but so profound was the influence of the Kantian philosophy upon subsequent intellectual history, an influence which incidentally persists in the German sociological tradition, that no contemporary contributor to any of the sciences can afford to ignore altogether the Kantian problems. The way of the methodologist is hard. Once a sociologist asks a methodological question he is enticed, as by a Circe, into the inner recesses of epistemology where he becomes, perforce, a traducer of common sense.

issues remain, however, and it is one of these to which we wish
to address the remarks which follow. It has to do with the relative roles of empiricism and rationalism as avenues of approach
to sociological knowledge. The virtues of empiricism, as over
against the virtues of rationalism, is a question that has informed
the entire history of philosophy, particularly post-Cartesian
philosophy, and it is no part of our present project to pursue it in
epistemological detail. But it is worthy of more than an incidental note that contemporary sociology has capitulated almost completely to empiricism and that its method adheres as closely as
possible to the empirical pole. It may be of some importance to
survey the reasons for this preference and to report upon its
consequences.

The reasons are easy enough to discern. They are primarily
historical in a sense that has significance for the sociology of
knowledge. Sociologists, like poets and criminals, are products
of the socio-cultural environment that has nurtured them. In this
country we have all been trained in the empirical tradition. We
have uniformly been taught to believe that observation and
experiment are the twin touchstones of the scientific method. It
has been impressed upon us, in all our schools, that the scientific
method began its spectacular conquest of the fields of human
knowledge when men like Copernicus, Kepler, Galileo, and
Newton stopped reading the books of Aristotle and taught themselves to read the book of nature. Our response to dialectic in
any form, including the Socratic, is a negative one. We entertain
an abhorrence of scholasticism. We are amused at the ignorance
of the medieval thinkers and their "unnatural" views on the fauna
and flora that surrounded them. For the philosophy of an Anselm
or a Scotus we have no respect; the *Sic et Non* of Abelard
depresses us. We note with condescension St. Thomas's efforts to
prove, by refuting a complex constructive dilemma, that the
adornment of women was, under certain circumstances, devoid
of mortal sin. We accept as an historical curiosity, nothing more,
the employment of intellectual energy to decide whether a thousand angels can dance on the head of a pin, whether the mouse
that steals into the cathedral and eats the consecrated wafer has

partaken of the body of Christ, and whether a prostitute can become, through divine intervention, a virgin again. And we cannot contain our contumely for the medieval man who, wanting to know how many teeth the mouth of a horse contains, consulted Aristotle rather than the horse.

As for rationalists of a later period, we are ready to agree that the famous sorites constructed by Leibniz in order to prove the immortality of the soul could not command conviction from anyone, including those who have a prior disposition in its favor.[4] And for the "ghostly ballet of bloodless categories" which comprise the Hegelian philosophy most American sociologists have something akin to contempt.

But these are the excesses of rationalism, excesses of a kind that can be found in any period of history. In the medieval cases we are plagued not so much by an excess of rationalism as by an excess of authority. Authoritarianism as a method is assuredly no approach to valid knowledge of either nature or society. It was Descartes who first broke clearly and definitely with the scholastic tradition in philosophy, and Descartes was no empiricist. The source of our contemporary emphasis upon empiricism is to be sought not solely in our reaction to scholasticism but also, and perhaps primarily, in our view of the origin of modern science. It rests in our respect for the observations made by

---

[4] This "proof" appears in the second part of his *Confessio Naturae contra Atheistas* (1668) and is reproduced by H. W. B. Joseph in the following form: "The human soul is a thing whose activity is thinking. A thing whose activity is thinking is one whose activity is immediately apprehended, and without any representation of parts therein. A thing whose activity is apprehended immediately without any representation of parts therein is a thing whose activity does not contain parts. A thing whose activity does not contain parts is one whose activity is not motion. A thing whose activity is not motion is not in space. What is not in space is insusceptible of motion. What is insusceptible of motion is indissoluble. What is indissoluble is incorruptible. What is incorruptible is immortal. *Therefore*, the human soul is immortal." See Joseph, *An Introduction to Logic*, second edition, revised, Oxford: Clarendon Press, 1916, pp. 355–356.

Copernicus and Kepler and Tycho Brahe and for the experiments performed by Galileo in what was one of the most exciting periods in the entire history of science.

It is easy, however, to over-estimate the reliance which these men placed upon observation and experiment. It is especially easy because most of the contemporary texts in the history and philosophy of science erroneously reiterate it. Ignoring the fact that Copernicus probably found his great idea not in watching the planets but in reading Aristarchus and that Kepler, a "desk-mathematician," indulged in very little observation and no experimentation, let us consider the case of Galileo. No myth is more prevalent in our day than that Galileo disproved Aristotle's belief that bodies fall with a velocity directly proportional to their weights by dropping light and heavy balls from the campanile at Pisa. This "experiment," which is reputed to be a turning point in the history of science, (1) probably never happened;[5] (2) if it did happen it would not have proved what it was intended to prove;[6] and (3) if it did happen and if it did

---

[5] There is no reference to it in any of his extant works. Recent scholarship, particularly that of Lane Cooper, has cast considerable doubt upon the historical authenticity of the incident, as it has upon Galileo's whispered "Eppur si muove" at the Inquisitorial court.

[6] Morris R. Cohen has the following comment on this point: "Suppose that Galileo had actually performed the experiment, what would it have proved? Popular philosophers who praise Galileo for resorting to observation and experiment seldom think of repeating the experiment, and it never occurs to them to remark that feathers, snowflakes, rain drops, hail, and pebbles do not all come down with the same speed. The most obvious fact is that the resistance of the air, as of any other medium, is not the same for all bodies. It is a commonplace of physical science that only in a vacuum would bodies of unequal weight come down with the same velocity, and that the retardation due to the friction of any medium, such as the air, does depend on the mass as well as on the shape of the falling bodies. Now, Aristotle (who did not believe in the existence of a vacuum) was doubtless wrong when he thought that in the air the velocities of falling bodies would be simply proportional to the masses. The functional relation is more complex than that. But Aristotle's error in this respect was generally recognized in antiquity (for instance by his commentator Philopoemen); and Lucretius

prove what it was intended to prove, it proved no more than was known to many of Galileo's contemporaries, and predecessors extending back into ancient times.[7]

Another figure to whom our monolithic method owes allegiance is Francis Bacon. Bacon is in fact the high priest of modern empiricism with John Stuart Mill, in a more recent century, as his busiest acolyte. Now one may grant to Bacon considerable credit for his originality in identifying knowledge and power, for his classic statement of the four "idols" which introduce bias into efforts to acquire knowledge, and for his view that man's dominion over nature is one proof of his understanding of

---

gave a true and simple statement of what does happen." *Studies in Philosophy and Science*, New York: Henry Holt, 1949, p. 55. It is difficult to resist the temptation to quote another paragraph from Cohen on this general issue: "In support of the empirical myth in the conventional history of science are the assertions that Kepler discovered the laws of planetary motion by looking at Tycho Brahe's tables. . . . I venture to assert that one who does not already have the geometry of conics in mind cannot possibly see Kepler's laws in Tycho Brahe's, or any other, astronomical table." *Ibid.*, p. 54. Cohen uses many other examples from the history of science to exhibit this same error, for example the work of Leeuwenhoek on his "little animals," Hertz on electric waves, and Roentgen on X-rays.

[7] Among these contemporaries and predecessors Lane Cooper lists a large number, with quotations from their works, including Philoponus, who flourished in the Sixth Century and Hipparchus who lived in the Second Century B.C. See his *Aristotle, Galileo, and the Tower of Pisa*, Ithaca: Cornell University Press, 1935. The view of Lucretius is quite clear and correct: "All things that fall through the water and thin air, these things must needs quicken their fall in proportion to their weights, just because the body of water and the thin nature of air cannot check each thing equally, but give place more quickly when overcome by heavier bodies. But, on the other hand, the empty void cannot . . . support anything; . . . wherefore all things must needs be borne on through the calm void, moving at equal rate with unequal weights." *De Rerum Natura*, 2.230–9. Quoted *ibid.*, p. 49; translated by Cyril Bailey, *The Greek Atomists and Epicurus*, Oxford, 1928, p. 216. For the views of Philoponus see Cooper, pp. 47 and 68, and W. A. Heidel, *The Heroic Age of Greek Science*, Baltimore: Williams and Wilkins, 1923 (Pub. 442 of the Carnegie Institution), pp. 186–187.

it. But the notion that he outlined a method, namely the inductive method, whereby men could arrive without undue difficulty and without the risk of error at valid conclusions concerning either the natural or the social universe is one that surely requires rejection. Cohen contends, for example, that on the basis of the Baconian canons scientific knowledge would be impossible, and there is every reason to concur in Cohen's conclusion. Many who believe in the efficacy of this method are possibly unaware of the odd results that Bacon himself achieved in trying to use it. His notebook records of observations classified under the heading of "Heat" include not only fire and friction, but also manure, animal heat, the heat produced by quicklime, and the heat of acids and pepper on the tongue. Under the rubric "Swelling" we find notations on gases, soap bubbles, turkeys, insect bites, women's breasts, priapism, the pupil of the eye, ice, the apparent expansion of the stars on cold nights, and, as Preserved Smith says, "many other equally futile subjects."[8]

One could easily invoke more examples from the history of science to exhibit the limitations of observation and experiment in the production of scientific knowledge when these activities are carried on in the absence of rational methods. But these will suffice for the present purpose.

If there is little historical warrant for an excessive reliance upon empiricism in the scientific enterprise, there is perhaps even less logical warrant for it. In the first place, as an epistemological doctrine empiricism has nowhere received the philosophic support that would justify its exclusive use in the social sciences. In the second place, the ultimate logical consequences of a pure empiricism are either Berkeleian idealism or solipsism. In the third place, it can be demonstrated, on logical grounds, that observation and experiment are never sufficient for the construction of generalizations, laws, and principles in any of the sciences, except in cases where the universe of data is so limited as to allow for a complete induction. Consider, for example, one of

---

[8] *A History of Modern Culture*, New York: Henry Holt, 1930, Vol. I, p. 158.

the laws of physics, a science that is frequently exhibited as a paradigm for sociology. Leaving Galileo and his history aside, let us examine the formula for the velocity of freely-falling bodies. This formula—$V = \frac{1}{2}gt^2$—is as valid a scientific law as any other. As a generalization, however, it cannot be attained by experience alone, and this for a number of reasons. In the first place, inasmuch as the generalization is, in logical terms, a universal affirmative proposition, it applies to *all* cases of freely-falling bodies, and it would be forever impossible to observe or to "experience" all cases. In the second place, there is no such thing on earth as a freely-falling body; bodies fall freely only in a vacuum.[9] In the third place, the generalization contains symbols whose referents it is impossible to sense. There are no halves in the universe, no "g"'s, and, whatever may be said about time, it is difficult to imagine the possibility of having a sense-experience of time-squared. This example, of course, introduces logical and epistemological problems of a nice complexity, but it does illustrate the methodological fact that experience alone does not suffice for the construction of scientific laws. In our eagerness to assert that sociology is a natural science we have forgotten that natural science is not synonymous with empirical science and that empiricism does not exhaust the resources of the scientific method.

If some of the reasons for this empirical emphasis are clear, so are the results in sociology. At the moment no word has more honorific connotations than the adjective "empirical." All American sociologists, no matter what their implicit philosophic affiliations, pay obeisance to it. Indeed, the word, and all of its congeners, has become so sacrosanct in current sociological

---

[9] It is one of the merits of the modern logic to have shown that the proposition "All freely-falling bodies have a velocity of $\frac{1}{2}gt^2$" can be true, the proposition "Some freely-falling bodies have a velocity of $\frac{1}{2}gt^2$" false. In other words, one cannot now infer the truth of a subaltern particular affirmative proposition from the truth of its superaltern universal affirmative without an additional existential assumption.

literature that the radical positivism of Lundberg, the "quantic" formalism of Dodd, and the critical exegesis of Parsons all contend for the label. The case of Parsons is singularly instructive. In introducing his highly abstract expositions of the theories of Marshall, Pareto, Durkheim, and Max Weber, he was moved to insist that his inquiry was an empirical one.[10] Both in that place and in his more recent papers he uses this adjective with an unusual frequency, and sometimes in expressions like "empirical analysis," "empirical interpretation," and "empirical insights," which an epistemologist would find it somewhat difficult to decipher. Of the three sociologists mentioned, only Lundberg, of course, is a consistent empiricist and one, let it be said, who is courageous enough to follow the doctrine through to its ultimate logical consequences. But it is interesting, and possibly significant, that such disparate writers as Dodd and Parsons should also announce their allegiance to an empirical method.[11]

Now it is no part of our present intention to renounce the uses of observation and experiment in sociology. To do so would be to commit the same sin for which we are indicting the empiricists. Observation and experiment are necessary components of the scientific method. It is necessary to build our hypotheses and theories on the firm foundation of hard, solid, durable, obdurate, stubborn, and irresistible facts and never to let them wander into the empyrean of unsupported speculation. It is important, furthermore, to hold the ground we have won against all forms of authoritarianism, scholasticism, and dialectic—"methods" which have often exercised an hegemony over our intellectual disciplines. But empiricism, like rationalism, is susceptible to the excesses of enthusiasm, and in such periods as our own we tend

---

[10] The Structure of Social Action, New York: Macmillan, 1937. See especially pp. 11, 21, 26, and 697. This unfortunate emphasis led the author of this work into the contradiction of asserting both that scientific theories are empirical phenomena (p. 697) and that they are not empirical phenomena (p. 754).

[11] All three writers have in addition pledged a clear allegiance to "operationalism," which is a radical variant of empiricism.

to forget that reason too has an integral role to play in the socio-logical enterprise.

When we consider now the consequences of an excessive devo-tion to empiricism in sociology, certain unavoidable conclusions present themselves. The first of these is that the more a piece of sociological investigation resembles a collection of facts, no matter how comprehensive, complete, and accurate they might happen to be, the less is its scientific significance. Let us examine a collection of what must surely be called social facts. With a minimum of research we can discover a large number of "em-pirical" facts about the consumption of bread in the United States. We learn, for example, that in 1908 95% of the bread consumed in this country was baked at home, and that in 1948 only 5% was. We learn that 80% of Americans prefer white bread to any other kind. We learn that the average per capita consumption of bread is 54.9 pounds per year. People who live in Rhode Island and the District of Columbia, however, eat twice that amount of the bakery-produced bread and citizens of the states of Mississippi and South Carolina half that amount. Annually Americans spend one and a half billions of dollars for bread. The highest consumption of bread occurs in the range from twelve to nineteen years of age. Men eat more bread than women, colored men more than white men, the poor more than the rich, and rural-dwellers more than urban-dwellers. The early part of September is the period of the year when bread consump-tion is at its highest and the month of January when it is at its lowest. Before the war the profit on bread averaged 5 to 10%; today it is more than 18%. Bakers and retailers receive, on the average, 9.7 cents of a retail price of 14.5 cents a loaf and only 3 cents remains for the farmer who grows the grain.

It will be noticed that all of these facts fit into orthodox socio-logical categories—the regional, age, sex, ethnic, class, residen-tial, seasonal, and economic. It is now appropriate to ask, do we now, with these facts, have a social science of bread? And if we add these facts to a myriad others would we have a science of sociology? The question answers itself. In order to have a science something more than facts is required.

The contrast is clear also when we compare the sociological stature of a John Howard, a Charles Booth, or even a Frédéric Le Play with that of a Marx, a Comte, or a Spencer. Few factual investigations in sociology are superior to the Pittsburgh Survey, the Springfield Survey, the New York Survey, and the equally well-known crime surveys in Missouri and Illinois, to say nothing about the decennial census of the United States. But a survey or a census, no matter what its intrinsic merit or utility, does not contribute to a science, except in its function as a laboratory for testing the tools of research and as a source of data upon which to construct rational scientific theory. In this connection one may invite attention to the fact that Arisotle's *Politics* is one of the classic works of Western civilization not because of what it tells us about the electoral machinery of the Greek city states in the fourth century before Christ, but because of its observations on the origins and functions of government. And *The Polish Peasant in Europe and America* is a sociological classic not because of what it tells us about Polish immigrants but because of what it tells us about human social behavior. Few contemporary sociologists are interested in the Polish peasant; all are interested in *The Polish Peasant*.[12]

A second, and perhaps more immediately noticeable consequence of a rampant empiricism in sociology is that it determines the direction that research will take and emphasizes the importance of some kinds of research at the expense of others. This is particularly apparent in community research. Community studies have, in recent years, and under the powerful stimulus supplied by Robert and Helen Lynd,[13] come to be increasingly

---

[12] On *The Polish Peasant* in particular, see the brilliant recent paper by Robert Redfield, entitled "The Art of Social Science." *American Journal of Sociology*, Vol. LIV, No. 3, November, 1948, pp. 181–190.

[13] Few sociologists seem willing to acknowledge that the overwhelming superiority of the Middletown studies over all others which have succeeded them rests not in a superior collection of facts about an American community but in their striking proof of the discrepancy between what might be called economic realities and economic ideologies in American culture. Muncie is really irrelevant here in the sense in which Newburyport, for example, is not in the Yankee City studies.

popular and are, in many places, considered to be examples of sociological research *par excellence*. We currently labor under the impression that for some reason it is important to invade American communities with a battery of schedules and questionnaires and to compile as many facts about them as it is possible to stuff into a filing-cabinet. Under the influence of the now fashionable anthropology the community study has taken a position of predominance. As a result, sociologists are coming to confuse their discipline with ethnography.[14] Now there is some warrant for anthropologists to pursue this kind of research. Because of wide disparities and extreme variations in culture, it is useful to have complete descriptions of the way of life of peoples unlike ourselves, especially since there is considerable danger that these cultures will shortly disappear under the impact of Western European and American civilization. But these studies are primarily idiographic and not nomothetic. From most of them we have already learned the lesson they have to teach—the lesson of cultural relativity which was, incidentally, already appreciated by Boethius. Insofar as sociology is concerned, community studies have probably reached the point of diminishing returns. We do not need another Middletown or Plainville or Yankee City nor indeed studies of Ypsilanti, Escanaba, Kokomo, and points west, unless we have an intrinsic practical interest in these communities.[15] The United States Department of Agriculture has every reason to study more communities; the contemporary sociologist almost none. Although it is doubtless a radical statement, there is substantial ground for the assertion that the sociologist, insofar as he is a scientist, has no present business in the field, unless he is testing an hypothesis or trying to corrobo-

---

[14] On this point see the recent comment by Robert M. MacIver and Charles H. Page in their new *Society*, New York: Rinehart, 1949, p. 167.

[15] T. H. Marshall has suggested, somewhat slyly we may suppose, that one reason why some of these research activities are "somewhat intemperately pursued" is the "vast number of sociologists in America looking for something to do." See his *Sociology at the Crossroads*, an Inaugural Lecture delivered at the London School of Economics, February 21, 1946. London: Longmans, Green, 1947, p. 19.

rate one. And even in this case it is doubtful if detailed examination of a single case or community will provide him with the corroboration he needs.

A third result of empiricism is that the relative roles of research and theory have insidiously become reversed. Writers like Parsons and Merton imply in recent papers that theory is subordinate to research and justifies itself only to the degree to which it is useful or "usable" in research. Of the sociological theories of the past, for example, Parsons says, "Generally speaking as total systems they have not proved *usable* by the contemporary research social scientists, and those smaller elements of them which are *useful* have for the most part become incorporated into more recent work in more *usable* form than the original."[16] And Merton declares, "The theories of a Comte or a Spencer, of a Hobhouse or a Ratzenhofer are chiefly of historical interest—little of what they wrote remains pertinent today. . . . They testify to the large merits of talented men, but they do not *provide guidelines* to the present analysis of sociological problems."[17] Sociological theory is thus subordinated to sociological research and justifies itself only insofar as it assists research by serving as a source of hypotheses or as fabricator of "analytical tools." This emphasis is unfortunate. Scientifically speaking, we do not arrive at the formula $V = \frac{1}{2}gt^2$ *in order to* have the pleasure of dropping bowling-balls off the Empire State Building and to know in advance how fast they will fall. On the contrary, we perform experiments like these, when we do, in order to learn something about the relationship between velocity and time and mass. It is the latter knowledge that is the goal of scientific inquiry. And similarly in sociology; we do not construct sociological theories

---

[16] "The Position of Sociological Theory." *American Sociological Review*, Vol. 13, April, 1948, p. 157, note 3; italics not in original.

[17] "Discussion," *ibid.*, p. 165; italics not in original. Merton has, however, expressed views in accord with the thesis of the present paper. See his remarks under "The Hazard of Empiricism" in "The Social Psychology of Housing." "Preprint" from *Current Trends in Social Psychology 1948*, University of Pittsburgh Press, pp. 11–15.

in order to learn something about the rooming-house district in Chicago, but study the rooming-house district in order to contribute to our understanding of the nature of urban societies.

A fourth consequence of an excessive emphasis upon empiricism in contemporary sociology is that, in the United States at least, the construction of systematic sociological theory has been relegated to the writers of textbooks intended for use by introductory students, and only in that place permitted. It is a sobering reflection that the best sociological theory extant in the twentieth century is to be found not in monographs but in textbooks. The authors of these texts have received altogether too little credit for the formidable theoretical tasks they have, in their various ways, undertaken, and in many instances successfully pursued. A similar observation can be made about no other science. Indeed, of the four pre-eminent analyses of the social structure we have in recent American sociology, those of Hiller, MacIver, Sorokin, and Znaniecki, three of them appear today in the form of textbooks.

A fifth consequence of the current empirical emphasis appears in the difficulty of exhibiting, amid a welter of facts, sociological principles, generalizations, and laws. Since we have discussed this point in more general terms earlier in this paper we shall not elaborate upon it here, except to say that the absence of laws in our science is a perennial source of embarrassment to all of us. This situation encourages us to observe that it might be possible to learn as much about society from valid rational inferences derived from sociological theories themselves, including the "grand" but forgotten theories of yesterday, as we can from inductions from a space-limited, time-bound, and culture-constricted experience.[18]

----

[18] T. H. Marshall reminds us in addition that "Even the failure of a powerful mind attempting the impossible may be more fruitful than the successes of lesser minds in grasping things that are within the reach of all." *Loc. cit.*, p. 18. In his enlightening lecture Mr. Marshall pleads for more "stepping stones in the middle distance," *i.e.*, between vast syntheses on the one hand and concrete sociological investigations on the other.

We may summarize our conclusions as follows: First of all, an exclusive dependence upon empiricism in sociology has neither historical nor logical warrant. It nevertheless persists as a kind of methodological orthodoxy and results in the following consequences: (1) it places an inappropriate emphasis upon what T. H. Marshall calls an "aimless assembly of facts"; (2) it determines the kinds of research that are pursued and particularly exaggerates the scientific, as separate from the practical, importance of community studies; (3) it illogically reverses the roles of theory and research in sociology; (4) it places an undue burden upon the writers of textbooks; and (5) it makes of sociology a disorderly science in which principles, generalizations, and laws are distinguished by their scarcity. Other consequences, which we have not undertaken to discuss, include a reliance upon statistical data as a privileged category of facts, a preference for descriptive rather than causal inquiries, and the neglect of historical materials because they are not amenable to sense experience. In short, an adherence to a pure empiricism has helped us to forget that no mature science can remain in the statistical stage, it has induced us to surrender the quest for causes, and it has forced us to focus our researches upon the transient and specious present.

We may say finally that we have no disposition to emphasize rationalism *at the expense of* empiricism. Sociology is not mathematics, and cannot subsist on purely rational fare. Rationalism too has its excesses, as sociologists are happily aware. It is useful to remember Roger Bacon's "Argumentum non sufficit, sed experientia," William of Occam's "Entia non multiplicanda sunt praeter necessitatem," and Thomas Hobbes's "No discourse whatever can end in absolute knowledge of matters of fact." Nor is it advisable to forget John Locke's "Nihil in intellectu quod non prius fuerit in sensu," nor the immortal introductory sentence to *The Critique of Pure Reason.* When rationalism goes awry, however, as in the case of some of the "grand" sociologies, it often results in instructive error. When empiricism goes awry it results only in "busy work," and in trivial and unsystematic exercises. There is no doubt that an ordered empiricism is superior to an unbridled rationalism. But so also is a disciplined rationalism superior to a planless empiricism. It is reason, after all, which tells us what situations to study, what hypotheses to entertain, what conditions to observe, what operations to perform, what experiments to undertake, and what data to collect, and it is reason, finally, which helps us to weigh the accumulated evidence and to put it in its proper place. The argument is directed not against empiricism but only against its excess, an excess that violates not only the admonition of the Delphic oracle but the very spirit of science itself.

9

Wertfreiheit and
American Sociology

[1957]

It is now well over a hundred years since Auguste Comte coined
the word "sociology" and helped to launch a new science on an
independent career. Now, in the second half of the twentieth
century, sociology is an accepted and respectable discipline in
most of the world's universities, and it has taken its proper place,
along with psychology and anthropology, among those sciences
that explore the mysteries of human behavior in all its manifold
complexity and infinite detail. Sociology developed in somewhat
different directions, however, in different countries, and it exhibits, in consequence, some nationalistic traits and characteristics.

American sociology—meaning, in what follows, sociology in
the United States—experienced an initial period of hesitation
and uncertainty during which such disparate concerns as the
philosophy of history on the one hand and social welfare on the

other struggled for dominance. Indeed, at one time sociologists and social reformers were almost indistinguishable; both were people who wanted not so much to study society as to change it, to improve it, to cure it of its diseases, and even to revolutionize it in a manner reminiscent of an earlier utopian socialism. All these reformist strains later succumbed to a different ideology—the ideology of pure science—and it is this latter ideology which characterizes American sociology today.

American sociology apparently enjoys a contemporary repute in Europe for certain values ordinarily associated with the physical sciences in contrast to the more humanistic and philosophic disciplines. American sociologists in particular have rejected the Neo-Kantian distinction between the *Kulturwissenschaften* on the one hand and the *Naturwissenschaften* on the other, and the *verstehende* and *erklärende* methods, respectively, which the distinction entails. American sociology is known, for example, for the empirical quality of its investigations, the quantitative and statistical techniques that inform them, the accompanying distrust of broad and abstract generalizations, and the effort to apply to the study of social phenomena the same methods that have proved successful in the physical sciences. Indeed, the science of physics has served as an example for American sociologists to emulate. This "scientific" point of view has been accepted by the majority of sociologists in the United States, and as a result American sociology today is a heterogeneous collection of empirical studies, many of superior execution, but exhibiting perhaps little concern for the accumulation of individual results, the construction of systematic theories based upon these results, and the integration of these smaller systems into a general theory of society.

It would be erroneous, however, to suggest that American sociology is wholly empirical, wholly devoted to piecemeal research, or totally insensitive to the need for general theories of social structure and social change. The United States has produced its fair quota of sociological theorists also, and one need mention only the names of P. A. Sorokin, Robert M. MacIver, Florian Znaniecki, Talcott Parsons, Howard Becker, E. T. Hiller,

George A. Lundberg, Kingsley Davis, and Robert K. Merton to realize that the western shores of the Atlantic Ocean are not wholly barren of theoretical concerns. One must admit, of course, that not all these writers are American by birth. Sorokin is Russian, MacIver Scottish, and Znaniecki Polish. But they are nevertheless American by adoption, and all three produced their most important work in the United States. It would be instructive to devote a few paragraphs to the work of these American theorists and to discuss the nature of their contributions. In the space at our disposal, however, we want to address our remarks to another issue.

We suggested above that American sociologists have almost unanimously accepted the ideology of science and that they advocate the use of scientific method in their inquiries. It is not easy, of course, to say precisely what science is in this methodological sense, and here indeed we have a question that belongs to the philosophy of science rather than to the sciences themselves. The failure of the social sciences to duplicate the spectacular feats of the physical sciences, however, has required sociologists to devote a great deal of attention to methodological problems. It has almost certainly given them more methodological sophistication—and more methodological anxiety—than their colleagues in physics and chemistry. Some sociologists, it must be admitted, have even become idolaters of methodology and spend their time writing methodological essays rather than doing sociological research—forgetting altogether the admonition of the German logician Lotze that "the constant whetting of an axe is apt to be a bit tedious if it isn't proposed to cut anything with it."

Since American sociologists have dedicated themselves to the application of rigorous scientific method in the study and investigation of social phenomena, we should perhaps try to explain what is meant by "scientific method." One modest answer can be given in negative terms. As an American philosopher once remarked, just as it is not the function of a hospital to spread disease, so also it is not the function of science to disseminate error. Speaking positively, it is generally agreed that the scientific method is basically an attitude of mind, an attitude with which one can approach the investigation of any subject whatever, the phenomena of the social world as well as those of the physical world.

This attitude of mind has a number of specific characteristics. The first of these is that it is motivated by a quest for objectivity, that is, a desire to obliterate from inquiry the biases of time and place and circumstance which would distort both initial observations and the conclusions derived from them. Francis Bacon, of course, was the author of the classic statement of these biases, or "idols" as he called them—the idols of the tribe, the cave, the marketplace, and the theatre. An absolutely complete objectivity, although a methodological desideratum, is probably also a psychological impossibility. The scientist is also a person and a citizen, a person surrounded by others, the creature of a culture and a nation, and a person who is always in some sense too the prisoner of a personal philosophy of history. However difficult it is to avoid these biases, it is nevertheless desirable at least to be aware of them.

A second characteristic of this attitude of mind we associate with the scientific method is a respect for the law of parsimony. This rule, to which William of Occam gave expression in the fourteenth century—*Entia non multiplicanda sunt praeter necessitatem*—has come down to us as "Occam's Razor," and it is still sharp enough to shave the metaphysical stubble off the physiognomy of science.

A third attribute is the recognition that all scientific conclusions are only temporarily true, that science is therefore the only self-correcting discipline, and that a scientific law—itself only a statement of a uniformity in nature or society—is only a hypothesis that has resisted repeated attempts at falsification.

A fourth component is scepticism, a willingness to question all received opinion, no matter how highly placed or important the authority that supports it. Scepticism, as the Spanish-American philosopher George Santayana once remarked, is the chastity of the intellect and should be preserved through a long youth. Scientific method involves, therefore, not the suppression, but the cultivation of doubt.

Finally, scientific method involves—perhaps above all—an ethical neutrality, something the Germans call *Wertfreiheit*, that is unique to inquiry and characterizes no other endeavor of the human mind. Ethical neutrality means that the sociologist, as scientist, is concerned only with categorical judgments, not with normative ones; that he can know only what is, not what ought to be; and that he tries to discover the order that society exhibits, not to recommend the kind of order society should have. The sociologist, in short, agrees with the English philosopher Jeremy Bentham in saying that the word "ought" ought never to be used, except in saying it ought never to be used. The notion that sociology, a discipline that deals with society, can be value-free and have no goal but discovery is a difficult proposition for many to accept. But that is the view of the large majority of American sociologists.

No one knows whether sociology will ever achieve a genuine scientific maturity in the sense we have now suggested. It must be clear, however, that such attributes of mind as relativism, scepticism, and ethical neutrality do not harmonize well with allegiance to any monolithic doctrine or theory, whether political, religious, or economic. American sociologists, like other scientists, are most eager to find truth, but most reluctant to accept it—most reluctant to accept it, that is, as something ordained or sacred or permanent. In the lexicon of American sociology there is no such thing as a permanent truth. All truths are temporary and relative and are to be discarded at the first sign of contrary evidence. The degree to which any sociological theory resembles a fixed truth of the universe is precisely the degree to which it will be rejected by those who respect the scepticism of the scientific method.

If it be asked, therefore, whether there is any relationship between American sociology and the Marxian analysis of society and, if so, what this relationship is, the answer is a simple one. If sociology is ethically neutral, so also is it neutral with respect to politics and religion. The Marxian view, like the Thomist, is only one of a variety of approaches to society that entail a prior philosophic commitment and have thus surrendered their neutrality. Such commitments are useful for the purposes of political action—indeed for action in any sphere—but they are harmful to the processes of science and they interfere with the acquisition of knowledge.

The economic interpretation of society, for example, and the degree to which economic factors play a role in specific instances of historical change are always important questions—so important that no sociologist may ignore them. Similarly, the name of Karl Marx, along with other proponents of the economic interpretation of society, will always be an important and impressive name in the history of social thought. If a sociologist approaches an inquiry already committed to the view that economic factors are the only significant factors, however, and that factors of other kinds have only a subordinate significance, then he has surrendered any claim of making an objective contribution to the sum of sociological knowledge.

Prejudice is prejudice—whether it calls itself Marxism or Thomism or capitalism or materialism or anything else—and as such it is inimical to the pursuit of truth. Although the writer of these words can speak only for himself, it is probable that the majority of American sociologists, whatever their political preferences, would subscribe to this view of the nature of sociology.

Nominal and Real
Definitions in
Sociological Theory

[1959]

Some years ago, at a session of the American Sociological Society devoted to sociological theory, an argument developed between two eminent practitioners of the discipline. The details of the argument are no longer remembered with precision, but the subject of it was definitions in sociology. One of the protagonists, George A. Lundberg, maintained that it is important and indeed necessary to have clear and carefully articulated definitions of our concepts before we begin our inquiries in order that we may always know what it is that we are talking about. For this purpose he advocated, of course, the adoption of "operational" definitions, an advocacy he supported on the ground that, among other advantages, the meaning of the concept defined would always be closely associated with the procedures employed in investigating the phenomenon in question, metaphysical controversies over "real" essences or meanings would be avoided, and the progress of science in sociology would thereby be enhanced.

The other protagonist, Herbert Blumer, maintained on the contrary that clear and accurate definitions of our concepts can neither be "given" nor "constructed" at the beginning of inquiry, that in scientific procedure it is not always desirable to have exact definitions (because they may put a cloture on research), and that, in any event, a definition emerges properly only as one of the results and consequences of inquiry. Mr. Blumer contended, in short, that definitions increase in accuracy as a result of successive approximations and empirical confirmations, that they become increasingly definite as research and inquiry proceed, and that it is unrealistic therefore to insist that they be clear and precise at the beginning of the process.

The argument, as fallible memory recalls,[1] waxed warm at times. In the absence of an umpire or referee, however, and in the absence too of a court of final appeal, the issue remained unsettled at the conclusion of the meeting.

If we leave Chicago, the scene of the logomachy just described, and turn to Athens in the fourth century B.C., we shall find two ancients arguing, like Blumer and Lundberg, about a similar problem. Their names are Hermogenes and Cratylus and they appear in the Dialogue of Plato that bears the name of Cratylus. At the beginning of the piece, Hermogenes is insisting that words are purely arbitrary and conventional affairs, that they have no necessary or inherent relationship with their referents, and that custom is the sole arbiter of language. Cratylus, on the other hand, has a feeling that words somehow necessarily mean what they say, that the connection between words and their referents is neither haphazard, nor incidental, nor merely conventional,

---

[1] If the memory is too fallible, the writer begs the indulgence of both of the gentlemen mentioned, and offers apologies. For their views about this time, the reader is referred to Herbert Blumer, "The Problem of the Concept in Social Psychology," *American Journal of Sociology*, 45 (March, 1940), pp. 707–19; and George A. Lundberg, "Operational Definitions in the Social Sciences," *American Journal of Sociology*, 47 (March, 1942), pp. 727–43.

and that, consequently, a study of words can contribute to our knowledge of the nature of things. Unable to come to an agreement, they seek out Socrates and beg him to tell them who has the better part of the argument. Socrates, after an appeal to the names of the Athenian deities and to a series of improbable and over-ingenious etymologies, casts his lot with Cratylus and suggests that words do have more than a chance or incidental connection with the things to which they refer.

Because of the hegemony that words exercise over our intellectual domains it is the fashion today to reject the Socratic solution to this problem and to hold with Hermogenes that words, however necessary, serve merely a utilitarian function in the acquisition of knowledge, that definitions of them, accordingly, are wholly arbitrary and conventional, and that definitions therefore can neither be true nor false. We go further. Because of the errors that arise through a failure to estimate correctly the relationship between words and things, especially errors of hypostasis or reification, we assert that words have little or nothing to do with things and that our refusal always to recognize this constitutes a prime source of confusion in scientific communication. Since the operations employed in defining concepts, like words themselves, can apparently be arbitrarily selected, and since there is no independent criterion for selecting one operation rather than another, it appears that Hermogenes would be on the side of Lundberg, though the issues are not in all respects identical, with Cratylus and Socrates in support of Blumer.

Before we accept the minority view, however, let us stop a moment in the London of 1851, and particularly in Hyde Park, the scene of the Great Exhibition. If we stray into Crystal Palace we may happen to see there Augustus De Morgan, logician, and professor of mathematics at University College. The professor is listening to the playing of an organ by a performer who seems especially anxious to exhibit one of his stops. The rest of the story, in De Morgan's words, goes as follows:

"What do you think of that stop?" I was asked.
"That depends on the name of it," said I.

"Oh! what can the name have to do with the sound? 'That which we call a rose,' etc."

"The name has everything to do with it: if it be a flute stop, I think it very harsh; but if it be a railway-whistle stop, I think it very sweet."[2]

It is unfortunate that cosmic matters are not so arranged that Lundberg and Blumer, Hermogenes and Cratylus, the organist and Professor De Morgan can get together to discuss this problem.

In any event, before we leave the realm of the imagination and turn to the more sober concerns of logic and sociology, we should perhaps look in once, and hastily, on Adam and Eve in the Garden of Eden. The perennial human problems had their origin there, and the first pair did after all have a need to name the things they were the first to be privileged to see. Fortunately, we have Eve's diary, "translated from the original" by a latter day descendant named Mark Twain, and can learn how this initial issue was confronted and solved:

> During the last day or two I have taken all the work of naming things off his [Adam's] hands, and this has been a great relief to him, for he has no gift in that line and is evidently very grateful. He can't think of a rational name to save him, but I do not let him see that I am aware of his defect. Whenever a new creature comes along I name it before he has time to expose himself by an awkward silence. In this way I have saved him many embarrassments. I have no defect like his. The minute I set eyes on an animal I know what it is. I don't have to reflect a moment; the right name comes out instantly, just as if it were an inspiration, as no doubt it is, for I am sure it wasn't in me half a minute before. I seem to know just by the shape of the creature and the way it acts what animal it is.[3]

---

[2] Augustus De Morgan, *A Budget of Paradoxes* (Chicago: The Open Court Publishing Company, 1915), II, 91.

[3] "Eve's Diary," from *The $30,000 Bequest and Other Stories* (New York: Harper & Brothers, 1935).

Now so long as Eve is only gaily inventing names and applying them to the new animals, we have no logical problems with her. When she remarks, however, that the name that pops out instantly is the "right" name and that she knows by the shape of the creature—and how it acts—what it is, then we are again plagued by our little puzzle.

Fortunately, there is a solution to the puzzle that all of these stories pose, a solution that has rigor, elegance, and power—a solution, furthermore, that is taught in an introductory course in traditional logic. The general issue, moreover, is one that has ramifications in contemporary sociology, and particularly in that part of sociology known as "theory." It concerns what we shall call the vectors of inquiry. Before we examine the solution, however, let us attend to a situation in contemporary sociological theory.

A common and indeed facile observation in our field today concerns what everyone assumes to be the distressingly large gap between sociological theory and sociological research. Various writers, Merton for example, speak of a "codification" or "consolidation" of theory and research,[4] and followers of Parsons, as another example, tell us how useful his system of concepts is in helping them to see research problems, in directing their research, and in providing a conceptual frame in which to announce their conclusions. There is a feeling indeed that theoretical formulations need to justify themselves as useful in research and that unless the Parsonian architectonic, for example, is "usable" in research its justification disappears. Efforts to demonstrate utility thus increase in intensity out of respect for what must in the case of Parsons be regarded as an astonishing achievement of the human mind.

We have had occasion to remark before on this rather odd

---

[4] See Robert K. Merton, *Social Theory and Social Structure*, revised edition (Glencoe, Ill.: Free Press, 1957). See also "Discussion" of "The Position of Sociological Theory," by Talcott Parsons, *American Sociological Review*, 13 (April, 1948), pp. 164–68.

emphasis that would make theory subordinate to research.[5] Indeed, this same accent on utility then appears as a criterion in terms of which sociological theories in general are judged. In discussing the classical theories, for example, Parsons has remarked that "Generally speaking, as total systems they have not proved usable by the contemporary research social scientists, and those smaller elements of them which are useful have for the most part become incorporated into more recent work in more usable form than the original."[6] And Merton has supported this sentiment by saying, "The theories of a Comte or a Spencer, of a Hobhouse or a Ratzenhofer are chiefly of historical interest— little of what they wrote remains pertinent today. . . . They testify to the large merits of talented men, but they do not provide guidelines to the present analysis of sociological problems."[7] Utility is thus seen to be the bridge that will connect theory and research and make them more accessible to each other.

We want to contend in this paper that the issue as thus presented is misconstrued. The really distressing gap in sociology today is not that between theory and research—as serious as that may be—but between two different kinds of theory, to one of which the criterion of utility is relevant and to the other of which it is not. The important lacuna—to employ a less inelegant but more pedantic word—is that between metasociological theory on the one hand and sociological theory on the other or, stated differently, between methodological theory and substantive theory. Metasociological theory is now a highly developed discipline; sociological theory, on the contrary, is still a weak and pallid thing whose pursuit receives no special encouragement within the profession and whose major achievements frequently come not from academicians but from novelists, journalists, publicists, and those relatively few sociologists who are not afraid of

---

[5] Robert Bierstedt, "A Critique of Empiricism in Sociology," *American Sociological Review*, 14 (October, 1949), pp. 584–92.
[6] Talcott Parsons, "The Position of Sociological Theory," *American Sociological Review*, 13 (April, 1948), p. 157, note 3.
[7] Robert K. Merton, "Discussion," *op cit.*, p. 165.

epithets like "unscientific." One of the questions that concerns us is the distinction between metasociological theory and sociological theory. Indeed, we shall contend that the latter enterprise is vastly more significant for our discipline even when its conclusions fall short of the confirmation that is ordinarily required by the canons of scientific inquiry. Utility can of course serve as the criterion by which metasociological theory is judged, but of sociological theory cogency, not utility, is the measure.

The instrument we shall use in an effort to attack these problems is the instrument that solves the issues raised by the little stories with which we began. This instrument is the distinction between nominal and real definitions, a distinction accepted in contemporary logic but one relatively unknown in other disciplines. It is not the most powerful of our analytical and logical tools—it would do no good to overemphasize its merits—but it can remove some of the perplexities in the current sociological scene. It has a peculiarly apposite application to our puzzles.

The issue between Blumer and Lundberg, for example, is completely resolved by it. The most interesting aspect of their argument is not the enthusiasm with which they advanced their contrary views, but the fact that both were right—and both wrong. That is, Lundberg, who maintained that we ought to have our definitions clearly articulated at the beginning of our inquiries, was right if he was talking about nominal definitions. Blumer, who maintained that definitions can emerge only in the process of inquiry, was right if his subject was real definitions. There can be no question that, as Lundberg insisted, the adoption of precise nominal definitions is desirable at the beginning because they outline and delimit the ensuing research. As a matter of fact, loose and imprecise nominal definitions are to be countenanced at no stage of inquiry. On the other hand, as Blumer insisted, real definitions are not given at the outset of inquiry, either "operationally" or any other way, but result only from empirical investigation of the phenomenon in question. It is necessary to rely upon the investigation itself in order to determine whether or not the properties the definition ascribes to the concept actually do belong to it, whether, to put it bluntly, the *definiens* does in fact define the *definiendum*, whether, in short, the definition is "true." Attention here to an elementary distinction completely resolves an issue and ends an argument.[8]

In the same way we can referee the dispute between Hermogenes and Cratylus, this time without the help of Socrates. Hermogenes is right if he is talking about the nominal definitions of words, for these are wholly arbitrary and one has with respect to them a limitless range of choice. Cratylus, on the other hand, is right if he means that when a word once has a meaning, i.e., a connotation or an intension, it may not subsequently be applied in such a manner as to contradict that connotation. That way leads to madness, and to chaos in communication. And similarly for De Morgan and the organist. The organist can call his stop anything he desires, anything at all, but only, so to speak, if the word he chooses is not yet in the language. He is perfectly free to call it either a railway-whistle stop or a flute stop, as he likes. If these words are already in the language, however, the situation is somewhat different. If the sound is high and piping and somewhat aspiratory, he should not call it a railway-whistle stop; and if it is lonely, melancholy, and slightly disturbing in the distance, he should not call it a flute stop. In other words, once railway whistles and flutes have their characteristic sounds, and once, as words, they have their characteristic connotations, the organist has some obligation to call his new stop one or the other in accordance with his judgment of what it more nearly resembles. To do the reverse, though logically permissible, would add confusion rather than clarity to the language and to the processes of communication that it serves. And finally, Eve. She is at perfect liberty to call the new animal a dodo,[9] or anything else that

---

[8] This paragraph, like some of the others in this chapter, is taken with modifications from the author's unpublished doctoral dissertation, *Logic, Language, and Sociology.*

[9] "When the dodo came along he [Adam] thought it was a wildcat—I saw it in his eye. But I saved him. And I was careful not to do it in a way that could hurt his pride. I just spoke up in a quite natural way of pleased surprise, and not as if I was dreaming of conveying information, and said, 'Well, I do declare, if there isn't the dodo!'" Mark Twain, *op. cit.*

springs to her mind. If, however, the word "dodo" is already in her vocabulary as carrying a connotation of stupidity and if the creature appears to be intelligent, then she would be careless or capricious to do so. In this event, Adam should assert his authority and name the animal himself; and the Serpent should persuade her to eat yet another apple from the tree of the knowledge of good and evil.

It is necessary now to examine the distinction between nominal and real definitions a little more closely and a little more systematically. In doing so, we shall follow the discussion of Ralph Eaton in his *General Logic*,[10] because the distinction is treated there with both brevity and rigor. We shall first define each of these kinds of definitions, then consider their properties, and finally treat their functions, or uses. At the conclusion of the discussion we shall attend to certain rules that apply to both kinds of definition.

A nominal definition (sometimes called a verbal definition) "is a declaration of intention to use a certain word or phrase as a substitute for another word or phrase."[11] The word or phrase with which we begin is called the *definiens;* the word or phrase we substitute is the *definiendum.* A nominal definition has three important properties: (1) the meaning of the *definiendum* is dependent upon that of the *definiens;* that is, the expression or concept defined has literally no other meaning than that given arbitrarily to it; (2) the definition has no truth claims; that is, it can neither be true nor false, it is not a proposition, and therefore (3) it cannot serve as a premise in inference.

It is necessary to insist upon the literal truth of these three characteristics of nominal definitions. With respect to the first of them, as Eaton says, a concept defined nominally has no other

---

[10] Ralph Eaton, *General Logic* (New York: Charles Scribner's Sons, 1931), pp. 294–305. See also Morris R. Cohen and Ernest Nagel, *An Introduction to Logic and Scientific Method* (New York. Harcourt, Brace and Company, 1934), pp. 224–41.
[11] Eaton, *op. cit.*, p. 295.

meaning than that given arbitrarily to it. It has the form commonly used in algebra when we say, Let x stand for the unknown quantity. Throughout the working of the problem x has no other meaning whatever. Similarly, when Stuart Dodd, for example, develops a tension theory of societal action, he uses the symbol "E" to mean "equilibration index" and in this theory "E" means only that—nothing else.[12] As a third example, W. A. Anderson once suggested, in a communication to the *American Sociological Review*,[13] that the word "hurelure" might be adopted as a substitute for "human relationship structures." Since this neologism has no independent meaning in the language, it follows that its meaning is wholly dependent upon its *definiens*.

Attending now to the second characteristic of nominal definitions, it obviously makes no sense to inquire whether an "E" really is an equilibration index, or whether a "hurelure" really is a human relationship structure, whether equilibration indexes and human relationship structures are now correctly labeled. That is, a nominal definition has no truth claims and it is therefore senseless to ask whether it is true or false. It is merely a resolution, a stipulation, a convention, an agreement, an expression of volition to use a word or other symbol in a particular way. Of course, as Cohen and Nagel point out,[14] the assertion that a writer has conformed to his own resolution and consistently used a word in the sense that he himself has stipulated may be true or false, but this has nothing to do with the nominal definition itself.

Finally, such definitions as these examples, like all nominal definitions, cannot serve as premises in inference. This follows as a simple corollary of the second characteristic. Only propositions can serve as premises in inference and a nominal definition, being neither true nor false, is not a proposition. As an *a fortiori* consequence, of course, no nominal definition can contribute one iota

---

[12] Stuart Carter Dodd, *The Dimensions of Society* (New York: The Macmillan Company, 1942), pp. 265–71.
[13] W. A. Anderson, "A Note on the Phenomena of Sociology," *American Sociological Review*, 6 (December, 1941), pp. 882–84.
[14] Cohen and Nagel, *op. cit.*, p. 229.

to our knowledge of fact. It indicates only how we intend to use the language.

A real definition differs from a nominal definition in that it operates not only on the symbolic or linguistic level but also on the referential level. It may be defined as follows: a real definition is a proposition announcing the conventional intension of a concept. In more technical language, a real definition is a proposition predicating a distributed intension of its subject term. A real definition also has three important properties, as follows: (1) a real definition states that two expressions, *each of which has an independent meaning,* are equivalent to each other; (2) it has truth claims, i.e., it is a proposition; and (3) it can therefore serve as a premise in inference.[15]

It is convenient to illustrate these characteristics by means of an example that Eaton supplies, contrasting a real definition with a nominal definition. We can take the word "good," for example, and define it nominally as any object of desire; that is, we may submit the resolution, *Let the word "good" mean any object of desire.* It follows that "it would be vain—and meaningless—to question my statement that 'any object of desire is good,' for I am not asserting a truth about objects of desire or goods. All I am saying is that this is how to use the word 'good,' and one may use words in any way he chooses. However, I could not conclude from this definition that 'no objects of desire are evil.' The only legitimate process which the definition permits is verbal substitution; and all that this statement can mean is that 'no objects of desire are nongood, i.e., are not objects of desire.' "[16] On the other hand, quoting Eaton again, "If the term 'good,' for example, has a meaning of its own, the real definition—'the good is any object of desire'—might be false. We can ask, is it true that what is meant (independently) by 'good' is the same as what is meant by 'any object of desire'? And, if evil, as most religions maintain, can be desired, this definition cannot stand as 'a primary and indemonstrable truth.' "[17]

---

[15] Eaton, *op. cit.,* pp. 296–97.
[16] *Ibid.,* pp. 295–96.
[17] *Ibid.,* p. 297.

In other words, if it is true—and if it is a definition—that the good is any object of desire, it is also true that no object of desire is evil, a conclusion that can be inferred from a proposition but not from a resolution.

The logical danger here, and one we want to emphasize, is that when nominal definitions become familiar, as they tend of course to do, we sometimes forget they are nominal and begin to treat them as real. The word we have introduced by stipulation and to which we have arbitrarily given a meaning comes, through use and repetition, to be regarded as necessarily having that meaning. Once again we cannot refrain from quoting Eaton on this matter:

> Having introduced definitions as purely nominal, many writers tend later to treat them as if they were real—as if they conveyed some information about the concept defined, and so, analyzed this concept. Ethical philosophers who nominally define "the good" as "any object of desire" often end by arguing that this is the only meaning "good" can have, since everything that is good is an object of desire, and there is no object of desire that is not good. Tacitly they assign an independent meaning to the term "good," and their erstwhile nominal definition becomes an important truth in their minds.[18]

One may suspect, of course, that this human tendency to transform nominal definitions into real ones is to be found not only among ethicists but also among those who construct systems of sociological theory. It seems hardly necessary to add that one does not in this fashion "create" new truths about society.[19]

Let us consider some additional examples. Suppose we are constructing a coinage system and that we have already decided to call ten cents a dime. We are now ready to introduce the next larger unit and want a word for the amount equal to ten dimes. We may choose any word we want for this purpose. Suppose we

---

[18] *Ibid.*, p. 299.
[19] For that matter, logicians themselves sometimes succumb to this temptation. See Eaton's strictures on Whitehead and Russell, *ibid.*, pp. 299–300, and note.

hit upon the word "dollar." We then say, in effect, let the amount represented by ten dimes be called a dollar. This is a nominal definition. It makes no sense, of course, to question its truth because we are not asserting anything. All we are doing is resolving to call the amount of money equal to ten dimes or one hundred cents a dollar. The definition is neither true nor false. If, however, we have already placed the word "dollar" in our system, defining it as an amount equal to one hundred cents—i.e., if it has an independent reference before we equate it with ten dimes—then the definition is real, and it is true. If we now say that a dollar is ten dimes we are asserting the equivalence of two expressions, each of which has an independent meaning. The definition is a proposition. The simple act of multiplication demonstrates its truth and now we may not, on pain of contradiction, define a dollar as nine dimes, eleven dimes, or any other number of dimes except ten.

Consider, on the contrary, the definition of man as a rational animal. Under no present circumstances may we consider this a nominal definition. When we define "man" as a rational animal," we do not imply merely that we resolve to call a rational animal by the shorter expression "man" in any discussion in which we might be engaged. We imply that a man actually is a rational animal and that whatever "man" may mean, "rational animal" means the same, i.e., this time, that they have the same denotation. It makes sense, furthermore, to inquire whether or not man really is a rational animal and indeed there might be some dispute over the matter. Consider, finally, the purely nominal definition mentioned above—a hurelure is a human relationship structure. Here the word "hurelure" has no independent meaning. Mr. Anderson simply resolves to use it as an abbreviation for the longer expression, "human relationship structure." To inquire whether a hurelure really is a human relationship structure is not an intelligible question.

Nominal definitions have four important functions which are usually listed as follows:

1. Nominal definitions offer the only possible way of introducing new words into a language and, *pari passu*, new concepts into scientific terminologies.

2. Nominal definitions indicate the special importance of certain concepts in scientific schemata, implying, as they do, that the *definiens* is worthy of careful consideration—so worthy in fact that it has been given an equivalent expression.

3. Nominal definitions permit us to economize space, time, and attention, in the same way that abbreviations do.[20]

4. Nominal definitions permit us to substitute new concepts for the familiar words of ordinary speech that have emotional or other nonlogical connotations and thereby enhance the emotional neutrality of scientific discourse.

The functions of real definitions, as distinguished from nominal definitions, follow directly from their properties. Real definitions not only indicate the meaning of a word, as nominal definitions do, but they also assert something about the referent of the concept defined. They predicate, in propositional form, the conventional intension of the concept—that is, the essential or most important property of the concept to be associated with it in scientific communication. A real definition, furthermore, can serve as a premise in inference and, possibly more important, as an hypothesis concerning the nature of the phenomenon under investigation. It has all of the general functions of propositions and in addition the specific functions of a definition; it operates both on the referential level and on the symbolic level.

We judge nominal definitions, in short, by their utility; real definitions by their truth.

In what sense now is the intension announced in a real definition conventional?[21] It is conventional in the sense that it is a

---

[20] Cohen and Nagel comment on this function as follows: "If we continued to use ordinary words and did not introduce such technical terms of higher mathematics and physics as 'differential coefficient,' 'entropy,' and the like, our expressions would become so long and involved that we could not readily grasp the complex relations indicated by these terms. Thus it is easier to read Newton's *Principia* translated into the technical language of the modern calculus than in the more familiar language of geometry in which Newton wrote." *Op. cit.*, p. 229.

[21] On the intension of terms, and the distinction between subjective, objective, and conventional intension, see Eaton, pp. 235–72, or Cohen and Nagel, pp. 30–33.

matter of agreement or resolution which of various properties comprising the objective intension of a concept we choose to use as the *definiens;* that is, which property we shall regard as central for the purpose at hand. This depends upon our interest in general and the criterion of classification in particular, and may be different in separate treatments of the same subject matter. Although the choice may in one sense be arbitrary—in the sense that we decide to focus our definition upon one rather than another of the properties—the question whether or not the referent of the concept actually has this property is neither a matter of choice nor of convention. It is still appropriate and necessary, therefore, to inquire into the truth of a real definition. Thus, it is possible to define a triangle either as a plane figure in Euclidean space bounded by three straight lines, or as a plane figure in Euclidean space containing three angles whose sum is 180°. Both definitions are real, and both are true. It is a matter of convention, relative to the purpose for which the concept "triangle" is employed, which of the two definitions is used, but both must be true. This is what is implied, and all that is implied, in the word "conventional" when we say that a real definition is a statement announcing the conventional intension of a concept.

The adjective "conventional," traditional in discussions of this subject in the logic texts, also helps us to understand what committees can and cannot accomplish in the direction of clarifying and standardizing concepts and conceptual usages. Some years ago, for example, a "Committee on Conceptual Integration" existed within the American Sociological Society, a committee devoted to the purpose indicated by its name. The distinction between nominal and real definitions helps us to understand what a committee of this kind can—and cannot—do. It can do much to encourage the adoption by sociologists of uniform *nominal* definitions of the concepts sociologists employ, to aid in the establishment of uniform practices in the use of words that have risen to the prominence of concepts, and even to assist in the organization, classification, and "integration" of concepts. All of these activities, if successfully pursued, could theoretically at least contribute to the linguistic facility and accuracy of sociological communication.

By no stretch of the imagination, however, can such co-opera-
tive endeavor succeed in establishing uniform *real* definitions of
sociological concepts. In order to arrive at real definitions, as
the discussion above suggests, it is necessary to leave the level
of verbal equivalence and enter the field of sociological research.
When we seek a real definition of any sociological concept we
no longer want to know what the word stands for, in terms of
other symbols, but what the referent of the concept actually is,
and what its properties are—especially those properties that
enable us to use *this* word, with its own independent meaning,
as a terminological and logical equivalent. And this discovery
cannot be the work of a committee but constitutes instead the
task in which all sociologists are engaged as they pursue their
separate labors.

Again, we may inquire into the efficacy of a dictionary of
sociological terms, such as the one now in progress under the
auspices of UNESCO. Those who were engaged in the preparation of preliminary documents for this project recognized quite
clearly that there is room for improvement in the terminologies
of the social sciences, that science advances as it is able to
standardize these terminologies, and that regularity and consistency in conceptual usage is of vast assistance in hastening
the maturity of a discipline. Their estimate of the current situation in these respects was not sanguine. They expressed the
opinion that the terminology of the social sciences continues to
be vague, that social scientists spend a great deal of their time
in vocabulary construction, and that the net result is more words
and fewer standardized concepts than before. It is for these
reasons apparently that the dictionary project has been undertaken.

There is no doubt that these sentiments are correct. Sociologists
who have been invited to participate in the project can contribute a great deal to the discovery of the conventional intension of concepts now in use—and this in itself is a meritorious
and altogether praiseworthy enterprise. Such discoveries, and the
definitions associated with them, can help to reduce the wholly
subjective intensions frequently found in contemporary vocabularies. But no finite number of contributors, however competent,

and no board of editors, however expert, can establish uniform real definitions of sociological concepts. The dictionary can select and support one conventional intension over another, but it cannot determine the truth or falsity of the real definition that contains and announces it. This again is the job of all sociologists as they go about their professional duties.

We want now to list the standard rules of definition and then to comment on one of them. They are usually given in some such manner as the following:

1. A definition should be *per genus et differentiam,* wherever possible. (This is still a useful rule when Aristotelian assumptions regarding fixed essences are relinquished.)

2. A definition must be commensurate with that which is to be defined; i.e., it must be applicable to everything included in the concept defined, and to nothing else. In short, a definition must be convertible *simpliciter.*

3. A definition should not, directly or indirectly, define the subject in terms of itself; i.e., it should not be circular.[22]

4. A definition should not be stated negatively when it can be stated positively.

5. A definition should not be stated in obscure or figurative language.[23]

The second rule is the one most relevant to our present purpose, the rule that requires that definitions be convertible *simpliciter.* We have said that a real definition is a proposition. It is also a particular kind of a proposition, namely, a universal affirmative proposition. Thus, when we define man as a featherless biped we are asserting that all men are featherless bipeds. Now,

---

[22] All definitions, of course, are ultimately circular and for this reason there remain undefinable or primitive terms in any system. The circle need not be "vicious," however, unless it is too small.

[23] It is not very helpful, for example, to define "network," as Dr. Johnson did, as "anything reticulated or decussated, with interstices between the intersections."

all students of logic know that a universal affirmative proposition is not convertible *simpliciter* but convertible only *per accidens,* or by limitation.[24] That is, from the truth of the proposition just expressed we can infer, by conversion, not that all featherless bipeds are men but only that some are. The rule, however, states that a definition must be convertible *simpliciter;* in other words, the relationship established by the copula is not one of class inclusion or of class membership but of equivalence. In order to be a definition, it must also be true that all featherless bipeds are men.

A nominal definition, of course, is convertible by fiat. We simply resolve to use the *definiendum* as the equivalent of the *definiens.* The situation with respect to real definitions, however, is a little more complicated. Since, in order to be a definition, the proposition must be convertible *simpliciter,* and since we cannot so convert it formally, it follows that we must know *on other than formal grounds* that its converse is true. It is vital to recognize that these other grounds cannot be formal. They must be empirical.

The conclusion follows that no real definition of any concept in any field can be constructed without empirical knowledge of the phenomenon in question. Thus, if we want to define man as a featherless biped, and want our definition to have ontological and not merely symbolic implications—i.e., if we want it to be a real and not a nominal definition—we have to know not only that all men are featherless bipeds but also that all featherless bipeds are men. And if a plucked chicken is a featherless biped, as the ancient story has it, then some featherless bipeds are not men and we may not declare as a real definition that man is a featherless biped. Thus, in more general terms, all real definitions are propositions but not all propositions are real definitions. The universal affirmative proposition, *All men are mortal,* is true, but we may not define man as a mortal being because it does not conform to

---

[24] Without the existential assumption a universal affirmative proposition is not formally convertible at all; nor can we, without this assumption, infer the truth of a particular affirmative proposition from the truth of its superaltern universal affirmative.

the rule requiring unlimited convertibility. Real definitions, in short, have ontological and not merely logical consequences; they have empirical and not merely rational implications; and it is these characteristics that give to the distinction itself a certain relevance to contemporary sociological theory.

We want to contend in what follows that the distinction we have been discussing can do more than solve the vexatious little puzzles with which we began this essay, and more too than articulate the logical limitations upon the enterprise of making dictionaries. It can be of major assistance in addition in helping us to evaluate systems of sociological theory and in determining what kind of theory these systems represent. That is, the more nearly a given sociological theory resembles a set of nominal definitions, the more easily can we recognize that it has no truth claims. The more nearly it resembles a collection of real definitions—i.e., the more real definitions it contains—the more easily can we recognize it as a contribution to sociological knowledge. To state the matter in a different way, the more we are tempted to judge a system of theory in terms of its utility, the more likely it is that it is a nominal system and has methodological or metasociological significance. The more we are tempted to judge it in terms of its truth, the more likely it is that it is a "real" system—in the sense of real definitions of course—and has substantive and sociological significance. Let us apply these criteria to two contemporary examples of sociological theory, the one constructed by Stuart Carter Dodd and the other by Talcott Parsons.

The *Dimensions of Society*,[25] of course, is a work of prodigious effort and of almost incredible ingenuity. Motivated by the wholly meritorious goal of introducing mathematical methods into sociology, Dodd has worked out in detail one of the most consistent and comprehensive systems of symbols in existence. It is apparent, however, almost upon immediate examination, that the "S-system" is not a collection of propositions about society but

---

[25] *Op. cit.*

rather an ingenious set of nominal definitions. It makes no sense to inquire, for example, whether the symbol "S" "really is" a social situation, and the same for the symbols "T," "I," "L," and "P," whether they "really are" time, characteristics of people, space, and number of people. These are literally meaningless—and improper—questions. It is certainly the case that Dodd may express quantitatively recorded social situations in terms of a combination of four indicators, although it is not the case, as his front papers lead one to suggest, that this is a rigorous statement of the proposition that people and their characteristics change. In any event, most of the book is devoted to an elaboration, with multitudinous examples, of the way in which sociological data may be expressed in terms of these particular symbols which are, in turn, related to one another through a minimal set of "operators."

Needless to say, Dodd does not assert that his controlling equation is true, nor that it says anything about society. He inquires, rather, as we do, into its utility. The uses of "S-theory," or "S-system" as he later came to call it, are the subject of a separate paper. Among these uses are that it is (1) a contribution to the nomenclature of sociology, a nomenclature in some instances susceptible to mathematical manipulation; (2) a method for guiding "the inductive and deductive manipulations, the analysis and synthesis, in various operationally defined ways, of the recorded observations" of sociology, and (3) a system of second-order symbols "for making summaries and conclusions, for defining concepts and stating relations, for interpreting and predicting, in short for helping to convert recorded observations into laws." [26]

The interesting thing about these claims is that most of them are valid. There is no question that Dodd's S-system can do many

---

[26] "Of What Use Is Dimensional Sociology?" *Social Forces*, 22 (December, 1943), pp. 169–82. See also the note to p. 179 where Dodd takes Talcott Parsons to task for failing in his review to grasp the essential nature of the enterprise. Parsons' review is in the *American Sociological Review*, 7 (October, 1942), pp. 709–14. Read Bain's "Communication," *American Sociological Review*, 8 (April, 1943), 214–16, is also pertinent.

of these things—and do them very well. The degree of *system* that characterizes the *Dimensions* is almost phenomenal. Everything has its place, and there is a place for everything. The S-system is comprised of versatile symbols and they can express many things. So, in the same sense, can any series of nominal definitions. No such series is a theory, however, and none is a "system" in any logical or scientific sense. To be a system in the latter sense means to be a system of propositions, including real definitions, each one related to another and each asserting something that can be inferred from other propositions in the system. And if real definitions are included, as they must be, evidence is needed in addition to inference—that is, evidence from the empirical world in order to validate the convertibility *simpliciter* of the definitions.

Although Dodd's formulae, like abbreviations, help to conserve time, space, and energy, and although they may greatly assist the processes of classification, they are not real definitions. In one of his passages, he recognizes this and indeed discusses the difference between what he calls descriptive equations on the one hand and calculative equations on the other—a distinction that appears to be identical to that between nominal and real definitions:

> In a descriptive equation one member is observed and defines the other member which is set equal to it. Thus here, the left-hand member, S, is not directly observed independently of the right-hand member. In a calculative equation both members may be independently observable. If a term is unknown in the calculative equation, it can be solved for. As many unknowns can be solved for as there are independent simultaneous calculative equations. But in a descriptive equation the term defined is the unknown, and a second unknown in the same equation, taken alone, cannot be solved for. Defining concepts by descriptive equations based on objectively observable quantities is the first step, however, in manipulating them and discovering and testing relationships among the concepts.[27]

---

[27] *Dimensions of Society, op. cit.*, p. 59.

It is Dodd's hope, of course, that his system will be increasingly productive of calculative equations and that some day he will be able to solve them for "sociological unknowns." Surely there is no more respectable ambition than this. The goal, however, is not yet achieved. The basic difficulty with such an invention as Dodd's lies in inducing others to adopt it. Unfortunately, his colleagues in the sociological enterprise seem to prefer their own nominal definitions to the systematic set that he has supplied. In any case there is a danger here, as in any system of nominal definitions, that a growing familiarity with them, on the part of their author or anyone else, will in time encourage the misconception that they are real definitions.

To suggest the nominal character of the symbol structure contained in the *Dimensions of Society* in no way reduces the merit of Dodd's achievement in creating so consistent and comprehensive a scheme for the classification of quantified data in sociology. It needs only to be remembered, as outlined in great detail in the foregoing paragraphs, that nominal definitions are not real definitions and that the characteristics of the two types of definition are fundamentally dissimilar. To make the point almost platitudinous, one might simply say that it is forever impossible to get more out of a nominal definition than is put into it in the first place. And so with a symbol system, a system of notation, however ingeniously contrived. Whatever important and indeed necessary functions it may perform on the nominal level, it is sterile in itself. Whatever it contributes to the nomenclature of sociology, the S-system of Dodd is not a calculus. It cannot inseminate the data it embraces and it can play no intimate creative part in the ongoing processes of science. Like the mule, an amiable beast, it has no pride of ancestry, no hope of progeny.

Nevertheless, we may not conclude that nominal definitions are unimportant simply because they are not real definitions. Nominal definitions have their own important functions to perform. If, as some sociologists believe, the prime task of current methodology in sociology, and indeed in all the social sciences, is to adopt a common system of symbolic notation, the notation constructed so painstakingly in the *Dimensions of Society* may be regarded as an outstanding contender for that position. In terms of its precision, its parsimony, its consistency, and its comprehensiveness, the S-system possesses high qualifications, and one cannot help but admire the labor that Dodd has expended upon it and the zeal with which he has brought it to public attention.[28]

We turn now to Talcott Parsons in an effort to discover whether the distinction between nominal and real definitions has any relevance to the vast theoretical structures he has contributed to contemporary sociology. The enterprise on which Parsons has been engaged for upwards of twenty years has often seemed a puzzling one not only to those who have not had the benefit of personal participation in his seminars at Harvard but even to some of those who have enjoyed this privilege. Fortunately, Parsons, like Dodd, is a sophisticated methodologist, one who is thoroughly aware of what it is he is trying to do and who often stops to explain it to his readers. Although couched in different language from that employed in the present chapter, many of his observations are directly relevant. We shall not pursue these through the impressive corpus of his work, but confine our attention at the moment to certain statements that appear in *The Social System*.[29]

Parsons is quite clear, in fact, that the content of this book is sociological theory in a very special sense of the term. He does not intend to offer the book as a critique of the literature of sociological theory,[30] as a codification of empirical knowledge, or as a theory of any concrete phenomenon in society. It is, on the contrary, an essay in systematic theory, a logically articulated conceptual scheme, a frame of reference explicitly defined, an

---

[28] Nothing in the above discussion implies that Dodd's sociological writings are limited to nomenclatural concerns. Among his many substantive contributions we should like to mention especially his work on message diffusion.

[29] Glencoe, Ill.: Free Press, 1951.

[30] Except for references to the unpublished dissertations of his own students and an occasional bow to Weber, the work in question makes almost no mention of the work of other sociological theorists.

effort at theory construction.[31] The following comments are so suggestive that they require direct quotation:

> The book is thus an essay *in* systematic theory but the suggestion is quite explicitly repudiated that it attempts in one sense to present a system of theory, since it has been consistently maintained that in the present state of knowledge, such a system cannot be formulated. Put a little differently, it is a theory of systems rather than a system of theory.[32]

This engaging juxtaposition of the two words "theory" and "system" helps us enormously in understanding what it is that Parsons is "about" even though we may not share his optimism concerning the utility of a general theory of social action—nor his pessimism that a system of theory, as contrasted with a theory of systems, cannot now be formulated. It appears in particular that the distinction so neatly articulated here has more than a little in common with that treated in this chapter—namely, the distinction between nominal and real definitions—and, in addition, with the distinction between methodological (or metasociological) theory on the one hand and substantive (or sociological) theory on the other.

In this respect, it is interesting to observe and, we hope, not unfair to either author to note that the general methodological intent of Parsons' work is basically similar to Dodd's, however dissimilar the symbols in the two systems. To a very large degree both authors have supplied—and both with prodigious labor—a set of nominal definitions for sociological use. Both authors, curiously enough, in spite of their many obeisances to empiricism (in Dodd's case to "operationalism," a radical variant of empiricism; and in Parsons' to an especial fondness for the word "empirical"), have taken a highly formal and indeed taxonomic approach to sociology. Both authors have built their nominal definitions into

---

[31] All of these expressions are to be found on p. 536.
[32] *Ibid.*, pp. 536–37.

elaborate conceptual schemes. Both authors contend, finally, that these conceptual schemes can embrace multifarious phenomena from other disciplines. Dodd, as we have seen, suggests that symbolic logic, the equations of mathematics, the formulae of statistics, and the categories of Aristotle and Kant can be translated into the S-system—a claim we have conceded. Parsons has recently maintained, for his part, that the body of economic theory is a special case of his general theory of social systems and of his general theory of action, a claim we have also conceded.[33] It remains only, perhaps, to translate the "pattern variables" and their companions into the S-system and Dodd into "Parsonian," and we have little doubt that both translations are possible.

In any event, there is a vector of inquiry involved here that Parsons and Dodd tend to share. Inquiry in general has two vectors: it proceeds, in short, in two directions, and these directions can be characterized by the differences between nominal and real definitions. Sometimes we begin with our observations of objects, phenomena, or properties that have something in common and we want to apply a name either to this common characteristic or to the class of objects in question. In this case, we move from *definiens* to *definiendum* and the result is a nominal definition. At other times, we begin with a concept and want to discover and to articulate the properties associated with its referent. In this case we move from *definiendum* to *definiens* and the result is a real definition. In the first case, that of a nominal definition, we have a conceptual scheme that may or may not be useful. In the second case, we have a real definition that may or may not be true.[34] In moving along one of these vectors we aim at a continuously improved conceptual scheme; in moving along the other we aim to contribute true propositions to the sum of sociological knowledge. Both vectors of inquiry are important. But they are different. In the one direction, we are constructing the instru-

---

[33] See Talcott Parsons and Neil J. Smelser, *Economy and Society* (Glencoe, Ill.: Free Press, 1956) and the writer's review of this book in the *American Sociological Review*, 22 (June, 1957), p. 345.

[34] And if it is false, of course, it can no longer be a definition.

ments of inquiry and the categories of classification; in the other, we are building substantive sociological theory.

There is, of course, a certain artificiality in the first of these enterprises when carried on in independence of the second. It can lead to a system, or even a "theory of systems," that, however aesthetically satisfying and logically imposing, is sterile. The creator of a set of tools can admire their shine and their cutting edge, and can go on polishing and sharpening forever. The inventor of a generalized conceptual scheme can obviously be quite prolific in the multiplication of concepts (one cannot say that Parsons is altogether free of this tendency) and can spin out increasingly complex and elaborate series of nominal definitions. We shall ultimately have to require of such a system, however, that it produce progeny in the form of propositions.

As in the case of Dodd, we do not wish to imply that the corpus of Parsons' work is devoid of substantive theoretical propositions. Indeed, the latter are quite numerous, not only in his papers directed to special topics,[35] but also throughout *The Social System*. In the latter place, for example, we find illuminating discussions of kinship, of the socialization of the child, of the institutionalization of scientific investigation, of the role of the artist in society, of the problem of social change, and, most especially perhaps, of modern medical practice. Most of these discussions, however, appear largely as incidental suggestions (e.g., the penetrating observations on the use of family symbolism in fraternities and in the Catholic Church[36]) rather than as carefully worked out propositions, hypotheses, or theses. In view of the finely wrought systematic quality of his nominal definitions, it is somewhat surprising to see his real ones presented so haphazardly. The explanation is that they are introduced in fact not on their own account but as illustrations of the utility of the schema that is being constructed. They are, literally, "cases," and not conclusions.

---

[35] See, for example, his *Essays in Sociological Theory*, revised edition (Glencoe, Ill.: Free Press, 1954) for a representative collection.
[36] *The Social System, op. cit.*, pp. 406–07.

As helpful as the distinction between nominal and real definitions is, it should not be supposed that it is powerful enough to solve all of our problems. It contains certain residual difficulties of its own, of which we shall mention two. There is a sense, in the first place, in which real definitions can appear in purely formal systems even though they have no contact whatever with an empirical content. Equivalences introduced by fiat can be related to other equivalences also introduced by fiat in such a way that *definiendum* and *definiens* could, in the process of construction of a system, acquire independent meanings. In these cases, the new definition would have a truth claim but no reality claim. The "truth" involved would be a purely formal matter and would depend upon two prior sets of nominal definitions. In other words, although nominal definitions do not appear as empirical propositions, formal systems can be co-ordinated with real definitions, as, for example, in applied mathematics.

Secondly, there is a sense in which it is impossible to give a nominal definition to a word or phrase that has a structure. Eaton, for example, holds that "where any phrase has a structure, it cannot be nominally defined by a phrase with a structure," and again:

> Only a single word (or symbol) could be given a nominal definition in the strict sense, for it has no structure. The existence of a structure in a propositional expression is already the existence of an independent framework of meaning; that which has an independent meaning can be analyzed, or shown to be equivalent to, some other independent meaning, but it cannot be nominally defined.[37]

On this reasoning, for example, it would be impossible to offer a nominal definition of a concept like "consciousness of kind." But single words too would fall under this proscription if they

---

[37] Eaton, *op. cit.*, p. 300, note.

have prefixes or suffixes, especially the former, with independent connotations. It would thus be impossible to give a nominal definition of Dodd's "presuperdescript" because this word, prior to definition, has a structure that connotes a locus—namely, before and above—and one cannot therefore resolve to let it stand for an exponent, which would be a "postsuperdescript," without contradiction. The word "triangle," used in an earlier illustration, presents a similar case. The question arises whether the hyphen in such a concept as "pattern-variable" in Parsons gives the expression a structure that would prohibit its nominal definition. We should be inclined to answer in the negative; but the issue, as can be seen, is a difficult one.

Finally, we cannot use the distinction between nominal and real definitions as an infallible guide to, nor even as a criterion of, a "reality claim" on the part of the concept defined. There is no question but that at some point a real definition assumes not merely a logical but also an ontological significance. This problem cannot be treated in anything less than an essay in metaphysics, but we want to invite attention at least to Edel's paper in this volume[38] and particularly to his discussion of "locus-candidates." He suggests that even though locus-candidates "may have been advanced as categories for an analytical framework structuring the whole field of study [as, one presumes, in Dodd and Parsons, for example—R.B.], they still must exhibit some empirical content and maintain a material status." Edel's paper in fact involves, as he says, "treating locus-candidates seriously as empirical or material categories descriptive of level qualities, rather than as abstract categories structuring the inquiry prior to beginning it."

Similarly, Gouldner, in an incisive paper on recent sociological theory, insists that key postulates have a substantial empirical base:

---

[38] Abraham Edel, "The Concept of Levels in Social Theory," in Llewellyn Gross (ed.), *Symposium on Sociological Theory* (Evanston, Ill.: Row, Peterson and Company, 1959), pp. 167–195.

It is particularly necessary to raise questions concerning the empirical status of even key postulates in a theoretical system, and to treat this as an independent problem when the system is not a truly deductive one, as, for example, in the case of Parsons' theory.[39]

And again:

Even if one sets aside questions of the logical niceties of Parsons' analysis of "social action," there still remain important empirical issues. A specification of the elements of social action is no more attainable by formal definition alone than are the attributes of "life," which the biologist regards as the "subject matter" of his discipline. Znaniecki, almost alone among the systematic theorists who have raised the question, has stressed that the characteristics of social action cannot be taken as *a priori* data but are also to be inductively sought and empirically validated.[40]

The distinction we have been discussing is not, unfortunately, powerful enough to guarantee the ontological status of locus-candidates, nor can it confirm the independent empirical presence of *definienda*. It may be, therefore, that we have over-emphasized its importance to sociological theory. We find it, however, a suggestive and helpful device in the respects we have noted, and especially in exhibiting the two primary vectors of inquiry.

Mention of mathematics above in relation to formal systems induces us to include a brief comment on one methodological matter in which it appears that Parsons is almost certainly in error. In an early paper on sociological theory, a paper whose

---

[39] Alvin W. Gouldner, "Some Observations on Systematic Theory, 1945–55," in *Sociology in the United States of America,* Hans L. Zetterberg, ed. (Paris: UNESCO, 1956), p. 35, note.
[40] *Ibid.,* p. 37.

arguments he apparently still supports,[41] he disputes the views of the extreme empiricists that a science can be "purified of theoretical infection" and consist only of collections of heterogeneous and unrelated facts, although we should be surprised if anyone subscribes to this view. In his discussion he emphasizes the importance of mathematics in the natural sciences and insists that "mathematics in physics is theory."[42]

It seems doubtful, however, if this is a position that Parsons would want permanently to defend. He may have forgotten Bertrand Russell's witty and yet obviously correct remark that the mathematician never knows what he is talking about or whether what he is saying is true. It is possible to develop all kinds of mathematical systems, based upon postulates that have nothing to do with the actual world, as both Euclidean and non-Euclidean geometries testify. Nor is there any clear sense in which it can be maintained, for example, that the binomial theorem expresses a proposition about the physical world. Propositions in physical theory are quite another matter. The most fateful equation of our time—$E = mc^2$—is an apparently true statement about the universe and it is true in independence of the symbols used in order to give it expression. It may be doubted that this equation could ever have been discovered without mathematics, but the relationship it expresses has an ontological status in the world as we know it and is not something, like the binomial theorem, that is true only within a formal system. It is, in short, a proposition about the universe and not merely about some formal system in which the symbols "E," "m," and "c" have been given meanings. And it is as true in English as it is in mathematical symbols.

John Stuart Mill was doubtless the last philosopher to hold seriously to the view that mathematics is an empirical science. Contemporary writers, whatever their philosophical orientation, take, on the contrary, the view just expressed. Furfey, for exam-

---

[41] "The Present Position and Prospects of Systematic Theory in Sociology," reprinted in *Essays in Sociological Theory*, revised edition, *op. cit.*, pp. 212–37.

[42] *Ibid.*, p. 224.

ple, is quite explicit in saying that "The concepts of the mathematician are not limited by existing reality," and that the nature of mathematical entities "is determined by arbitrary decision, not by experience."[43] And von Mises writes, "One can construct in many ways tautological systems in which there exist, according to fixed rules, absolutely correct statements; but if one wants to state anything about relations between observable phenomena, e.g., in astronomy, then one is subject to control by future experiences. The application of mathematical methods can never guarantee the correctness of a nonmathematical proposition."[44] With respect to the use of mathematical models in sociology, a recent statement by Peter H. Rossi, too long to quote, is both accurate and comprehensive.[45] Models alone are not enough,[46] and mathematics itself is neither physical theory nor sociological theory. The analogy between mathematical models and nominal definitions, though not perfect, again illuminates the issue with which the present paper is principally concerned.

In conclusion, we may say again that, just as nominal definitions and real definitions are two different things, and illustrate different vectors of inquiry, so also are methodological theory and substantive theory in sociology. If utility is the test of the first,

---

[43] Paul Hanly Furfey, *The Scope and Method of Sociology* (New York: Harper & Brothers, 1953), pp. 113–14. This superior treatise, candidly metasociological, should be consulted on a number of matters relevant to the present discussion. See especially the treatment of formal and nonformal sciences, pp. 112–15; the inverse interpretation of formal systems, pp. 250–58; and the whole of Chapter 9, "The Logical Structure of Science," pp. 199–216.

[44] Richard von Mises, *Positivism* (Cambridge: Harvard University Press, 1951), p. 6.

[45] Peter H. Rossi, "Methods of Social Research, 1945–55," in *Sociology in the United States of America, op. cit.,* p. 24.

[46] On some of the studies of Simon and Rashevsky, for example, Rossi comments that they are "of interest almost solely as examples of mathematical virtuosity; they do not specify how the variables used may be given empirical definition." *Ibid.*

truth is the test of the second.[47] It is one thing—and an important thing—to develop a language, a schema, a system of symbols for use in sociology. It is quite another thing to develop a theory. A theory is a point of view and requires an assertion. A conceptual scheme is a language, and requires only a stipulation. A schema is sterile unless it can produce a theory. Substantive theory, in short, is propositional. Its propositions are assertions about society. Its concepts have referents in the empirical world. Its definitions are convertible *simpliciter*. Its conclusions have truth claims. And it is the ultimate goal of sociological inquiry.

---

[47] "Truth" is so complex a problem in philosophy that "cogency," a word used earlier, would be the superior criterion in sociological theory. We touch here, however, an issue that can be developed only in a separate paper. The reason for this observation, however, may be briefly indicated. We regard Max Weber's thesis on capitalism and Protestantism as one of the most distinguished of all contributions to sociological theory, and yet we have no idea whether or not it is true. Its truth may forever elude us. Certainly it escapes the ordinary methods of confirmation used so successfully in the experimental sciences. Our judgment, in short, is based not upon its truth but upon its cogency.

II

The Ethics of Cognitive Communication

[1963]

In a talk on David Hume given last year on the Third Programme of the BBC, Stuart Hampshire, Grote Professor of Philosophy at London, suggested that there is an ethic of argument to which philosophers have an especial obligation to conform.[1] He thought that Hume himself was particularly careful to subscribe to this ethic and indeed reflected it in his writing. Almost all of philosophy is argument and the philosopher therefore has a moral obligation to see that his words are clear, consistent, and correctly used. There is an ethic of communication too, of which argument is only one of the forms, and in this brief paper I should like to discuss some of its implications.

---

[1] *The Listener,* June 21, 1962, 1063–1064.

One can recognize first of all that there are different kinds of communication, and that different standards apply to them. The language used in the conversations of lovers has a different ethic surely than the language used by astronauts in their arcane communications. Communication has different goals and is carried on in different contexts. A spy under interrogation by hostile police almost certainly—given the propriety of spying in the first place, which no one seems to question—has a moral obligation to lie, to be evasive, to indulge in as much deceit as he can muster. A teacher in the classroom has exactly the opposite obligations.

It may be helpful therefore to distinguish between different modes of communication. In one mode the purpose is to persuade, to influence, to convince, and this mode is clearly seen in politics, in advocacy at law, and in advertising. This mode of communication clearly has ethical implications, but these are not the concern of the present paper.* The second mode appears in literature, and especially in poetry, where style takes precedence over—or at least equal rank with—substance and where the ethic of communication assumes rather less importance than its aesthetic. A third mode, the one that here engages our attention, is the use of language for cognitive purposes, as in journalism, literary criticism, scholarship, and science. There are other modes as well, including the communication for concealment referred to above.

That there is an ethic of cognitive communication can hardly be doubted. One need not dwell upon the obvious impropriety —not to say plain immorality—of indulging in misquotation or in willful misinterpretation in order to score a point against an opponent who holds a theory contrary to one's own. Less obvious perhaps is the construction of straw men whose easy destruction then is used to demonstrate one's own critical skill. Thus a great deal of polemical energy is wasted upon heroic demolitions of positions that nobody holds. Another example is to attack an

---

* If advertisers refuse to conform to the norms of grammar, it may be too much to ask that they conform to moral norms.

opposing theory in its weakest rather than its strongest form and to seize upon an opponent's infelicitous expression as evidence of a lack of cogency. *Argumentum ad hominem* also represents a departure from the highest standards of ethical communication and this fault made notorious—rather than merely interesting—the attack that F. R. Leavis recently mounted against C. P. Snow. Still another departure would be the adoption of something less than a moderate tone in one's critical writing. On this one need only agree with G. K. Chesterton, who remarked that his principal objection to a quarrel was that it interrupted an argument. One might contend finally that one has a moral—and not only a logical—obligation to be consistent, that consistency in fact is a form of honesty, and that inconsistency, except when inadvertent, is the reverse. One might even say more succinctly that one has a moral obligation to be logical.

All of these norms have ramifications which it would be instructive to explore. Here, however, I should like to address myself to a rather different issue. It concerns the use and abuse of the specialized languages that arise in intellectual intercourse in the arts and sciences. In these languages words are used in other than their publicly accepted sense, and concepts are developed that are intelligible only to those who are on the inside, as it were, and have been trained to use them. The ethical problem is that a necessary use invites an almost inevitable misuse. In order to introduce this problem let us consider for a moment the peculiar relationship that obtains between language and knowledge.

That knowledge depends upon language is an almost self-evident proposition. Knowledge of any kind—cognition, that is, not recognition; *wissen nicht kennen*—is comprised of true propositions, and propositions require expression and communication in sentences. Sentences are made of words, however, and words suffer from a variety of defects and debilities. They are vague, obscure, ambiguous and otherwise unclear. . . . [W]e have here an antinomy no less perverse than any of the classical antinomies of Immanuel Kant. The antinomy achieves a Kantian flavor in fact if we say that human knowledge has this peculiar fate, that it is impossible without language and imprecise because of it.

One way to overcome this imprecision is to construct conceptual schemata in which words or other symbols are given by nominal definition—i.e., by fiat or stipulation—specific connotations. The development of such schemata has taken different forms in different disciplines. In the physical sciences mathematical symbols largely serve this function. Chemistry has its own symbolism for the names of the elements and their combinations. Latin words make up the taxonomic concepts of the biological sciences. The social sciences, less fortunate, have had to take the words of ordinary speech and assign technical connotations to them.

The hope that mankind would be able to invent one technical language for all intellectual intercourse, a hope shared by Leibniz and others, has unfortunately had to be surrendered—although one must admit that the description David Hartley gave of such a language in his *Observations on Man* (1749) is most attractive:

> If we suppose mankind possessed of such a language, as that they could at pleasure denote all their conceptions adequately, *i.e.*, without any deficiency, superfluity, or equivocation; if, moreover, this language depended upon a few principles assumed, not arbitrarily, but because they were the shortest and best possible, and grew on from the same principles indefinitely, so as to correspond to every advancement in the knowledge of things, this language might be termed a philosophical one, and would as much exceed any of the present languages, as a paradisiacal state does the mixture of happiness and misery, which has been our portion ever since the fall.

It may be, as Hartley speculates, that Adam's disobedience has deprived us of a perfect and universal language. We should still, however, have need of developing special terminologies for our arts and our sciences. There are at least four reasons why this should be the case. In the first place, as the arts and sciences advance they are inevitably informed by new notions. New notions require new names and new names, in turn, constitute new vocabularies. In the second place, ethically neutral notions, which are the kind desired in cognitive discourse, also require new names in order to avoid the emotional and otherwise undesirable encumbrances of ordinary speech. Thirdly, systematic knowledge in any discipline, including musicology and the history of art, requires a uniformity of usage, and this only a technical and standardized terminology can supply. Finally, clarity and precision are especial desiderata in cognitive communication and these are the attendant virtues of a specialized vocabulary. Innovation and neutrality, uniformity and clarity—these are the needs that a technical terminology can serve.

In spite of manifest advantages, suspicion always accompanies these special languages, these conceptual schemata, these privileged vocabularies. Cicero, for example, demanded to know "What sort of a philosophy then is this, which speaks the ordinary language in public, but in its treatises employs an idiom of its own?" And George Bernard Shaw, both cynical and suspicious, declared that every profession is a conspiracy against the laity. We face, therefore, a dilemma that has both cognitive and ethical consequences. As is usually the case, we have to choose not between right and wrong but the greater over the lesser good. It is possible, in short, to pay too high a price for precision.

Against these obvious advantages of a technical language we have to juxtapose several genuine defects:

1. Terminological concerns can entrap their votaries on a treadmill of an eternal dialectic, and separate the verbal from the substantial to such a degree that the discipline disappears, leaving empty words as a residue. Knowledge is not acquired, after all, by shining and polishing words.

2. Neologisms sometimes encourage other irregular and bizarre usages which can easily result, as an end product, in a cult of unintelligibility.

3. Specialized terminologies, when *too* specialized, contribute to academic parochialism and to the isolation of every discipline— every art and science—from its neighbors, and render interdisciplinary intercourse difficult and even impossible.

4. Familiarity breeds hypostasis. There is a danger that language

will conceal an absence of substance, that the human tendency toward reification will encourage the belief that when we have a name we also have a "thing," that the richness of the vocabulary will conceal a poverty of knowledge. Some of our most familiar concepts, as some perceptive person has said, may be only "fig leaves that conceal the nudity of our ignorance."

5. Technical vocabularies, like other "institutions," may be susceptible to a precocious *rigor mortis*. Premature "routinization," as Max Weber would have called it, may interfere with future innovation, and the technical language may operate as a conservative influence and obstruct the advancement of inquiry. The problem of vested interests, in short, can be a plague to any discipline. A powerful and prolific writer, a terminological "entrepreneur," who has taken the time and trouble to construct a systematic schema may be reluctant to entertain other schemata than his own. One is wedded after a while to one's own words; one thinks in terms of them; one regards them as old and familiar servants whom it would be heartless to retire and replace. And thus the old, in familiar ways, repels the new and fixes a discipline in an accustomed mold.

It appears that we have here five arguments in the negative as against four in the affirmative. Our conclusion therefore should be to seek in this instance, as in so many others, an Aristotelian mean. We need technical languages in intellectual discourse but we need also to recognize the temptations they contain. Advantages accompany them—and also dangers. We need to acknowledge—this time in reverse Kantian language that they are instruments only, and never ends in themselves. We need finally to remember, with appreciation, the sentiment to which John Locke gave such eloquent expression:

> For language being the great conduit whereby men convey their discoveries, reasonings, and knowledge from one to another, he that makes an ill use of it, though he does not corrupt the fountains of knowledge, which are in things themselves; yet he does, as much as in him lie, break or stop the pipes whereby it is distributed to the public use and advantage of mankind.

PART 3

ON SOCIAL ORGANIZATION

The three essays in this section all seem easily to fit the same rubric. They all concern sociological phenomena as such, phenomena that belong to no other discipline, phenomena that could themselves—if indeed it were necessary—give to sociology its *raison d'être*. It has been contended, for example, that sociology is the residual discipline of the social sciences, that it appropriates only those subject matters that are "left over" by economics, political science, and jurisprudence. Not so. Majorities, social power, and authority are purely sociological in essence and emphasis, and none of them can be exhausted by analysis that is only economic, only political, or only legal. It has similarly been contended, by W. G. Runciman for example, that the content of sociology cannot usefully be distinguished from either history or anthropology. Again, not so. If Runciman's own essays do not refute his contention—as in fact they do—attention to these three phenomena can readily do so. Elaboration would be supererogatory. It is no longer necessary to proclaim or to defend the autonomy of sociology or the "purity" of its central concepts.

"The Sociology of Majorities," the first of the essays, presents a case in point. The juxtapositions of majorities and minorities, both in groups of all kinds and in the larger society, have implications that go far beyond those that normally attract the attention of the political scientist. They affect not only the organization of government but the organization of society itself. They affect not only organized groups but unorganized groups as well. If the history of sociology prior to Comte is indistinguishable from the history of political philosophy, it is for the reason primarily that the Greeks made no distinction between state and society, between the polis and the community. It is one of the many merits of the late Robert M. MacIver, a political philosopher and a sociologist, to have seen in depth the quality and significance of this distinction, to have seen that there is an order —a social order—that lies beyond the realm of government.

In this connection it occurred to me that majorities had received less than condign consideration in the literature of sociology. Sociologists knew a great deal about minorities and even had an especial affection for them, but who except Simmel had said anything about majorities? Here was an omission that required repair, here a phenomenon that invited analysis, and it was to this task that I devoted a preliminary effort. I was surprised to discover that so much needed to be said and disappointed that so much of that became obvious in the saying of it.

In the paper on majorities I had occasion to comment upon the power that a majority exercises, not only in organized groups but in society at large. I used the word "power" rather freely, especially toward the end, where I also refer to such phenomena as strength, force, and control. The more I thought about this the more dissatisfied I became. I had caught myself in the act, so to speak—the act of using a concept whose meaning was more than a bit obscure, a concept I was unable to define. Something had to be done to relieve the discomfort. Accordingly, I wrote the paper entitled "An Analysis of Social Power" in order to clarify the meaning of the word for myself. It seems also to have been of some help to others because it is my most reprinted paper. The version that appears here, a slight revision of the original, is from the third edition of *The Social Order*.

The article entitled "The Problem of Authority" is a corollary of the one on power. Since I insisted, in the latter, that power is always "potential," I had to account in some way for its expression in society. This I did by suggesting that power is expressed either as force or as authority and that authority might usefully be conceived of as institutionalized power. In order to do this I distinguished authority from competence and authority from leadership, in the latter case again dissenting from Max Weber and his concept of charismatic authority. The essay goes on to show that authority is ubiquitous in complex societies and that its locus is always in associations, never in the interstices between them or in the unorganized community. Finally, I worried about the rationale of authority—whether it operates by coercion or consent—and decided, with certain qualifications, on the side of the former. I concluded with the suggestion that authority is always a power phenomenon (or, less dogmatically, that it is more useful and consistent so to conceive it) and that it has something to do with majorities, which are one of the sources of social power. The article was written as a contribution to a *Festschrift* in honor of Robert M. MacIver. It appears here in its original form.

An attentive reader of this section may notice a conspicuous omission. Although the concepts of power and authority are treated in detail, there is no comparable treatment of the concept of force. Here I have to confess to failure. Again and again I have tried to analyze it, but nothing has emerged that did not collapse at the first exposure to my own criticism. I should want to mean by "force" something that Bertrand Russell called "naked power," but unfortunately a synonym is no substitute for an analysis. I have tentatively defined it as "the reduction or limitation or closure or even total elimination of alternatives to the social action of one person or group by another person or group." But by what means? Is force always physical, or can it appear in sundry social forms? Are force and coercion identical, or is it necessary to distinguish them? Why do we call the police a "force?" And how, if at all, does the concept of force fit into a system of sociology? Is it, like power and authority, one of the components of the social order? Is it in fact, as Russell and MacIver both contended, the *ultima ratio* of society, the ultimate ground on which the order and stability of society repose? To these questions I have so far been able to supply no satisfactory answers.

12

The Sociology of
Majorities

[1948]

A casual but not uninterested observer of the current sociological
scene could not fail to notice the serious concern within the field
for problems of minorities and minority groups. If he pauses to
reflect upon this phenomenon the thought may occur to him that
nowhere is there a similar or even comparable concern for majorities and majority groups. Systematic treatments of this latter
subject are distinguished by their scarcity, and this may seem
doubly strange in view of the fact that some of the societies in
which sociology has reached its highest development accept as
almost axiomatic the political principle of majority rule.

The proposition that majorities have been neglected requires
no more than negative evidence. Even those sociologists like

Simmel,[1] von Wiese,[2] and MacIver,[3] who have touched upon the subject, have done so largely in a political rather than a sociological context.[4] Without implying that political and sociological concerns are mutually exclusive, it may nevertheless be suggested that the latter might be broader in significance than the former and may present issues that a political emphasis obscures. Some of these issues we should expect to see treated in sociography. When we turn to the sociology of groups, however, a subject that has properly been regarded as of central and indeed of pivotal concern,[5] we find an almost infinite number of classification of types of groups, but no mention of majorities. There are open groups and closed groups, organized groups and

---

[1] "Exkurs über die Uberstimmung," in *Soziologie*, Leipzig: Duncker & Humblot, 1908, pp. 186–197.

[2] Leopold von Wiese and Howard Becker, *Systematic Sociology*, New York: Wiley, 1932, pp. 267–268, 431–432, 598.

[3] See *Leviathan and the People*, Baton Rouge: Louisiana State University Press, 1939; *The Web of Government*, New York: Macmillan, 1947; and *The Elements of Social Science*, London: Methuen, 1921, pp. 174–176.

[4] Political treatments of the principle of majority rule embrace almost the entire literature of political philosophy, and particularly the philosophy of democracy. For an excellent recent discussion, with carefully selected bibliography, see Willmoore Kendall, *John Locke and the Doctrine of Majority Rule*, Urbana: University of Illinois Press, 1941. Kendall suggests that although in one sense no political scientist can avoid the problem of majorities, in another sense it is the " 'dark continent' of modern political theory" (p. 16). See also von Gierke, "Über die Geschichte des Majoritätsprinzipes," *Schmollers Jahrbuch für Gezetsbegung Verwaltung und Volkswirtschaft im Deutschen Reiche*, 39:565–587, 1915; and Ladislas Konopczynski, "Majority Rule," *Encyclopedia of the Social Sciences*, 10:55–59.

[5] For a comprehensive summary of this subject see Logan Wilson, "The Sociography of Groups," in *Twentieth Century Sociology*, Gurvitch and Moore, eds. New York: Philosophical Library, 1945, pp. 139–171. Also Florian Znaniecki, "Social Organization and Institutions," *Ibid.*, pp. 172–217; Wiese-Becker, *op. cit.*, pp. 488–555; G. A. Lundberg, *Foundations of Sociology*, New York: Macmillan, 1939, pp. 339–374, and "Some Problems of Group Classification and Measurement," *American Sociological Review*, 5:351–360 (June, 1940).

unorganized groups, primary groups, "A" groups and "B" groups, in-groups and out-groups, "real" groups and "nominal" groups, horizontal groups and vertical groups, voluntary groups and involuntary groups, large groups and small groups, long-lived groups and short-lived groups, "unibonded" groups and "multibonded" groups, and many others in terms of sociological form, and others still, such as age, sex, ethnic, occupational, economic, educational, class, religious, linguistic, territorial, and so on,[6] in terms of sociological content.[7] In all these classifications the majority-minority distinction is conspicuous by its absence. If not in sociography at least in the general texts on sociology one would expect the majority-minority distinction to have achieved some prominence, particularly in view of the heavy emphasis upon minorities, but again the distinction fails to appear, and there is no discussion of majorities as such. Finally, one would expect to find treatments of majorities in texts on social control, but once again a cursory examination leaves the expectation un-

---

[6] For a recent discussion of the problem of group classification see P. A. Sorokin, *Society, Culture, and Personality*, New York: Harper, 1947, pp. 145–255.

[7] In view of the difficulty of finding a *fundamentum divisionis* for a logically rigorous classification of groups, the question arises as to whether a classification can serve any useful purpose, even if an adequate construction could be achieved. Ogburn and Nimkoff, for example, contend with some cogency that all such classifications are of limited usefulness. See *Sociology*, Boston: Houghton Mifflin, 1946, p. 251. In support of this view it may be said that a good deal of so-called formal or structural sociology, whatever its intrinsic merit or logical appeal, has little or nothing to do with sociological theory. Taxonomy is not theory, although the two are often confused. Sociological taxonomy belongs to methodology, sociological theory to sociology itself; taxonomy deals with the logical relations between sociological concepts; sociological theory deals with the spatio-temporal and causal relations between social variables. Logical order is the goal of the former inquiry, scientific truth of the latter; the former issues, ideally, in a modified Tree of Porphyry; the latter in universal propositions. On the other hand, in opposition to the view of Ogburn and Nimkoff, classifications, like nominal definitions, are, if not systematically necessary, at least a desirable propaedeutic to the construction of sociological theories.

fulfilled.[8] Social control is treated almost exclusively in terms of such cultural factors as folkways, more, institutions, laws, and so on, rather than in terms of such social factors as the influence of majorities. It is almost as if sociologists had unanimously agreed to leave the subject of majorities to the devices of political scientists.

The subject, however, is worth considering for several reasons. The first of these is that number is a necessary category in sociology and that phenomena of many different kinds change not only in degree but also in their nature as they vary in size. Certainly small groups, for example, are different from large groups in other ways than that the former are small, the latter large.[9] In like manner, majorities differ from minorities in other ways than that they are larger, and it is these other ways that it is instructive to analyze. Differences of this kind have an intrinsic sociological interest and, difficult as they may be to discern, comprise an integral part of group theory. In this connection von Wiese has the following comment:

> It is difficult to assign the proper place to the concepts of majority and minority. They are primarily expressions of a purely numerical relation, and they therefore belong among the other colorless terms here discussed [swarm, band, pack, and herd]. The social relationships between majority and minority, however, play an extremely important part in many plurality patterns. . . . The circumstance

---

[8] On this subject see L. L. Bernard, *Social Control*, New York: Macmillan, 1939; Paul H. Landis, *Social Control*, Philadelphia: Lippincott, 1939; Jerome Doud, *Control in Human Societies*, New York: Appleton-Century, 1936; E. A. Ross, *Social Control*, New York: Macmillan, 1916, (Ross notes, however, that "The prestige of *numbers* gives ascendancy to the crowd," p. 78); and Joseph S. Roucek and Associates, *Social Control*, New York: Van Nostrand, 1947. On the other hand, there is relevant material in William Albig, *Public Opinion*, New York: McGraw-Hill, 1939, although not couched specifically in terms of majorities and minorities. See especially Chapters I, II, and XVI.

[9] On the influence of number and size upon social groups see Simmel, *op. cit.*, pp. 47–133, and Wiese-Becker, *op. cit.*, pp. 498–501.

that these two categories taken in conjunction denote a proportion and not a mere summation makes them sociologically important. Majority and minority are not primarily or usually purality patterns, but in certain situations they may become groups, and hence should receive attention for this reason as well.[10]

Secondly, it is apparent that the majority-minority distinction differs in principle from distinctions based upon number and size. As von Wiese says in the passage quoted immediately above, a proportion is different from a summation. Groups of whatever size differ from other groups of the same size when the former are majorities and the latter are not. Furthermore, it is obvious that a majority may be relatively small, a minority relatively large, although not, of course, when they are in opposition in the same context. It is also obvious that majorities may vary considerably in size, in relation to their conjoint minorities, without ceasing to be majorities. In a group of 100, 51 and 99 both constitute majorities. For these reasons the majority-minority distinction is not comprehended by any other formal categories of groups and the distinction is, in fact, unique.

In the third place, majorities and minorities are universal in all societies and in all groups, except those which have an even number of members evenly divided and those which are unanimous. In all complex societies, where integration is imperfect and unanimity non-existent, majorities and minorities are constant phenomena.

A fourth reason for studying majorities has both theoretical and practical consequences, and the latter outweigh the former. For it has often been observed by writers concerned with oppressed minorities that the problems are essentially not minority problems at all, but majority problems. Writers on the Negro in the United States, for example, and especially Myrdal, have

---

[10] Wiese–Becker, *op. cit.*, pp. 431–32. These few lines, under the section on "Concepts and Categories: Numerical," are unfortunately all these authors have to say about majorities, with two minor exceptions.

insisted that there is no such thing as a Negro problem, that the problem is actually a "white" problem. In a sense, of course, this is only a manner of speaking, but there can be no doubt that the problem, whether Negro or white, would have a dramatically different impact upon American life if (a) the Negro population were not so large as it is, (b) the Negro population were not so small as it is, (c) the white population comprised not a majority but a dominant minority, (d) the Negro population were the same size but comprised a dominant minority, (e) Northern whites were not a majority and Southern whites not a minority, and so on through many diverse combinations. Whatever the way in which the issue is phrased, it is easy to agree that there is something about majorities that causes and creates minority problems and that a knowledge of the nature and characteristics of the former may contribute to an understanding of the latter. We know, for example, that people become prejudiced not through contact with minority (i.e., oppressed) groups, but through contact with prevailing attitudes toward minority groups.[11] Attitudes "prevail" in a society when they are held by majorities.

---

[11] There is a vast literature that can be invoked in support of this point. See, for example, Murphy, Murphy, and Newcomb, *Experimental Social Psychology*, New York: Harper, 1937; Murphy and Likert, *Public Opinion and the Individual*, New York, 1938; Theodore M. Newcomb, "The Influence of Attitude Climate upon Some Determinants of Information," *Journal of Abnormal and Social Psychology*, 41:291–302, 1946; Arnold Rose, *Studies in Reduction of Prejudice* (mimeographed) Chicago: American Council on Race Relations, 1947; Robin M. Williams, Jr., "The Reduction of Intergroup Tensions," *Bulletin* 57, Social Science Research Council, 1947; and Robert M. MacIver, *The More Perfect Union*, New York: Macmillan, 1948. For psychological studies of the influence of majorities in the formation of opinion see H. E. Burtt and D. R. Falkenburg, Jr., "The Influence of Majority and Expert Opinion on Religious Attitudes," *Journal of Social Psychology*, 14:269–278 (1941); and C. H. Marple, "The Comparative Suggestibility of Three Age Levels to the Suggestion of Group vs. Expert Opinion," *Journal of Social Psychology*, 4:176–186 (1933). These last two studies, unfortunately, were made with very small groups and are not conclusive. In short, the experimental evidence on the influence of majorities upon opinion is meager.

Finally, as suggested above, a sociological approach to the subject of majorities may assist in discerning attributes and properties that are not insignificant for the purposes of political science and that tend to be obscured in the latter approach. It may be suggested, for example, that political majorities and what we are unfortunately forced to call societal majorities (*i.e.*, the majority of all the people in a society) do not necessarily coincide, either in personnel or in political predilections. Even under conditions of universal suffrage a political majority may represent only a small societal minority. Of even greater significance, however, is the fact that majorities have so often been conceived of in purely political terms that the broader sociological nature of the subject has suffered neglect. Political majorities are only one kind of majority and, even if they are the most important kind, it does not follow that other kinds are unimportant. Nor does it follow that the nature and characteristics of majorities in general can be discerned in an investigation of political majorities or, for that matter, of any particular kind of majority. In other words, as in most cases affecting the relationships between sociology and the other social sciences, certain phenomena appear that have a more generic and universal significance than can be grasped in any inquiry more specialized than the sociological. It is not inconceivable that a general sociological analysis of majorities may illuminate some of the more special political implications of majorities.[12]

These five reasons, among others, support the opinion that the subject merits attention by sociologists. In the present place it is naturally not possible to inquire into all of the problems presented by majorities, but it is at least desirable to indulge in some preliminary observations of a formal and necessarily hypothetical nature.

A preliminary analysis may begin with the recognition that majorities, like other groups, may be large or small (both abso-

---

[12] Kendall, for example, says that Simmel's "Excursus," cited *infra*, note I, is "a discussion which no student of the social sciences can read without subsequently paying to it the unusual compliment of wishing that it had been many times as long." *Loc. cit.*, p. 27.

lutely and relative to their conjoint minorities), open or closed, primary or secondary, active or inactive, cohesive through one or many bonds, relatively permanent or relatively impermanent, and so on. Indeed, many additional adjectives of this polar kind may be attached to them. These adjectives will not, however, contribute anything substantial to an investigation of their specific characteristics. One aspect of groups, on the other hand, is significant. This is the aspect that determines whether group, or the majority, is organized or unorganized. There has been a tendency in sociology, not dominant perhaps but nevertheless discernible, to consider organized groups, often called associations, to be of greater significance than unorganized groups. Attention to majorities may help to dispel the opinion that this is always, or even usually, the case. For majorities, in many situations of interest to sociology, are unorganized, and this absence of organization does not diminish their significance.

The distinction between organized and unorganized groups, however, is insufficiently discriminating when applied to majorities. It is doubtful, in fact, if it is wholly satisfactory when applied to groups. A consideration of majorities illustrates that there are four general kinds, as different one from the other as the kinds of groups of which they are a part. In attempting to delineate these kinds one is embarrassed, as so often in sociology, by the paucity of terms with which to label them and by the consequent necessity of utilizing words already burdened with connotations. In spite of this hazard, we may distinguish four kinds of groups as exhibited in the accompanying somewhat crude "table." These four may be called the statistical, the societal, the social, and the associational. Statistical groups are synonymous with logical classes. They have only an "analytical"

Classification of Groups

	Consciousness of Kind	Social Relations	Social Organization
A. Statistical	No	No	No
B. Societal	Yes	No	No
C. Social	Yes	Yes	No
D. Associational	Yes	Yes	Yes

existence and are "formed," if one may be permitted the expression, not by people themselves but by people who write about people—in other words by sociologists, statisticians, demographers, and so on. Whether they have members or not is immaterial, and we may accordingly have null groups in sociology in the same sense in which we have null classes in logic. Statistical groups, therefore, have no social organization, they have "members" in a logical but not in a sociological sense; and consciousness of kind, in the absence of a social stimulus to evoke it, is only potential. Similarly, the "members" do not enter into social relations with one another on the basis of the trait in terms of which they constitute a group. They may have one or several traits in common, but they have no interests in common, nor any like interests.[13] Examples of such statistical groups are right-handed persons, red-headed persons, persons fifty years of age, persons who are five feet tall, persons who have had the measles, persons who have died of tuberculosis, persons who prefer soap operas to Italian operas, and so on.

Societal groups differ from statistical groups in that they do have members and these members are conscious of their kind, of the similarity or identity of traits they all possess. There are no null groups here and the trait itself may be single or multiple. Here appear external signs by means of which the members recognize one another, such as skin color, language, accent, grammar, response to patriotic symbols, appearance, and so on. The members, in short, are or may easily become "visible" to one another. They have like interests but not common interests. They do not, however, in the absence of a social stimulus, enter into social relations with each other. Examples of societal groups are males, females, Negroes, whites, Southerners, New Yorkers, golfers, the blind, college professors and indeed all occupational groups.

Social contact and communication appear in the third category. The social group differs from the societal group in that its

---

[13] For a distinction between the like and the common see R. M. MacIver, *Society*, New York: Farrar & Rinehart, 1937, pp. 28, 30.

members have social relations with one another and from the statistical group both in this respect and in that consciousness of kind is present. Social relations are the distinguishing additional characteristic. The members may have like but not common interests, common but not like interests (*e.g.*, an assortment of persons on a life-raft after a shipwreck), or both like and common interests. Examples are groups of acquaintances, relatives, cliques, audiences, spectators, crowds, mobs, passengers on board a small ship, and many other unorganized groups discussed in the texts.

When a group has these characteristics and is, in addition, organized, we have the fourth kind of group indicated above, the associational group or, more simply, the association. Examples are a fraternity, a lodge, a club, a team, an orchestra, a committee, and so on. In these groups it is the formal organization which is the prominent characteristic and membership in them in itself confers consciousness of kind and generates social relations in accordance with procedural norms. Here, finally, the members usually have both like and common interests.

Before commenting upon its uses, it is necessary to say that this is not an inclusive classification. Some groups find no place in these categories; for example, groups that involve social relations but no necessary consciousness of kind, and groups comprised not of individuals but of other groups. It should also be recognized that none of these groups is stable, and that in the process of social life they may become transformed into groups in other categories under the impress of events. Red-headed people, a statistical group, would become a societal group with the improbable passage of legislation taxing them, a social group if they entered into social relations on the basis of the color of their hair and attended a meeting, for example, to which only red-headed people were invited, and an associational group if they organized a Red-Headed League for the purpose of resisting the legislation. Finally, the classification is a logical but not a temporal continuum; a statistical group may become an association immediately, without passing through the intervening categories; and the reverse could happen on the occasion of the dissolution of an association.

When we return from this digression on group classification in general to the question of majorities in particular, an interesting reflection emerges. For it immediately appears that all four of these groups, the statistical no less than the associational, have sociological significance when they are majorities. And in many cases it is only because they are majorities that they acquire general social significance in the societies in which they occur. This significance can be illustrated by a number of examples. Consider the significance of the majority first of all when it is a statistical group, where no social relations are involved. A society or group in which the majority of the population were of age fifty and above would be a different kind of a society from one in which the majority were fifty and below. Substitute any age categories and the generalization retains its cogency. Similarly, societies differ when or if right-handed persons or left-handed persons are in the majority, urban-dwellers or rural-dwellers, literates or illiterates, and so on. In other words, statistical groups do have sociological significance when they are majorities. They determine to an extensive degree the general characteristics of a society and of a social group. Statistical majorities always have more than a statistical significance. It is therefore a mistake to limit sociology, as formal sociologists are sometimes inclined to do, to a study of social relationships as such, if that term implies social contact and communication between people. For it is apparent that many phenomena of the highest import for sociology, those responsible for the character of an entire society, are determined by the juxtaposition within it of majorities whose members have never met, who do not know one another, and who may, in fact, be unaware of the individual existence of one another.[14]

---

[14] It is similarly a mistake to emphasize the role of organized groups in a society at the expense of the unorganized, and especially of those in the latter category which are only statistical groups, i.e., as defined above, groups the sociologist himself constructs in the process of classifying people in various ways. It may be safe to say, incidentally, that the conclusions of demographers have not been integrated into formal sociology and that chapters on population remain somewhat logically separate from those on social structure, even though frequently bound together in the same book.

Comparable observations are relevant to the role of societal majorities. Men's college communities are different from women's college communities, and the differential status of "faculty wives" in the two situations is striking. Of more importance, however, is the fact that minority group problems, problems involving ethnic and national minorities, appear in societies when consciousness of kind and consciousness of difference characterize majority and minority groups. Tension in such situations, in the absence of compensating factors, is directly proportional to the size of the minority and inversely proportional to the size of the majority. That is, majority-minority tension appears to be least when the majority is large, the minority small, and greatest when the minority threatens, by increase in size, to become the majority. Meanwhile, ethnic minorities are oppressed largely in proportion not to their absolute but their relative size. Conversely, a very small minority, again relatively speaking may suffer the satiric sanction but no specific social disability. This point unfortunately requires more development than can be offered here, but it is noteworthy that it is amenable to empirical research.

The social group also, the group that is unorganized but in which social relations occur, is dependent for its function upon a majority. Whether a group of friends goes to a play or to a musical comedy, to an expensive nightclub or to an inexpensive tavern, drinks coffee or beer on a given occasion, and so on, depends, often unconsciously, upon majority desires. Similarly, in larger groups, a lynching can occur only if it is at least tacitly sanctioned by a majority of those present, and a panic can occur only if a majority of the persons involved in a situation fail to "keep their heads." A clique clearly operates under the influence of the majority of its own members and an elite, although a minority, suffers no discrimination only because it embodies social values of which the majority approves and would like to emulate.

It is in the organized group, the association, in which majorities seem, on the surface, to have the least significance. As social organization introduces an hierarchical structure into a group the significance of numbers, and therefore of majorities, diminishes in proportion. The more highly organized the association the fewer functions belong to the majority. Here majority action is, in fact, constrained and limited by organization, by rules and regulations, and by the creation of authority. It would be an error to assert that the majority exercises any official influence in a tightly organized, hierarchically ordered association like, for example, the Roman Catholic Church, the United States Navy, or the Communist Party, three associations which, whatever their diverse goals, exhibit a remarkable sociological similarity in internal organization and structure.[15] There are many more priests than cardinals, seamen than admirals, and party-workers than members of the Politburo, and it is the latter, not the former, who possess the power. This, of course, is true in varying extent of all associations, even the most "democratic." The power structure is always pyramidal.

But even here majorities play a role. This role appears with the recognition that all associations have two types of organization, a formal organization and an informal organization,[16] and that, although majorities exercise no formal function whatever—

---

[15] One interesting similarity, among others, is that the distinction between "associational" and "private" statuses of the functionaries tends to disappear and extra-associational statuses have little importance. Such associations differ in this respect from the "corporate groups" delineated by Max Weber which exemplify "rational-legal" authority and in which distinctions between official and private statuses are maintained. On this point see *Max Weber: The Theory of Social and Economic Organization*, edited by Talcott Parsons, New York: Oxford, 1947, pp. 324ff, and especially Parsons' Introductory essay, "The Institutionalization of Authority," pp. 56–77. See also E. T. Hiller on the professions and on the office, *Social Relations and Structures*, New York, Harper, 1947, pp. 544–596.

[16] Although E. T. Hiller has not used these concepts, his distinctions between intrinsic and extrinsic valuations of persons and between personal and categoric social relations are directly relevant. See *Ibid.*, pp. 191–213; 631–645. The interrelations between formal and informal organization represent an important junction of formal sociology and social psychology and require, perhaps, more intensive analysis than they have as yet received.

except when they constitute a legitimate party[17]—they often exercise covert and sometimes even overt informal control in associations. Utilizing only the most extreme and rigid cases for illustration, that is associations in which majorities would seem to have the least influence, it can be demonstrated that they are not immune from the pressures of majorities. A clear example is afforded by the Navy during the recent war. Not even the highly inflexible rules and regulations of the service, enforced by Regular Navy officers in command positions, were impervious to the pressure of the large majority of Reserve officers who considered some of the niceties of naval etiquette, particularly with respect to salutes, ceremonies, and relations with enlisted men, to be more than a little ridiculous. The exodus of Reserve officers after the war, their declining majority and ultimate minority, contributed increasing conformity to the rules and reduced the discrepancy between the formal and informal organization.[18]

The Roman Catholic Church offers another illustration in a totally different sphere. The long struggle with "modern errors" began in 1543 with the publication of *On the Revolutions of the Celestial Orbs* by Nicolai Copernicus and became intense when Galileo was summoned once in 1616 and five times in 1633 to the bar of the Inquisition. This story is well known. What is not so well known is that a license to print a book espousing the heliocentric hypothesis was refused as late as 1820 and that not until September 11, 1822 was the following decree quietly issued by the Holy Office:

---

[17] In sociological terms a party is a device for recruiting a majority and can, as Max Weber suggests, exist only within an organized group or association (Weber: *Verband*; Parsons: "corporate group"), even though it operates, as do political parties in the United States, without specific constitutional sanction. See Max Weber, *loc. cit.*, p. 407. See also R. M. MacIver, *The Web of Government, op. cit.*, pp. 208–224 and especially p. 213.

[18] For an excellent analysis of formal and informal organization in the Navy see Charles H. Page, "Bureaucracy's Other Face," *Social Forces*, 25:88–94, October, 1946. For an implicit fictional treatment of the same theme see *Mister Roberts*, by Thomas Heggen, Boston: Houghton Mifflin, 1946.

There is no reason why the present and future Masters of the Sacred Palace should refuse license for printing and publishing works treating of the mobility of the earth and the immobility of the sun, according to the common opinion of modern astronomers.[19]

What scientific evidence was unable to accomplish, majority and "common" opinion finally did, even though several centuries were consumed in the process.[20] One is tempted to say that no association, no matter how rigidly organized, is able to withstand the permanent pressure of a majority and that an organized majority is the most potent social force on earth. There is a certain authority in a majority which no hierarchy can wholly obliterate.

From these instances and others another principle can be induced. It concerns the nature of formal and informal organization in any association and the role of majorities with respect to these two forms of organization. First, however, it is appropriate to clarify the meaning of these terms which have appeared in preceding paragraphs. The formal organization of an association consists of the formally recognized and established statuses of the members in accordance with the rank of the offices and other positions they occupy, together with the rules and regulations that set out the obligations, duties, privileges, and responsibilities of these positions. The status of non-office holding members, their duties and privileges, is also, of course, a part of the formal organization—formal because formally recognized and concurred in as a condition of membership. Social relations between the members are conducted formally in terms of these statuses, in conformity with explicit norms, and in accordance with "extrinsic" and "categoric" evaluations of persons. In the formal

---

[19] Quoted in Preserved Smith, A History of Modern Culture, New York: Henry Holt, 1930, Vol. I, p. 58.

[20] Illustrations for the third example, the Communist Party, are more difficult to exhibit because of lack of information. It is possible, however, that increasing anti-semitism in the high councils of the Party in Russia, as reported by Drew Middleton in articles in the New York Times in February, 1948, may be concessions to majority opinion even though in direct opposition to both constitutional and doctrinal orthodoxy.

organization, statuses have differential prestige in independence of the persons who occupy them.

Since this independence is difficult if not impossible to maintain in the dynamics of associational life, however, an informal organization arises to exist coevally with the formal. The informal organization consists of roles rather than statuses, of patterns of dominance and ascendancy, affection, hostility, or indifference of the members in accordance with their intrinsic and personal evaluations of one another. These role patterns may or may not coincide with or conform to the status hierarchy of the formal organization. In the informal organization social relations occur on the basis of the esteem that the members have for one another in independence of their statuses. In short, in formal organization social relations proceed in terms of the prestige of statuses in accordance with explicit associational norms; in informal organization they proceed in terms of the esteem for persons in accordance with implicit societal (*i.e.*, extra-associational) norms. Prestige attaches to statuses; esteem to persons.[21] The former is a component of formal organization, the latter of informal organization.[22]

Now it is apparent that in some associations there may be a close coincidence between the formal and the informal organization and that this coincidence may be relatively permanent. In such cases the statuses that carry the greatest prestige are occupied by the persons who are held in the highest esteem. On the other hand, an association may exhibit a wide discrepancy between its formal and informal organization. In these cases the prestige continues to attach to the status while esteem is withheld from the person who occupies the status and who there-

---

[21] The writer is indebted to Kingsley Davis for this distinction between prestige and esteem.

[22] It is not altogether clear in what respect it may be appropriate to refer to these informal elements in terms of "structure" or even "organization." In some respects they may be antithetical to organization and in that case the concept "informal organization" becomes an oxymoron. This is particularly true because it is these informal elements which are susceptible to frequent change in contrast to the formal which are, by comparison, relatively stable.

upon becomes a figurehead. The officers then have the formal authority of their positions but not the informal authority sustained by esteem. Now, whether or not offices are filled by "democratic" vote, it is within the power of the majority to confer actual as well as statutory authority upon the officers or to retain authority residually in the informal organization. Similarly, it is within the power of the majority to determine whether social relations in the association shall proceed only in terms of the formal rules and regulations, which are explicit norms, or in terms of informal norms which may or may not coincide with the former. Here then is the principle to which attention is invited, that the discrepancy between the formal and informal organization of any association will be least when the majority gives full support and sanction to the former and greatest when this support is for any reason or in any particular withheld. That this power of determination is a function of the majority rather than of any aspect of social organization itself is clear from the consideration that it is prior to social organization and determines the form that social organization takes. Finally, it is the support of the majority which sustains the association, the absence of this support which moves it in the direction of change or of ultimate dissolution.

We may now inquire whether some of these observations have a similar relevance in the larger society. Here the problem becomes involved in the more general question of the nature and kinds of social power, especially when we attempt to probe the source of the power that the majority exercises. Unfortunately, the subject of social power is not one that has received a comprehensive analysis in the literature, and to discourse on majorities in terms of power is like pronouncing the words of a language one does not fully understand.[23] MacIver defines it

---

[23] R. M. MacIver observes that "There is no reasonably adequate study of the nature of social power," although he himself contributes some highly pertinent remarks. See *The Web of Government, op. cit.,* p. 458, and especially Chapter 5, "The Pyramid of Power," pp. 82–113. E. A. Ross's discussion, though short, is still suggestive. See *Social Control, op. cit.,* pp. 77–88.

variously as "the capacity in any relationship to command the service or the compliance of others,"[24] and "the capacity to control the behavior of others either directly by fiat or indirectly by the manipulation of available means."[25] Among the sources of power MacIver lists property, status, office (apart from status[26]), special knowledge, managerial and executive function, financial resources, artistic, religious or other eminence, publicity, and so on. It is clear from his discussion that social power, whatever its sources and manifestations, is "responsive to the *mores* of the society."[27] And it is the majority which sustains the mores. Here then we find the authority that lies "beyond the realm of government," the authority that community and society retain, which they may or may not confer upon the state, and which, even when it is wrested from the community, wells up again and restrains the actions of governments. Not even an autocrat can remain unresponsive to the will of a majority.[28]

It would, of course, be highly unrealistic to assert that the power of the majority always manifests itself, or is always successful when it does. Majorities are frequently inert and frequently too have no means of expression. Indeed, it is one of

---

[24] *Ibid.*, p. 82.

[25] *Ibid.*, p. 87.

[26] That is, the power that proceeds from the *possession* of status.

[27] *Ibid.*, p. 98.

[28] In an eloquent passage, MacIver has described this situation as follows: "The authority of government does not create the order over which it presides and does not sustain that order solely by its own fiat or its accredited power. There is authority beyond the authority of government. There is a greater consensus without which the fundamental order of the community would fall apart. This consensus plays a different role under different forms of government. Sometimes it has nothing to do with the processes that make or unmake the princes or potentates who rule the people. Sometimes it has no mode of expression, should the ruler get out of hand and violate the fundamental order he is presumed to protect, save the rare violence of revolution. Sometimes it is alert and sensitive to all that government does and sets its seal of approval or disapproval on the policies that government pursues. But always, whether mainly acquiescent or creatively active, it is the ultimate ground on which the unity and the order of the state repose." *Ibid.*, p. 85.

the lessons of history that majorities of one kind or another have long suffered oppression. Nevertheless, it is of sociological significance to note that majorities remain the source of so much residual power, even in these situations, that autocrats and oligarchs bend every effort to prevent them from organizing. It is the power of a majority that gives meaning to the imperial command, "Divide and rule."

We find, thus, in the larger society the same principle that was found in the association. Where there is no organization, the majority determines. In the absence of stratification, likewise, the majority determines. When there is formal organization there is also informal organization, and in the latter the majority plays an important role. Indeed, society itself is an informal organization, the state a formal organization; the laws belong to the formal structure, the mores to the informal. It is the majority which sustains the mores, the minority which initiates changes in them which are then either resisted or finally sanctioned by the majority. In all societies of any complexity there is a discrepancy between the laws and the mores. This discrepancy will be wide or narrow depending upon the position of the majority. Where it is wide it will be found that the majority supports the mores, a minority supports the laws. It is the role that majorities play in societies which gives point to what is one of the most profound and cogent of all sociological principles—"When the mores are adequate, laws are unnecessary, when they are inadequate, laws are useless." The mores are adequate when they are supported by a large majority; they are inadequate when they lack this support. There is a power in the majority that can contravene any law.

It is the majority, in short, which sets the culture pattern and sustains it, which is in fact responsible for whatever pattern or configuration there is in a culture. It is the majority which confers upon folkways, mores, customs, and laws the status of norms and gives them coercive power. It is the majority which guarantees the stability of a society. It is the majority which requires conformity to custom and which penalizes deviation—except in ways which the majority sanctions and approves. It is the majority which is the custodian of the mores and which defends them against innovation. And it is the inertia of majorities, finally, which retards the processes of social change.

Throughout the preceding discussion we have, except for several incidental references, omitted from consideration the question of the size of majorities. Here it is possible to note only one implication of size, one that relates to the general problem of social and cultural integration. Reflection upon majorities enables us to see that cultural integration is a function of the size of the majority that conforms to a single set of patterns, that subscribes to the same myths, and that aspires to attain the same societal goals. When this majority is large, the culture is integrated, no matter how extensively the society is stratified. When it is small the culture lacks integration. When it dissolves into competing minorities all vestiges of integration disappear. A culture is in fact dependent upon the existence in a society of a majority. Without it the society is split into partial and fragmented cultures. Whatever the value of the cultural approach in sociology, when used exclusively it sometimes obscures the *social* factors that create and sustain a society and that determine both its coherence and its cohesion.

What, finally, is the ultimate ground for the power that the majority exercises? The answer is so deceptively simple as to discourage ready acceptance. It rests in the elemental fact, a fact so formidable as to seem incontrovertible, that the majority is stronger than the minority or, in Simmel's words, *"dass die Vielen mächtiger sind als die Wenigen."*[29] It is certainly incontrovertible that two men can force one man to do what they want, and that ten men can do it even more easily. Given the same organization, the larger number can always control the smaller, can command its service, and secure its compliance. This, incidentally, is a social and not a cultural fact.[30]

---

[29] *Loc. cit.*, p. 190.
[30] For an expansion of this thesis see John Dollard, "Culture, Society, Impulse, and Socialization," *American Journal of Sociology*, 45:53–56 (July, 1939).

In summary, we have noted the neglect of majorities in contemporary sociology and have introduced, in a very preliminary fashion, some hypotheses that a sociology of majorities might subject to further investigation. We have observed that the majority-minority distinction is a distinction *sui generis* which requires inclusion in any comprehensive group theory; that majorities play significant roles in both organized and unorganized social groups, and particularly in the informal aspects of the former; that majorities play a similar role in the larger society; that majorities constitute a residual locus of social power; that they sustain the mores; and that they are responsible for whatever cultural integration a society exhibits. Majorities doubtless have in addition multifarious characteristics and functions that we have neglected to mention. But these will suffice to show that the subject merits sustained sociological analysis.

13

An Analysis of Social Power

[1950]

Sociological inquiry provides few problems as perplexing as the problem of power. It is as perplexing in its way as the problem of electricity in physics. As a matter of fact, social power is like electrical power. We see the effects and manifestations of both but not the phenomenon itself. Social power is transformed into order, force, and authority; electrical power into light, heat, and motion. The misapplication of both, to be macabre for a moment, can result in death. But the essence of these phenomena is elusive. Not even the dictionary can give us a satisfactory definition of electricity and indeed can only call it "a fundamental entity of nature." We can similarly—and truthfully—say that power is "a fundamental entity of society," but with an awareness that we are not saying very much, if indeed we are saying anything at all. Our relative ignorance of the nature of power is itself a curious phenomenon. The word has been in our vocabularies for as long as we can remember and we frequently use it. But we find ourselves unable to define it. We here confront the dilemma of St. Augustine who confessed that he knew perfectly well what time was—until someone asked him. (*Si non rogas, intelligo.*) In this essay, however, we shall dare to ask what social power is, and we shall try to offer an answer. In the process we shall also hope to communicate the notion that power is a matter of central sociological importance.

1. Power and Society

The power structure of society is not an insignificant problem. In any realistic sense it is both a sociological (*i.e.*, a scientific) and a moral (*i.e.*, a social) problem. It has traditionally been a problem in political philosophy. Like so many other problems of a political character, however, it has roots that lie deeper than the *polis* and reach into the community itself. Its primitive basis and ultimate locus are to be sought in society, and not only in government, because in government it is already institutionalized. It is apparent, furthermore, that not all power is political power and that political power—like economic, financial, industrial, and military power—is only one of several and various kinds of social power. Wall Street, for example, can compete with the government of the United States in exercising power over foreign trade and in affecting the exchange rate of foreign currencies.

Society, in fact, is shot through with power relations—the power a father exercises over his child, a master over his slave, a teacher over his pupils, the victor over the vanquished, the blackmailer over his victim, the warden over his prisoners, the judge over the convicted defendant, an employer over his employee, a general over his lieutenants, a captain over his crew, a creditor over a debtor, and so on through an impressively large number of social relationships. Some of these are examples of authority. But all of them are examples of power because authority is a species of power. It is worth an incidental note that not all of these examples of power enjoy the support of the state. To some of them the state is indifferent, to others it is opposed.

Power, in short, is a universal phenomenon in human societies. It is seldom absent except from those social relations in the narrower sense that the sociologist Georg Simmel called relations of "polite acquaintance," the kind of interaction that appears at cocktail parties and at wedding receptions. Most other social relations contain elements of power. What, then, is this phenomenon? In trying to answer the question we shall first distinguish it from other phenomena with which it has often been associated and often confused.

2. Power and Prestige

Social power has variously been identified with prestige, influence, eminence, competence, dominance, rights, strength, force, and authority; and it was the distinguished Lord Chancellor of England, Francis Bacon, who identified it with knowledge. Since the intension of a term varies, if at all, inversely with its extension—i.e., the more things a term can be applied to the less precise its meaning—it is necessary to distinguish power from most of these other phenomena. Let us begin by separating power from prestige.

A close association between power and prestige was made by the American sociologist E. A. Ross in his classic work on social control. "The immediate cause of the location of power," he said, "is prestige." And further, "The class that has the most prestige will have the most power."[1] Now prestige may certainly be construed as something that is sometimes related to power, in the sense that powerful groups tend to be prestigious and prestigious groups powerful. Prestige clearly separates man from man and

---

[1] *Social Control*, The Macmillan Company, New York, 1916, p. 78. Dennis Wrong is most enlightening on the relationship between power and social control. See his "Some Problems in Defining Social Power," *American Journal of Sociology*, Vol. 73, May, 1968, pp. 673–681.

group from group and it has, as one of its consequences, one kind of stratification that appears in human societies. But we can always escape confusion if we can find, no matter how close the relationships, one phenomenon in the absence of the other. We can do this with respect to power and prestige and consequently the two phenomena are not identical. They are in fact independent variables. Prestige is frequently unaccompanied by power, as in the case of scholars elected to membership in the American Academy of Arts and Sciences, and power may similarly be unassociated with prestige, as in the case of a group of gangsters preying upon the small independent stores in the Bronx in New York City. Physicists, in our world, have great prestige, but not much power. Policemen, on the other hand, have significant power but—except perhaps in London—little prestige. The Phi Beta Kappa Society has high prestige in American academic circles, but no power. Prestige, in short, does not suffice to create power, and the two phenomena, both sociologically important, are not identical and may or may not appear together.

Similar observations may be made about the relationship of knowledge, eminence, skill, and competence to power. All four of these may contribute to prestige, but they may be quite unaccompanied by power. When power does accompany them the association is incidental rather than necessary. Thus the most erudite archaeologist, the most famous sculptor, the most talented pianist, and the most competent automobile mechanic in the world might all four be devoid of power. Knowledge, eminence, skill, and competence, although they may accompany it, have nothing intrinsically to do with power.

3. Power and Influence

When we turn to the relationship between power and influence we find a more intimate connection, but once again it is necessary to make a distinction. It is necessary because influence is persuasive whereas power is coercive. We submit voluntarily to influence but power requires our submission. The mistress of a king may influence the destiny of a nation, but only because her paramour permits himself to be swayed by her designs. In any ultimate reckoning her influence may be more important than his power, but it is inefficacious unless it is transformed into power. The power a teacher exercises over his pupils stems not from his superior knowledge (this is competence rather than power) and not from his opinions (this is influence rather than power), but from his ability to apply the sanction of failure to the student who does not fulfill his requirements and meet his standards. The competence may be unappreciated, and the influence may be ineffective, but the power may not be gainsaid.[2]

Furthermore, power and influence can occur in isolation from each other and so they also are independent variables. We should say, for example, that Karl Marx exerted an incalculable influence upon the twentieth century, but this poverty-stricken exile who spent so many of his hours in the British Museum was hardly a man of power. Even the assertion that he was a man of influence is an ellipsis. It is the ideas that were—and continue to be—influential. The Soviet dictator Stalin, on the other hand, was a man of power, but he had few if any influential ideas. Influence does not require power, and power may dispense with influence. Influence may convert a friend, but power coerces friend and foe alike. Influence attaches to an idea, a doctrine, or a creed, and has its locus in the ideological sphere. Power attaches to a person, a group, or an association, and has its locus in the sociological sphere. Plato, Aristotle, St. Thomas, Shakespeare, Galileo, Newton, and Kant were men of influence, but none of them exercised any noticeable power. One need only compare Aristotle, for example, with his famous pupil, Alexander the Great. Napoleon Bonaparte and Abraham Lincoln were men of both power and influence. Genghis Khan and Adolf Hitler were men of power. Archimedes was a man of influence, but the soldier who slew him at the gates of Syracuse had more power.

When we speak, therefore, of the power of an idea or when

---

[2] In this case, however, the power is transformed into authority.

we are tempted to say that ideas are weapons or when we assert, with the above-mentioned Napoleon, that the pen is mightier than the sword, we are using figurative language, speaking truly as it were, but metaphorically and with synecdoche.[3] Ideas are influential, they can change the course of history, but for the sake of logical and sociological clarity it is preferable to deny to them the attribute of power. Influence in this sense, of course, presents quite as serious and as complex a problem as power, but it is not the problem we are now discussing.[4]

4. Power and Dominance

It is relatively easy to distinguish power from dominance. Power is a sociological, dominance a psychological phenomenon. The locus of power is in both persons and groups, and in almost all of the important cases it is in the latter. The locus of dominance, on the contrary, is only in individuals. Power is a function and resource of the organization and opposition of associations, of

---

[3] We frequently speak of the power of the press. The President of the United States, for example, to say nothing of the Cabinet, the Congress, and even the Court, listens intently to the voice of *The New York Times*, and *The Times* of London is not known as "The Thunderer" for nothing. But neither newspaper can elect a single candidate to political office, and neither editor nor columnist, however influential, can issue an order that will alter a governmental policy or force a change in one. To revert to our earlier analogy, power is lightning, not thunder.

[4] For sophisticated treatments of influence, see William A. Gamson, *Power and Discontent*, The Dorsey Press, Homewood, Illinois, 1968; Talcott Parsons, "On the Concept of Influence," *Public Opinion Quarterly*, Vol. 27, Spring, 1963, pp. 37–62; James S. Coleman, "Comment on 'On the Concept of Influence,'" *Ibid.*, pp. 63–82; and Parsons' rejoinder to Coleman, *Ibid.*, pp. 87–92. For an unusually clear and correct use of the concepts of influence, leadership, power, and authority in the study of a United States congressman, in this case the Chairman of the Ways and Means Committee of the House of Representatives, see John F. Manley. "Wilbur D. Mills: A Study in Congressional Influence," *The American Political Science Review*, vol. LXIII, no. 2, June, 1969, pp. 442–464.

the arrangement and juxtaposition of groups, including classes, and of the structure of society itself. Dominance, on the other hand, is a function of personality or of temperament. It is a personal trait. A timid robber, who flaunts his gun, has more power than his unarmed victim, however dominant or aggressive the latter may be in his normal social relationships. Furthermore, and one of the most interesting facets of this distinction, dominant individuals play roles in powerless groups and submissive individuals play roles in powerful ones. Some groups indeed acquire an impressive power in society, especially political power, because there are so many submissive individuals who are persuaded to join them and who meekly agree to the norms and ideologies that membership imposes. A clear example of this is the growth of the National Socialist Party in Germany in the 1930s. We can easily see, therefore, that dominance is a problem in social psychology, power a problem in sociology.

This distinction, among others, illustrates once more the impropriety of associating sociology too closely with psychology, or even social psychology. Individual and group phenomena are fundamentally different in character. The subjective factors that motivate an individual to participate in social action, the ends he seeks and the means he employs to achieve them, have little to do with the objective social consequences of the action. A man may join the army, for example, for any number of reasons—to achieve financial independence, to earn early retirement, to conform with the law, to escape a delicate domestic situation, to withdraw from an embarrassing emotional commitment, to see the world, to escape the pressure of mortgage payments, to fight for a cause in which he believes, to wear a uniform, to do what his friends are doing, or to do what he believes is right. None of these motivations will affect very much the power of the army that he joins. Similarly, people do not have children because they wish to increase the birthrate, to raise the classification of the municipal post office, or to contribute to the military strength of the state. The births, however, may have all three of these consequences, and many more besides. And finally, to return to our subject, a dominant personality does not confer power upon the man who possesses it. Power, in short, is one thing, dominance quite another.

5. Power and Rights

It is a little more difficult to distinguish power from rights because the latter term is itself ambiguous. It appears indeed in two senses that are exactly contradictory—as those privileges and only those that are secured by the state and as those that the state may not invade even to secure.

A complex example of the latter concerns the work of the Federal Communications Commission in the United States. The commission is committed by law to observe and enforce a so-called "fairness doctrine." This means, in view of the limited number of television channels available, and in view also of the fact that the airwaves belong to the people and not to private corporations, that all points of view and the entire spectrum of opinion on any subject should receive full and equal treatment. This requirement has caused serious difficulty and embarrassment in giving equal time to the very small political parties that could not otherwise gain access to television except at prohibitive expense and that, in any case, have no chance of winning an election.

But there is a more serious problem involved. Some television stations in smaller communities, properly qualified, and owned or subsidized by particular religious denominations, devote almost all of their time to the propagation of their own particular faith. The fairness doctrine would seem to require that other religious denominations have an opportunity to answer and to advocate their own doctrines. But who, if the local supply of channels is exhausted, is empowered to decide? Who will determine the allocation of time? The First Amendment to the Constitution of the United States constructs a famous wall of separation between church and state and it can be argued therefore that no official agency of the government, including the Federal Communications Commission, can make a decision on religious grounds, even in the interest of fairness. We may encounter here a prohibition of the kind that has often been sustained by the Supreme Court of the United States. This example is introduced only to illustrate the complexity of the problem and to show that there are certain rights—in this instance the right of access to the air —which, as we have said, it can be argued that the government may not invade even to secure.

We do not, fortunately, need to pursue the ramifications of this particular problem. Nor do we need to pursue the distinctions between various kinds of rights, including "natural rights" and natural law (like fairness for example) which are elaborated in the history of jurisprudence, in the sociology of law, and in theology, to recognize that a right always requires some support in the social structure. No individual can successfully claim a right that is unrecognized in the law and nonexistent in the mores.[5] Rights in general, like privileges, duties, obligations, responsibilities, perquisites, and prerogatives, are attached to statuses both in society itself and in the separate associations of society. One may have a right without the power to exercise it—for example, the right to vote in certain communities in the American South— but in most cases power of some kind supports whatever rights are claimed. Rights are more closely associated with privileges and with authority than they are with power. A right, like a privilege, is one of the perquisites of power and not power itself. There is, of course, a further distinction between rights and privileges. Military leave, for example, is a privilege and not a right; it may be requested but it may not be demanded. Similarly, promotion in any association, except sometimes for reasons of seniority, is a privilege and not a right.

---

[5] Odd and extravagant claims, of course, are sometimes made. A woman once claimed the right of using the house of the president of a Middle Western university, and indeed on one occasion lodged herself in the living room, on the grounds that the university and all of its buildings belonged to the taxpayers of the state and that the president's house was therefore a public facility.

6. Power, Force, and Authority

We have now distinguished power from prestige, from influence, from dominance, and from rights, and the three concepts of strength, force, and authority remain. Physical strength detains our analysis only for a moment because it has almost no sociological significance. Hard muscles can conquer flabby ones and a big man can usually defeat a small one (unless the latter knows karate) in physical combat, but two men—the Herculean feats of television detectives notwithstanding—can almost always subdue a single man when all other resources of the three are equal. As Thomas Hobbes noted long ago, "One man is not much stronger than another." It is ludicrous to suppose that anyone exercises authority over another because of his size. Size and strength are both negligible factors in civilized societies. Physical strength, however, is a form of power, and its use is force, as we shall now proceed to see in a larger perspective.

It is the concepts of force and authority that give us a solution to our problem. Power is not force and power is not authority, but it is intimately related to both. We want, therefore, to propose three definitions and then examine their implications: (1) power is latent force; (2) force is manifest power, and (3) authority is institutionalized power. The first two of these propositions may be considered together. They look like circular definitions and, as a matter of fact, they are. If an independent meaning can be found for one of these concepts, however, the other may be defined in terms of it and the circularity will disappear.[6]

---

[6] As a matter of purely technical interest, it may be observed that all definitions are ultimately circular. Every system of inference contains undefined or "primitive" terms in its initial propositions because, if it were necessary to define every term before using it, it would be impossible ever to talk or write or reason. There would be no word with which to begin. An undefined term in one system, however, may be defined in another. Although we may still perhaps have a logical deficiency here, it is not necessarily a practical deficiency if the circle, so to speak, is not too small. When we find an independent meaning for one of the terms in a couplet of circular definitions we are, in effect, enlarging the circle. The problem involved here has engaged some of the best minds in the history of logic, including Whitehead and Russell, who discuss it in the Introduction to *Principia Mathematica*.

We may therefore suggest an independent definition of the concept of force. Force in sociology is remarkably similar to force in physics and here we have an interesting linkage between nature and society. In both cases force means the production of an effect, an alteration in movement or action that overcomes resistance. It is an interference with a body at rest or in motion that changes its state or direction; an interference with a person that changes what he is doing or intends to do. In the sociological sense, where it is synonymous with coercion, it compels a change in the course of action of an individual or a group against the wishes of the individual or the group. It means the application of sanctions when they are not willingly received. It means, further, the reduction or limitation or closure or even total elimination of alternatives to the social action of one person or group by another person or group. "Your money or your life" is a threat that, when acted upon, becomes a situation of naked force, the reduction of alternatives to two.[7] The blackmailer who exacts his tribute from his victim as the price of silence is again limiting alternatives—pay or be exposed. The bouncer who throws an obstreperous patron out of a bar or nightclub is depriving him of the alternative of staying for another round of drinks. The execution of a sentence to hang represents the total elimination of alternatives. One army progressively limits the social action of its enemy until only two alternatives remain for the unsuccessful contender—to surrender or die.[8]

---

[7] The holdup man expresses his disjunction dramatically but incorrectly. What he really means is "Your money, or your life and your money."

[8] There is a further distinction to be made between force and violence. We should be inclined to say, although a continuum and not a dichotomy is involved, that violence is uncontrolled force, undisciplined force. A mob engaged in shooting, looting, and arson, as in the riots that occur in cities, is an expression of violence. The police that restrain, subdue, and finally control it are an expression of force. Unfortunately, as in the student demonstrations that have occurred in universities in the world's major cities, the police too have often become undisciplined—"lost their cool" as the slang phrase so aptly puts it—and have themselves indulged in violence. War, although fought by disciplined force on both sides, is always violent at the

Now all of these are situations of manifest power. Power itself is the predisposition or prior capacity that makes the use of force possible. Only groups that have power can threaten to use force and the threat itself is power. Power is the ability to employ force, not its actual employment, the ability to apply sanctions, not their actual application. Power is the ability to introduce force into a social situation; it is stance, not action; it is a presentation of the probability of force. Unlike force, incidentally, power is always successful; when it is not successful it was not, or ceases to be, power. The bankrupt corporation and the vanquished army are both powerless. Power symbolizes the force that *may* be applied in any social situation and supports the authority that *is* applied. Power is thus neither force nor authority but it makes both force and authority possible. Without power there would be no force and without power there would be no authority.

7. Power and Formal Organization

The implications of the preceding propositions will become clearer if we turn our attention to the locus of power. We discover it both in the organized sectors of society and in the unorganized; that is, it rests, latent, both in associations and in the unorganized community. Furthermore, in associations themselves, its presence is discernible both in the formal and in the informal organization. The first of these presents a fairly simple problem. It is in the formal organization of associations that social power is institutionalized and transformed into authority. If social interaction proceeded wholly in accordance with the

---

points where the opposing armies clash. Political assassination is always an act of violence and so, more generally, is the act of murder. In these cases it is the destruction of life, rather than the absence of discipline, that becomes the governing criterion. Violence is force used not to maintain or to restore order, but to destroy. It thus has a moral connotation whereas the concepts of power, force, and authority are morally neutral.

norms of the formal organization, and if the norms were always clear, then power would be dissolved without residue into authority. This would happen, however, only in a "perfect" or "ideal" association, and such associations do not exist in the actual world. In the real world uncertainties arise, some situations are unanticipated, penumbral areas appear in which the norms are unclear or inadequate. Strong leaders expand the authority attached to their statuses; weak leaders may diminish it. Questions occur about the distribution of authority, both horizontal and vertical. The table of organization becomes unstuck; it is something that looks good on paper, but only there. Miss Brewster, at the age of fifty-six, is being difficult. She is the secretary of the graduate department of economics, but she has survived five different department chairmen, she knows all the rules, and she is beginning to decide which of the graduate students will make it through to their Ph.D. degrees and which will not. She does this not ·by examining them in economics, which she has neither the competence nor the authority to do, but by a selective application of the rules. Something is happening here that disturbs the structure of authority. A good "petty officer," as seen in this example, can often make or break his superior, even in a military association.

Sometimes authority clearly vested in an associational status may not be exercised because it conflicts with a moral norm to which the larger and surrounding community subscribes. A naval officer who surrenders his ship, in opposition to ancient tradition and stringent law, may escape a court martial because his superiors recognize that—because he made his difficult decision in the interest of saving human lives—the sentiment of the nation supports him. Sometimes an official may remove a subordinate from office without formal cause and without formal authority because such action, now involving power, also finds support in public opinion. Public opinion may require the resignation of an associate justice of the Supreme Court, a requirement that the Chief Justice himself has no authority to impose. Sometimes, on the contrary, a superior may have the authority to discharge a subordinate, but not the power, because retention of the subordinate is demanded by the community. One example was the inability of both the general manager and the owner of the New York Yankees to "fire" Babe Ruth, or even to trade him, when he was at the height of his fame, although there were numerous occasions on which they wanted very much to do so. The Yankee fans would have been outraged.

These situations abound and they are often quite complex. In a university it may not be clear whether a dean has the authority to decline to reappoint a professor when this action has been recommended by the chairman of the department with the concurrence of the department's members; or, more subtly, whether, if he uses his authority to deny a salary increase to the professor in question in order to encourage him to resign, he will be accused of maladministration if he exercises it. It may similarly be unclear whether a Bishop of the Episcopal Church has the authority to remove a rector from his parish when the latter has the support of a large majority of his parishioners. In other words, opposing power often makes it a matter of unwise policy for an official to exercise the authority that is specifically vested in his status. In recent years we have have seen student power bring about student representation on policy-making committees, sometimes even on boards of trustees, and black power add to the curricula of many universities programs in Afro-American studies. In all of these cases we see power leaking into the joints of associational structure and affecting the formal organization.

8. Power and Informal Organization

Interaction in an association, as we have previously illustrated, does not proceed in precise or in complete conformity to the norms of formal organization. Power spills over the vessels of status, which only imperfectly contain it as authority. We arrive, therefore, at a brief consideration of informal organization, in which the prestige of statuses gives way to the esteem for persons and in which the social interaction of the members proceeds not only in terms of the explicit norms of the association but also in terms of implicit extra-associational norms whose locus is in the community and which may or may not conflict, at strategic points, with the associational norms. The examples we have already offered help us to anticipate what we have to say about the incidence and presence of power in informal organization.

No association is wholly formal in its social organization. Social organization, as we have seen, makes possible the orderly social intercourse of people who do not know one another and indeed can make personal acquaintance supererogatory. But in the continuity of associational life the members do become acquainted with one another and interact not only extrinsically and categorically, in terms of the statuses they occupy, but also intrinsically and personally in terms of the roles they play and the personalities they exhibit. Subgroups arise and begin to exert subtle pressures upon the organization, upon the norms that may be breached in the observance thereof, and upon the authority which, however firmly institutionalized, is yet subject to change. These subgroups may, as cliques and factions, remain within the association or, as sects and splinter groups, break away from it and form new and often competing associations. In any event, no formal organization remains wholly formal under the exigencies of time and circumstance. Power is seldom completely institutionalized as authority, seldom exhausted in organization. If power sustains the structure, opposing power threatens it, and every voluntary association is always at the mercy of a majority of its own members. It would be difficult to overemphasize the importance of this fact. In all associations, even involuntary associations, the power of people acting in concert is so great that the prohibition against "combinations" appears in the statutes of military associations and the right of collective petition is denied to military personnel.

Power appears, then, in associations in two forms, institutionalized as authority in the formal organization and uninstitutionalized as power itself in the informal organization. But this does not exhaust the incidence of power in the associations of society. It must be evident that power is required to inaugurate the association in the first place, to guarantee its continuance, and to enforce its norms. Here, in fact, we come close to the essence and etiology of social power. Half a dozen people, or a dozen, forming an association would not seem to represent much power. In agreement about the desirability of forming the association, for example, they represent only consensus. But in the association they form they do indeed represent power, a power that enables them to initiate the association in any case in which there is resistance or even inertia. And, once formed, power supports it against opposing power, both internal and external, that would challenge or threaten its continued existence.

Power, in short, supports the fundamental order of society and the social organization within it. Power stands behind every association and sustains its structure. Without power there is no organization and without power there is no order. The intrusion of the time dimension and the exigencies of circumstance require continual readjustments of the structure of every association and it is power that sustains it through these transitions. Authority itself cannot exist without the immediate support of power and the ultimate sanction of force.

9. Power and Conflict

As important as power may be in associations, it is even more important where it reigns, uninstitutionalized, in the interstices between associations and has its locus in society itself. Here we find the issues and conflicts of our time—labor versus management, Protestant versus Catholic, militant black versus reactionary white, radical student versus conservative administration, business versus government, Republican versus Democrat, Tory versus Labor, Israeli versus Arab, the Soviet Union versus the United States, hawks versus doves in both countries, and indeed one side versus the other in all the wars and revolutions in history. If it is power that supports the social order it is power also that rends it asunder.

It is not the task of the present essay to examine any of these conflicts but rather to confine the focus to the nature of power itself. And here we have two logical possibilities—power in the confrontations of like groups and power in the confrontations of unlike groups. Examples of the former are commercial companies competing for the same market, factions competing for control of a national student association, religious associations competing for adherents, newspapers competing for readers, magazines for advertisers, construction companies for contracts, political parties for votes, and so on through a large number of instances. Examples of the latter are conflicts between labor and management, between church and state, between the legislative and executive branches of government, between different subdivisions of the same bureaucracy, between the "Young Turks" and "the Establishment" in almost every large-scale association, and so on through an equally large number of instances. Power thus appears both in competition and in conflict and has no incidence in groups that neither compete nor conflict; i.e., in groups that do not share a common social matrix and have no social relations with one another, as for example, the American Council of Learned Societies and Rotary International. Power thus arises only in social opposition of some kind.

It is no accident that the noun "power" is related to the adjective "potential." It may seem redundant to say so, but power is always potential; that is, when it is used it becomes something else, in nature force, and in society either force or authority. It is, as we have said, latent force, potential force. It is the lion ready to spring, the leopard ready to pounce. It is the engine of a rocketship, still attached to its gantry, during the countdown that precedes blast-off. And so in society, on every level from the insignificant to the serious. Aces and kings in the hand represent power in the game of bridge. When played they represent authority according to the rules of the game, the authority to take tricks, and no one disputes the authority of the ace of trumps. Money and credit represent financial power; when spent or used they are transformed into property which, in turn, may become one of the sources of even more power.[9]

---

[9] For an ingenious, but highly complex, working out of the analogy between money and power, see Talcott Parsons, "On the Concept of Political Power," *Proceedings of the American Philosophical Society*, Vol. 107, No. 3, June, 1963, pp. 232–262.

Military power is the most awesome of all because its function, when necessary, is to be transformed into force. But it is power before it becomes force and indeed if it never does. This is the power that is attached to intercontinental ballistic missiles at rest in their silos or in submarines at sea. One desperately hopes that they will always remain at rest, but no one doubts that they represent power. It is a power that affects the destinies of nations. Indeed, the nations that have it are called "powers," and those that have the most of it are called "superpowers."

If power is one of the imperatives of society it may also be partly a pretense and succeed only because it is inaccurately estimated, or unchallenged. The encouragement of inaccurate estimates by the enemy, of course, is a familiar stratagem in war. But it occurs in many power relations. The threat of a strike may succeed when the strike will not. Blackmail may have consequences more dire than the exposure of the secret. The threat of a minority to secede from an association may affect it more than an actual secession. The threat of a boycott may achieve the result desired when the boycott itself would fail. In poker parlance—and indeed it is the same phenomenon—a "bluff" is powerful, but the power vanishes when the bluff is called.

10. The Sources of Power

We are at last in a position to locate the sources of power, which are three: (1) numbers of people, and especially majorities, (2) organization, and (3) resources.

It is difficult to overestimate the power that resides in numbers. As suggested before, other things being equal, two men can almost always force one man to do what they want, and ten men can do it even more easily. The power of a majority is so great that in many social situations there is a consensus about the right to express it as authority. This can be seen on many levels, from the trivial to the sublime. Thus, a group of three friends will ordinarily go to the movie that two of them want to see. On a larger stage, the party that wins the majority of votes is conceded the right to form a government. In a very profound sense, as Simmel once observed, this right is conceded because it can be taken. Majorities own so much power that they can be overcome only by dividing them into factions and "Divide and rule" (*Divide et impera*), therefore, is one of the oldest of imperial devices. Majorities are threatened, of course, when they are small, when the minority is increasing in size, and thus augmenting its power. For this reason it is the better part of wisdom to follow the admonition of Thomas Jefferson that slender majorities should not initiate large innovations. The tides of sentiment and opinion move too fast. But majorities are powerful, and the larger they are, both relatively and absolutely, the more powerful.

Given the same social organization, in short, and the same resources, the larger number can always control the smaller and secure its compliance. If majorities have frequently and for long historical periods suffered oppression and exploitation, it is because they have not been organized or have lacked resources. Finally, the power of a majority appears in all associations, except in the rare cases in history when charisma blinds all followers and bends them to the leader's will. It is the power of a majority, even in the most formally and tightly organized associations, that either threatens or sustains the stability of the associational structure.[10]

Important as numbers are, however, as the primary source of social power, they seldom operate alone. As suggested above, majorities may suffer oppression for long historical periods; they may, in short, be powerless or possess only the residual power of inertia. We arrive therefore at the second source of social power—social organization. A well-organized and disciplined body of marines or police can control a much larger number of unorganized individuals, as in a riot or insurrection. An organized minority can control an unorganized majority.

---

[10] For an elaboration of this theme see the author's paper "The Sociology of Majorities," *American Sociological Review*, Vol. 13, December, 1948, pp. 700–710.

But even here majorities possess so much power that there are limits beyond which this kind of control cannot be exercised. These limits appear with the recognition that the majority can organize and thus reverse the control. There is such a thing, after all, as a successful revolution. An organized majority—we are tempted to say—is the most powerful social force on earth.

Of two groups, however, equal or nearly equal in numbers and comparable in organization, the one with access to the greater resources will have the superior power. Political power, as Chairman Mao has observed, flows from the barrel of a gun. Similarly, Stalin once asked how many divisions the Pope was able to mobilize. And so resources constitute the third source of social power. Resources are of many kinds—money, credit, property, knowledge, skill, competence, cunning, acumen, deceit (as in the poker bluff), armament, and of course all of the things usually included under the term "natural resources,"—especially, at this moment of history, iron and uranium ore. They are all a part of the arsenal of power. Here, in fact, we are able to reintroduce the many phenomena we have previously distinguished from power. They are sources, not synonyms, of power. There are also supernatural resources in the case of organized religions which, as agencies of a celestial government, apply supernatural sanctions as instruments of control. It is apparent that, in any power conflict, they can tip the balance when the other sources of power are equal and comparable. Important as they are, however, as sources of power, they are not themselves power. Unless utilized by people who are in organized association with one another they are devoid of sociological significance.

Finally, it may be of more than incidental interest to note that there is one kind of social situation in which the power of opposing groups is completely balanced. The numbers on each side are equal, their social organization is identical, and their resources are as nearly the same as possible. This situation reveals itself in games and contests in which power components are cancelled out and the victory goes to the superior skill. Whether the game be baseball or bridge there is insistence, inherent in the structure of the game itself, upon an equalization and thus cancellation of power, and this is the universal characteristic of sport and the basis of the conception of "fair play."[11] It would be foolish, of course, to assert that resources are always equal. One professional baseball team has financial resources that may not be available to another, and one bridge partnership may have better cards than its opponent. But such inequalities excite disapproval because they deny the nature of sport.[12] In the former case recruitment of talent—the player draft—proceeds in inverse order of the previous year's standings of the clubs, and tournament bridge is duplicate bridge so that all partnerships will play the same hands. When resources cannot be equalized, a game loses some of its savor, and sentiment supports the "underdog." We have here a most familiar, but nevertheless peculiar, situation—one in which power is so balanced as to be irrelevant. Sport may be a moral equivalent for war, as William James wanted to believe, but it cannot unfortunately be a sociological equivalent. The situations are quite similar in many respects, but they are different in a crucial one. The difference between a conflict and a contest is that the former is a power phenomenon, and the latter is not.

11. Conclusion

In this chapter we have addressed our discussion to one of the most perplexing of sociological problems—the problem of power. We have taken a vague and ambiguous concept, a concept we all know but find difficult to define, and have attempted to sharpen the edges of its meaning. Among the propositions

---

[11] The game of poker is an exception. Here, unless there are betting limits, resources are not equalized among the contestants. And even with limits the player who can afford to lose the most has an advantage that represents power.

[12] About which, incidentally, a substantial sociological study has yet to be written. That none has appeared is surprising in view of the very great importance of sport in human life. Indeed, Honduras and El Salvador once went to war over the result of a soccer match.

offered the following may serve as a summary: (1) power is a social phenomenon par excellence, the analysis of which is a particular responsibility of sociology; (2) it is useful and necessary to distinguish power from other phenomena such as prestige, influence, dominance, rights, force, and authority; (3) power is latent force, force is manifest power, and authority is institutionalized power; (4) power has its incidence in social opposition of some kind and, unlike authority, appears both in associations and in the interstices between them; (5) power is always potential and has its issue, in society, in either force or authority; (6) the sources of power can be found in a combination of numbers (especially majorities), social organization, and resources, and finally, *passim*, (7) power is a fundamental support of the social order on the one hand and a constant threat to that order on the other. Some of these propositions will doubtless encounter qualification and even dissent. We hope, however, that they will stimulate the sociological reflection of the reader.

14

The Problem of
Authority

[1954]

In the vast complexity that is a human society the exercise of authority is a constant and pervasive phenomenon. Society indeed is impossible without order—in a larger sense society is synonymous with order[1]—and it is authority which serves as the foundation of much of the order which society exhibits. Every day thousands of persons interact with thousands of others in relationships that involve superordination and subordination, the issuance of commands and obedience to them, the announcements of decisions by some and the acceptance of

---

[1] On the problem of order in general, see Florian Znaniecki, *Cultural Sciences: Their Origin and Development* (Urbana: University of Illinois Press, 1952), Introduction and Chapters 1, 2, and 6.

these decisions by others. Here we have a phenomenon of considerable significance and one that requires serious sociological analysis. What is it, in short, that confers upon some men the right to command, upon others the obligation to obey? Why should anyone exercise this right, anyone owe this duty? How does authority contribute to the order that all of the members of a society desire, those who obey as well as those who exact obedience?

If we seek examples of the exercise of authority we shall find them in every sector of society. It is authority that enables the jailor to hand to Socrates the cup of hemlock with the rueful but reasonable expectation that he will drink it; authority that enables the elders of the synagogue to execrate, curse, and cast out Spinoza with all the maledictions written in the book of the law; authority that confers upon an American president the right to remove an imperious general from his commands. On less exalted levels it is authority that enables a vice-president to dictate to his secretary, a sales-manager to assign territories to his salesmen, a personnel manager to employ and discharge workers, an umpire to banish a player from a baseball game, a policeman to arrest a citizen, and so on through innumerable situations. All these can serve to illustrate the ubiquitous character of the phenomenon we are about to analyze.

In inaugurating an inquiry into the nature of authority, however, it is advisable to exercise several cautions. In the first place the sociological literature on this subject, astonishingly enough, is somewhat scanty. Indeed, Florian Znaniecki remarked as late as 1935 that he was unacquainted with any sociological monograph on authority, although he conceded that the historical and political literature was "very rich."[2] In the second place, Roberto Michels, in an article specifically devoted to this problem, an article rich in insights, says nevertheless that "It is futile to discuss the *raison d'être* of authority."[3] Observations like

---

[2] *Social Actions* (New York: Farrar and Rinehart, 1936), p. 673.
[3] "Authority," *Encyclopedia of the Social Sciences*, Vol. II, pp. 319–321.

these suggest at least some of the difficulties that an analysis will encounter.

A second caution concerns the fact that the problem of authority is susceptible to treatment on several different levels. One of these levels might be called the philosophic. Here the problem is the apparent opposition between liberty and authority. The literature here, of course, is voluminous, and it embraces in an important sense the entire history of political philosophy from Plato to MacIver. It is an issue, in fact, which is of continuing concern to philosopher and citizen alike. It is not, however, the problem we wish to pursue in this place. Another level might be called the political, that is, the level on which the competence of the political scientist is most relevant. Here we should meet, for example, problems of political obligation, of the particular kind of authority represented by the law, of the delegation of powers, of political power in general, and of public administration. On problems of this kind too there is a large literature and one which it would not be possible to examine in the space at our disposal. There is, however, a third level on which a discussion might proceed, and this level we shall call the sociological. It is less abstract than the first of the levels mentioned and less restricted in scope than the second. On this level we shall be interested in authority wherever we meet it and not only in the political organization of society.

One should not have to contend that the problem of authority in this last sense belongs to sociology. It is indeed obvious that the problem of authority rests at the very bottom of an adequate theory of the social structure. When MacIver, for example, seeks "the authority beyond the authority of government" he knows that even government, in a sense, is not merely a political phenomenon but primarily and fundamentally a social phenomenon, and that the matrix from which government springs itself possesses an order and a structure. If anarchy is the contrary of government so anomy is the contrary of society. Authority, in other words, is by no means a purely political phenomenon in the narrow sense of the word. For it is not only in the political organization of society, but in all of its organization, that authority appears. Each association in society, no matter how small or how temporary it may be, has its own structure of authority.[4]

Before discussing the nature of authority proper it will be convenient if we first distinguish it from two other phenomena with which it is sometimes confused. The first of these is competence. Thus, we commonly speak of a given person as "an authority" on a given subject. Branch Rickey, for example, is an authority on baseball, Lou Little on football, Emily Post on etiquette, Arturo Toscanini on music, Charles H. Goren on bridge, and every professor on the subject he teaches. In this sense authority is related to influence but not to power, and in this sense it has nothing to do with legitimacy and nothing with obligation. It is recognition of competence that encourages us to accept the opinions of those who have achieved prominence and prestige in their special fields of endeavor. There is nothing compulsory about this acceptance, and if we accede at all to opinions of this kind it is as a tribute to eminence rather than as an obeisance to authority. We voluntarily respect the competence of others, but authority requires our submission. When the situation involves competence, furthermore, one may choose one "authority" rather than another, Casey Stengel rather than Branch Rickey, for example, or Herman Hickman rather than Lou Little, and so on. Competence, in other words, exerts influence; authority exacts obedience.[5]

It is interesting to note in this connection that our language tricks us into error. When we speak of an order or a command having been issued by "competent authority," we do not,

---

[4] The word "association," throughout this paper, is exactly synonymous with "organized group."

[5] This distinction has more recondite consequences of a political character than can be considered in this place. Ernest Barker has suggested, for example, that the authority of science can be used to perfect the science of authority. *Reflections on Government* (London: Oxford University Press, 1942), p. 232. See his discussion of this issue, pp. 231–234, and especially the note to p. 232.

curiously enough, mean competence at all. We mean not that the authority is competent, but that it is legitimate. In an inferior position, for example, we may obey the command of a superior whose authority we recognize even when it seems unreasonable, and disobey a command that seems reasonable if we question the authority of the alleged superior to issue it. Superior knowledge, superior skill, and superior competence need not be involved in the exercise of "competent" authority. As Talcott Parsons points out, the treasurer of a corporation may have the authority to sign checks disbursing the corporation's funds, but this does not imply that the treasurer is a better "check-signer" than any one of hundreds of others.[6] The authority to sign checks, in short, has little relation to the capacities of individuals and much less to the caliber of their calligraphy. Robert MacIver, similarly, has said that "The man who commands may be no wiser, no abler, may be in no sense better than the average of his fellows; sometimes, by any intrinsic standard, he is inferior to them."[7]

In view of considerations like these it is difficult to determine why Roberto Michels should begin his discussion with the statement that "Authority is the capacity, innate or acquired, for exercising ascendancy over a group."[8] We shall contend, on the contrary, that there is no clear sense in which authority is a capacity, that it is certainly not innate, and that it is never acquired except in the process of social organization. We shall further contend that it always has an institutional and never, except indirectly, a personal origin.[9]

---

[6] Note 4 to p. 58 in Max Weber, *The Theory of Social and Economic Organization*, edited by Talcott Parsons (New York: Oxford University Press, 1947).

[7] *The Web of Government* (New York: The Macmillan Co., 1947), p. 13.

[8] *Loc. cit.*

[9] In one sphere, however, it is especially difficult to dissociate the authority of competence from the authority of legitimacy. This is the sphere of religious authority. It is clear that the authority of a philosopher, for example, is the authority of competence and that the authority of the praetor,

The second phenomenon with which authority is sometimes confused is the phenomenon of leadership. Here again, for reasons that have considerable cogency, it seems desirable to maintain a distinction. It cannot be said that Max Weber, who otherwise contributed so many penetrating observations on this problem, maintained complete clarity on this point. It is the introduction of charismatic authority into his treatment that prompts this reservation. Weber, as is well known, distinguished charismatic authority from traditional authority on the one hand and from rational-legal authority on the other. Charisma, of course, is a gift of grace which, imputed to a leader by his followers, gives a divine sanction, encouragement, and even justification to his actions. A charismatic leader is believed to be different from other men; he rises above them because he is touched with divinity; there is something of the celestial afflatus about him. It is interesting to notice that persons whose achievements are so impressive that they distinguish them from the multitude are frequently suspected of charisma,[10] and indeed it is of significance for the sociologist of religion that the attribution of charisma seems to be the initial stage in apotheosis.

But leadership is not authority. As in the case of competence,

---

on the contrary, is the authority of power. But what shall we say about the authority of the pontiff? What supports the decretal issued by a religious hierarch? Is it his competence, the unique capacity imputed to him of direct communication with the deity? Or is it his authority, which stems from his superior administrative position in the hierarchy? This situation introduces difficulties of a special and interesting kind and requires, unfortunately, a more elaborate analysis than we can give it here.

[10] The biographer of John Maynard Keynes, for example, permits himself to speculate as follows: "In making a final appraisement of Keynes' influence, some may seek to attribute it to a gift or special power that lies outside the range of normal human qualities; they may seek for some mysterious aptitude, some nameless gift, bestowed on him from the unseen world." From R. F. Harrod, *The Life of John Maynard Keynes* (New York: Harcourt, Brace & Co., 1951), p. 646. This suggestion is immediately rejected, but if sophisticated scholars can allude, however lightly, to such a possibility, it is easy to see how the multitude, in any society, might concede charisma to those whose extraordinary achievements win them extraordinary devotion.

no one is required to follow a leader and no one involuntarily satisfies a leader's desire or grants a leader's wish. The fiat of the leader lacks legitimacy. One may follow or not and no sanction except possibly the informal sanction of being regarded as odd by other followers is applied to those who abstain. The situation is different with respect to authority. A leader can only request, an authority can require. The person subjected to an order by "competent authority" has no alternative but to obey.[11] The examination must be taken at the appointed time, taxes must be paid, the draft induction notice must be observed.[12] Obedience to an authoritative command is not a matter of a subordinate's arbitrary decision. Leadership depends upon the personal qualities of the leader in the situations in which he leads. In the case of authority, however, the relationship ceases to be personal and, if the legitimacy of the authority is recognized, the subordinate must obey the command even when he is unacquainted with the person who issues it. In a leadership relation the person is basic; in an authority relation the person is merely a symbol.

We may summarize these observations by noting that an authority relationship is one of superordination and subordination; the leadership relationship, on the contrary, is one of dominance and submission. These are independent variables. Superordinates may or may not be dominant individuals in a psychological sense; subordinates may or may not be submissive.[13] The exer-

---

[11] Unless, as we shall subsequently observe, the situation is rearranged in such a manner that the subordinate is able to withdraw from it.

[12] An amusing story comes from England concerning the Londoner who, upon receiving his draft induction notice, replied, "See Luke 14:20." ("I have married a wife and therefore I cannot come.") To which the War Office answered, "Your attention is drawn to Luke 7:8." ("For I also am a man set under authority, having under me soldiers, and I say unto one, Go, and he goeth; and to another, Come, and he cometh.")

[13] Leadership qualities, of course, are frequently involved in a man's rising to a position of authority, but this is another process. Frequency is not necessity, as can be seen in countless illustrations, from the monarch to the sheriff, where no test of leadership—or of competence—is imposed.

cise of authority does not necessarily involve a personal relationship of any kind. As suggested immediately above, those who exercise authority, especially in the large-scale associations of complex societies, are frequently unaware of the individual identities of the persons over whom the authority is exercised and, conversely, the latter may be unaware of the personal identity of the former. In a military establishment, for example, thousands of men are sent to the far corners of the earth by an official whom they have never seen and whose name they may even fail to recognize. This official, in turn, is unacquainted with the men thus subjected to his command and he may not see or even sign the paper that dispatches them to their destinations. It would be inappropriate to contend that there is any leadership in this situation or that this kind of authority, as Michels has suggested, marks some kind of capacity, "innate or acquired," for ascendancy. Leadership, in short, like competence, is a species of influence; authority is a function of power.

Once we have distiguished authority from competence and from leadership we are prepared to indulge in some statements of a more positive character. Our first observation is perhaps the obvious one that authority is always a property of social organization. Where there is no organization there is no authority. Authority appears only in the organized groups—the associations—of society, never in unorganized groups or in the unorganized community. An absence of organization implies an absence of authority. There is authority only within an association, never in the interstices between associations. The exercise of authority, furthermore, never extends beyond the limits of the association in which it is institutionalized and which gives it support and sanction. The dean of women, for example, may require all women students to be in their domiciles at a certain hour in the evening, but such an order can have no effect upon the young women of the community who are not students at the university. The collector of internal revenue may not examine a candidate for the degree of doctor of philosophy, a policeman may not decide a close play at second base, and so on through all the situations of society.[14] This observation, of course, contributes nothing to the analysis of the phenomenon; it merely gives it a locus. But the locus is significant. If we ask where in society authority obtains, we shall reply in associations, and never anywhere else.

If authority is created in the organization of an association it is necessary, accordingly, to examine the process in which an unorganized group is transformed into an organized one. In this process several things happen. In the first place, informal procedures and patterns of interaction come to be standardized as norms. In the second place, roles come to be standardized as statuses. It is the institutionalization of procedures into norms and roles into statuses which results in the formal organization of the association. Norms and statuses then constitute the structure of the association; they are its organization. More particularly, the role of leader, which one or several members of the group have been playing, comes to be institutionalized in one or several statuses to which authority is now attached in accordance with the norms. These roles become statuses in order that the stability of the association may be assured and its continuity guaranteed.

It is apparent that no association of any size or degree of complexity can maintain a constant membership. The inexorable process of life itself determines that the personnel of the association will change over the course of time. Some associations, of course, cannot survive the individual departures of the people who comprise them because they have no method of recruitment.[15] Any association whose members wish it to survive and

----

[14] An instance of error in this respect concerns the late General Patton. On a tour of inspection at an army post he became annoyed at a telephone lineman who paid no attention to his passing and who continued to work at the top of the pole. The lineman refused in addition to obey the general's peremptory command to come down from the pole and stand at attention. At this point the general, near apoplexy as the story goes, demanded to know the man's name and company. The name is unimportant; the company was the Bell Telephone Company.

[15] This is Simmel's "broken-plate" pattern.

to gain an independence of particular personnel must institutionalize its roles into statuses and must create authority where initially there was only leadership. The leader who has been instrumental in organizing the association may subsequently be indisposed or withdraw from the circle of his followers. Unless his role has been institutionalized such a contingency would jeopardize the association's existence. After it has been institutionalized the leader may even be deposed from whatever position of authority he may occupy without damage to the group. A structure is thus necessary if associations are to survive the flow of individuals in and out of membership. The supreme test of the organization of an association, in fact, is satisfied when it can sustain a total turnover in personnel.

The formal organization of an association, in short, is constituted of norms and statuses. The norms are attached to the statuses and not to the persons who occupy them. The norms involve rights, duties, privileges, obligations, prerogatives, and responsibilities as they are attached to particular statuses in the structure of the association. The right to exercise authority, that is, the right to make decisions and to enforce them, is now attached to certain statuses, and this right receives the support of all those who belong to the association and who conform to its norms. But the exercise of authority is not only a right; it is also a duty. The occupation of certain statuses implies the obligation to make decisions in the name of the association and the obligation to enforce them.

It is important to recognize that authority is never exercised except in a status relationship. As a right and as a duty it is always attached to a status and is never a matter of purely personal privilege. When an individual issues a command in his own name rather than in the name of the status or position that he occupies, we have a sure indication that it is leadership, not authority, which is being exercised. Sometimes, of course, there is a penumbra of uncertainty with respect to the authority vested in a status, and the right to make a decision, as in jurisdictional disputes, may be more hotly contested than the policy that the decision involves. Similarly, the authority of one status is always exercised over another status and never over an individual as such. It is not the case that Mr. Jones, the vice-president, issues orders to Mr. Jackson, the cashier of a bank. It is the vice-president who issues orders to the cashier in independence of the identity of the individuals who occupy these statuses. Authority is thus a function of the formal organization of an association, and it is exercised in accordance with specific and usually statutory norms and statuses. It makes no appearance in the informal organization. The superordination and subordination of associational statuses is characteristic of all formal social organization and it is this hierarchical arrangement, this stratification of statuses, that permits and indeed makes possible the exercise of authority.

That authority involves a status and not a personal relationship can be illustrated in addition by some interesting cases of status reversal which alter the superordination and subordination of two individuals. One factory-worker may be subordinate to another in the status hierarchy of the factory. In the union local to which they both belong, on the other hand, the latter may be subordinate to the former. In the Navy a commander of the line exercises military authority over all lieutenant commanders, both line and staff, but when he occupies the status of patient he is subject to the orders of a lieutenant commander of the medical corps who occupies the status of doctor. On a civic committee an employer may occupy a status subordinate to that of one of his own employees. For that matter, the President of the United States, superior in several hierarchies, takes orders from the officers of the Secret Service who are charged with the protection of his person. It is obvious that examples of this kind could be multiplied.

In spite of this important distinction it would be improvident to ignore the fact that personal factors do enter into status relationships and that the latter are seldom "pure" except in cases where the two individuals involved are wholly unaware of each other's identity. It is a fact that persons evaluate each other "intrinsically" in terms of their personalities and not only "extrinsically" in terms of their conformity to the norms that their statuses impose upon them. It is an additional fact that the informal organization of an association sometimes takes precedence over its formal organization. Subordinates in these situations frequently exhibit capacities as leaders and begin to play leadership roles; superordinates, on the other hand, frequently withdraw informally from the responsibilities of their statuses and exercise only a nominal authority.[16] Nor can we ignore the familiar phenomenon by which the possession of a status involving authority exerts an influence upon personality. Otherwise submissive individuals, "dress'd in a little brief authority," sometimes assume an authoritarian air, and otherwise dominant individuals, stripped of the perquisites of status, sometimes exhibit a new humility. Recognition of the intrusion of psychological factors does not alter the fact, however, that authority is exercised in a status relationship and not in a personal relationship, and that the relationship becomes increasingly impersonal with increase in associational size.

What, now, sustains the authority exercised by some people over others? Why should a subordinate obey a superordinate when he disapproves of the command? Why, in fact, does subordination not imply agreement, insubordination dissent? Why does an inferior obey a superior whom he may obviously dislike, whom he may never have met, or to whom in other relations he may be totally indifferent? A preliminary answer to these questions has already been suggested: both the superior and the inferior recognize that they are operating in a status relationship and not a personal relationship and that personal sentiments are irrelevant to the exercise of authority in the situation. Indeed, a person is expected and even required to exercise the same kind of authority over friends and intimates that he does over enemies and strangers. In the ideal case the exercise of authority is wholly objective, impartial, impersonal, and disinterested. The judge

---

[16] On the intrinsic and extrinsic evaluation of persons see E. T. Hiller, *Social Relations and Structures* (New York: Harper & Brothers, 1947), Chapters 13, 14, and 38. For an illuminating article on formal and informal organization see Charles H. Page, "Bureaucracy's Other Face," *Social Forces*, Vol. 25, October, 1946, pp. 88–94.

who has violated a traffic regulation is expected to fine himself.[17]

This observation, however, does not answer the more general question. The reasons people submit to authority, in the larger focus, are the reasons that encourage them to obey the law, to practice the customs of their society, and to conform to the norms of the particular associations to which they belong. This question has received a comprehensive discussion in the literature of political philosophy and sociology and the treatment that Robert M. MacIver has given to it in several of his works is unexcelled.[18] This treatment requires no recital or repetition here. But the reason why men in general conform to the norms does not always explain why particular men accept particular authority especially in situations where the person who exercises authority introduces new norms, when he exercises, in effect, a legislative function. What supports the authority in these instances?

The only possible answer to this question is that authority in these, as in all other cases, is supported, sanctioned, and sustained by the association itself. The person who exercises it is recognized as an agent of the group. He represents the group. He acts not in his own but in the group's name. Insubordination now is a threat not to a personal relationship but to the continued existence of the group. It is an assault upon the group, a denial of the validity of its norms, and, even more significantly, an attack by an individual upon a majority. Since authority is attached to a status, in a system of statuses supported by the majority of the members, and since this system of statuses is synonymous with

---

[17] The writer is indebted to Talcott Parsons for the suggestion that in the ideal case authority is as impersonal as a traffic light.

[18] See particularly the section entitled "How and Why Men Obey," *The Web of Government*, pp. 73–81, *et passim;* and *Society: An Introductory Analysis* (with Charles H. Page) (New York: Rinehart & Co., Inc., 1949), pp. 142–146 and the whole of Chapter 9, pp. 189–209. For an interesting recent discussion, one that depends to some extent upon MacIver's, see F. Lyman Windolph, *Leviathan and Natural Law* (Princeton: Princeton University Press, 1951), Chapter 2. This problem ultimately becomes a problem in moral philosophy, the problem of the proper relationship between the individual and his society.

the organization of an association, it is apparent that any disinclination to accept the status arrangement and the exercise of authority involved in it implies a disinclination to accept the group itself. It is the majority of the members of an association who support its structure and who sustain the authority exercised in particular statuses in accordance with particular norms. If we seek the rationale of authority, therefore, we find it in the very factors that induce men to form associations in the first place, to band together in organized groups, and to perpetuate these associations. It is the desire for stability and continuity which guarantees that the exercise of legitimate authority will be maintained in the statuses of the association, not as an underwriting of particular decisions, but as a bulwark behind the organization of the association itself. An individual who rejects this authority is jeopardizing the continued existence of the association.[19] The ultimate answer therefore to the question of what sustains the authority exercised in an association of any kind is that this authority is sustained by a majority of the association's own members.[20]

We have finally to inquire whether authority is a phenomenon exercised by coercion or by consent. Does the person who accepts a command from superior authority do so, in short, because he has to or because he wants to? Both Barnard and MacIver seem to accept the latter alternative. Barnard, for example, speaking primarily of the nonpolitical associations of society (but including the army), says, "The existence of net inducement is the only reason for accepting *any* order as having authority," and, even more strongly, "The decision as to whether an order has authority

---

[19] Chester I. Barnard has noted in this connection that: "If objective authority is flouted for arbitrary or merely temperamental reasons, if, in other words, there is deliberate attempt to twist an organization requirement to personal advantage . . . then there is a deliberate attack on the organization itself." *The Functions of the Executive* (Cambridge: Harvard University Press, 1938), p. 171.

[20] For an elaboration of the role of majorities in organized groups see Robert Bierstedt, "The Sociology of Majorities," *American Sociological Review,* Vol. XIII, December, 1948, pp. 700–710.

or not lies with the persons to whom it is addressed, and does not reside in 'persons of authority' or those who issue these orders."[21] His discussion emphasizes the view that the direction of authority proceeds from the bottom up rather than from the top down in any associational hierarchy. MacIver, similarly, speaking of political authority and the governmental associations of society, says that the identification of authority with power is "inept" and further that "The accent is primarily on right, not power. Power alone has no legitimacy, no mandate, no office."[22] Kingsley Davis, on the other hand, refers to authority as "a system of normatively sanctioned power";[23] Horace Kallen calls authority "the sanctioned exercise of indirect coercion";[24] for Lasswell and Kaplan authority is synonymous with "formal power";[25] and the present writer has defined it as "institutionalized power."[26] Finally, Michels, meeting the dilemma head-on as it were, insists that "Even when authority rests on mere physical coercion it is accepted by those ruled, although the acceptance may be due to a fear of force."[27]

A possible solution to this apparent contrariety of opinions rests in a distinction between two kinds of associations, voluntary and involuntary. In a voluntary association membership is a matter of consent, and people voluntarily give their allegiance to it. They conform to the norms of the association for the same reason, let us say, that they conform to the rules of the games they play; that is, they conform because the desire to play exceeds the desire to win. Similarly, they accept the authority of others in voluntary associations because the desire to belong

---

[21] *The Functions of the Executive*, pp. 166, 163.

[22] *The Web of Government*, pp. 85, 83.

[23] *Human Society* (New York: The Macmillan Co., 1949), p. 48.

[24] "Coercion," *Encyclopedia of the Social Sciences, op. cit.,* Vol. III, p. 618.

[25] Harold D. Lasswell and Abraham Kaplan, *Power and Society* (New Haven: Yale University Press, 1950), p. 133.

[26] "An Analysis of Social Power," *American Sociological Review,* Vol. XV, December, 1950, pp. 733ff.

[27] "Authority," *Encyclopedia of the Social Sciences, op. cit.,* Vol. II, p. 319.

exceeds the desire to make independent decisions on matters of associational concern. This is doubtless what Barnard means above by "net inducement." The candidate for the degree of doctor of philosophy, for example, accepts the authority of his examiners to ask him questions, a student accepts the authority of the instructor to evaluate his academic work, and an employee accepts the authority of his employer to assign his duties. In voluntary associations, in short, authority rests upon consent, and it might be appropriate in these circumstances to define authority as institutionalized leadership.

In involuntary associations, however, the situation is somewhat different. A soldier may not defy the order of a superior officer, a citizen may not ignore the demands of the tax-collector, and a prisoner certainly may not refuse to accept the authority of his guards. In certain associations, in other words, voluntary withdrawal is impossible, and these are what we should be inclined to call involuntary associations. In associations like these it would be somewhat unrealistic to deny that coercion is present in the exercise of authority. It is in these situations that authority becomes a power phenomenon, and it is in these that we can define authority as institutionalized power. In voluntary associations, then, we could say that authority is institutionalized leadership; in involuntary associations that it is institutionalized power. In the former authority rests upon consent; in the latter, upon coercion.

This solution, however, is not quite satisfactory. In the first place it is not always easy to distinguish between voluntary and involuntary associations. The distinction is one of degree. There are many associations, in addition, which one may voluntarily join but from which one may not voluntarily withdraw. In the second place, and possibly more important, authority that may or may not be accepted hardly qualifies as authority in accordance with the ordinary connotation of the term. There is something mandatory, not merely arbitrary, about the acceptance of authority and no analysis can quite rationalize this mandatory element away and retain the full significance of the phenomenon. Furthermore, even in what we have called voluntary associations a member who refuses to submit to constituted authority is ordinarily required, in an exercise of authority, to resign. If he refuses to resign there must be still another exercise of authority to compel his withdrawal from the association and to repel the threat to the group as a whole that his insubordination entails. In view of these considerations it would seem as if our problem requires yet another answer.

In order to find this answer we have to dare an apparent disagreement with MacIver. In order to retain the central connotation of the concept we are examining it seems desirable to assert that authority is always a power phenomenon. It is power that confers authority upon a command. But it is sanctioned power, institutionalized power. The power resides in the majority of the members. It is the majority which supports and sustains the association and its norms. This observation enables us to say that authority is always delegated. Its ultimate source is the power of the majority. The formation of an association, its stability and its continuity, involves the formal delegation of the power that resides in the majority to one or several of the group's members as agents of the whole. It is true, of course, that an individual's membership in an association may be a matter of consent and he may similarly be free to withdraw. But so long as he remains a member, the authority exercised by his superordinates, supported by the majority of the members, is mandatory and not a matter of voluntary determination. The consent in these cases applies to membership in the association and not to the acceptance of the particular commands of constituted authority. Membership may be voluntary, but acceptance of authority is mandatory. It is one of the conditions of membership. Stated alternately, an individual may be free to belong or not to belong to a particular association, but as a member he is not free to question or to reject the authority exercised by other individuals in accordance with the norms of the association. Considerations like these encourage us to conclude that when consent is involved, as it is in voluntary associations, it applies to the fact of membership and not to the acceptance of authority.

The disagreement with MacIver, however, is only apparent

and stems from a slightly different conception of power. We can agree that "power alone has no legitimacy, no mandate, no office," and that authority is not simple power in this sense. But when we say that authority is institutionalized power we attribute a legitimacy, a mandate, and an office to its exercise, and with this proposition there is every indication that MacIver would agree.[28]

We have attempted in this essay to discover how this institutionalization occurs and how it characteristizes every association, every organized group, in society. We have suggested in addition that the institutionalization of power is a process that occurs in the formal organization of groups and that it is institutionalized in them as authority. Without the support of the power that resides in the majority of the members of associations there would be no such phenomenon as authority. MacIver's definition of authority as "the established *right*, within any social order, to determine policies, to pronounce judgments on relevant issues, and to settle controversies,"[29] is therefore quite in accord with the argument of this paper. We have merely attempted to show how this right becomes established and how it is sustained. We should maintain, in conclusion, that it is difficult to explain these processes without recourse to the concept of power.

---

[28] Although it involves an additional issue, and one that we have no space to discuss, authority is distinguishable from force in that it always makes some appeal to rationality. An act of authority is not susceptible to argument but it does, in contrast to an act of force, attempt to satisfy the criterion of reason.

[29] *The Web of Government*, p. 83. See also *Society*, pp. 146–147.

PART 4

ON CIVILIZATION AND
HUMANE LEARNING

The first paper in this section has to do with the concept of civilization. Prepared for a plenary session of the American Sociological Association, it is an effort to find an index of civilization that is both useful and objective. In order to do this I first mentioned the origin of the word in English and then described its use by such writers as Alfred Weber, Robert M. MacIver, Oswald Spengler, Arnold J. Toynbee, P. A. Sorokin, and Robert K. Merton. In their works, however, I found no unanimity. Differences are easy to discern, and they increase as writers are added to the list. Indeed, the concept suffers from all the afflictions that normally attend our terminologies. With respect to the indices of civilization, those characteristics that distinguish civilization from its opposite, I found an embarrassment of riches, too many to be able to take them all seriously. In conclusion, therefore, I put forth a proposal of my own.

The second paper, "Once More the Idea of Progress," treats another subject on which the literature is both voluminous and inconclusive. I wrote it on invitation of Ronald Fletcher, who had been commissioned by the British Sociological Association to edit a book of essays in honor of Morris Ginsberg, late Martin White Professor of Sociology at The London School of Economics. When I arrived at the School in the fall of 1966 to take up my appointment as Fulbright Senior Lecturer, I wrote Professor Ginsberg a note to ask if I might have the privilege of calling on him to pay my respects. (At that time, he had been retired for some years.) He promptly invited me to tea at his house on the edge of Hampstead Heath. We quickly discovered that we shared many sentiments and opinions (except that he had little regard for Weber on the Protestant ethic), and a warm friendship was born. We had a number of luncheons together during the year, and once we were joined by Robert MacIver on what was destined to be his last visit to London. (MacIver and Ginsberg died within a few months of each other in 1970.)

Professor Ginsberg had given his presidential address to the first annual meeting of the British Sociological Association only fifteen years earlier. As his subject he had chosen the idea of progress, a subject he expanded somewhat and later published in a small book. It seemed to me an appropriate subject to reexamine, and this I did with his address as a starting point. It turned out that my conclusions were not as sanguine as his. Wedded in some ways, however sophisticated, to an evolutionary doctrine and the inheritor, in some ways too, of a late Victorian tradition, Ginsberg professed to find some viability in the idea. He believed, or wanted to believe, that progress was discernible in the passage of history, especially in the increasing realization of such ideals as freedom, equality, justice, and truth. He had what I call a quiet but persistent moral optimism. It was an optimism I could not share. In my view, as the paper shows, the idea of progress is hopelessly normative; the abundant evidence that one can summon for and against it cancels out; and what masquerades as an idea, subject to truth claims, is in fact nothing but an attitude, a temperamental response to history.

The third paper, written also for a session of the American Sociological Association, is entitled "Sociology and General Education." The paper was prompted by the realization that the number of undergraduates who major in sociology is statistically small compared with those who take courses in the subject. What can sociology do for them, for those who have no intention of becoming sociologists? In answer to this question I advance the thesis that sociology has many purely pedagogical virtues, that it enriches the liberal arts curriculum, and that it can build a bridge between the hard sciences on the one hand and the humanities on the other. Marvin Bressler has since observed, in a generous reference to the article, that most of the virtues I claim for sociology are served by other liberal arts as well. This I readily concede. My only concern is to emphasize, for the reasons I enumerate, that sociology cannot be excluded from the arts that liberate the human mind. In this connection I invite attention especially to the lovely quotation from George Berkeley with which the article concludes.

This theme is expanded in my earlier presidential address to the Eastern Sociological Society, "Sociology and Humane Learning," an essay that is in many ways my favorite. I once shared "the dream of Comte," the desire to transfer to sociology the precision and objectivity of the physical sciences, and even served as a naïve propagandist for that point of view. A more mature reflection began to indicate that the methods of these sciences, however supreme in their own domain, could not exhaust the possibilities of discovery or the resources of scholarship in sociology. Sociology belonged not only to the "scientists" but also to those who wandered open-eyed and eager in the realms of humane letters. Indeed, there are good reasons for thinking that sociology, as I say in the paper, owns an important place in these domains and that, like history, philosophy, and literature, it is an inquiry worthy of a free man. I have the temerity to suggest that objectivity may not be the virtue we are universally taught to consider it and that something I call "the theoretic bias" has its own role to play in the construction of our theories of society.

15

Indices of Civilization [1]

[1966]

A treatment of the subject of civilization might appropriately begin with the recollection that the word itself is of fairly recent origin in both the French and the English languages. Dr. Johnson declined to include it in his dictionary of 1772, even though Boswell urged him to do so. Johnson preferred the word "civility." In French it appeared first, so far as research can disclose, in the year 1757, in a book written by the Marquis de Mirabeau, and later on in an unpublished manuscript by the same author in which he associates it variously with urbanity, comity (*la politesse*), the refinement of manners or customs, something that

---

[1] Paper read at the annual meeting of the American Sociological Association, Chicago, Illinois, August 31, 1965.

gives to societies the form and foundation of virtue and is the source of their humanity.[2] This is not, of course, the sense in which the word is used today in sociology and the philosophy of history, but it is related nevertheless to certain indices to which I shall later refer.

The concept of civilization, like the concept of culture, has had a variegated and colorful career in the literature, and both of these words have been defined and refined, compared and contrasted, by many writers. Indeed, although not used interchangeably by the same writer, they operate nevertheless like twins who are seldom found apart. One Frenchman, for example, can say that America has a civilization but no culture, another that America has a culture but no civilization, and both mean exactly the same thing.[3]

Sociologists and anthropologists, however, have generally preferred to maintain a distinction between these two concepts. One of these distinctions was developed by Alfred Weber and Robert M. MacIver and discussed also, incidentally, by Robert K. Merton in one of his early papers.[4] For Weber civilization appears to mean all of the practical and technical arts, including knowledge, that have been devised for the control of nature. Culture, on the other hand, consists of values, principles, and ideals, a unique set of which is represented by every historical society. Civilization is thus a means, culture an end; civilization is cumulative, culture is not; civilization is impersonal and objective, culture personal and subjective. The difference is illustrated by

---

[2] See E. Benveniste, "Civilisation: Contribution à l'histoire du mot," in *Eventail de l'histoire vivante (hommage à Lucien Febvre)* (Paris, 1953); and Lucien Febvre, *Civilisation, le mot et l'idée* (Paris: Publications du Centre International de Synthèse, 1930). Referred to in John U. Nef, *Cultural Foundations of Industrial Civilisation* (Cambridge: University Press, 1958), p. 79.

[3] I am indebted for this observation to William R. Dennes, "Conceptions of Civilization: Descriptive and Normative," *Civilization* (Berkeley and Los Angeles: University of California Press, 1959), p. 149.

[4] Robert K. Merton, "Civilization and Culture," *Sociology and Social Research*, XXI, No. 2 (November-December, 1936), 103–13.

an example suggested by Merton, namely, that "A profound study of the techniques of Shakespeare or of Rembrandt will not enable a modern litterateur or painter to duplicate the work of these masters. But any repetition of the operations defined by Newton in his *Principia* will enable the modern scientist to attain the same results, upon which he can build further developments. It is this basic difference between the two fields which accounts for the cumulative nature of civilization and the unique (non-cumulative) character of culture."[5] This is not to say, of course, that anyone else could have written the *Principia*. Indeed, a French commentator of the time remarked that Newton was not only the greatest genius who ever lived but also the most fortunate. Why the most fortunate? Because there is only one universe, he said, and it can therefore be given to only one person to discover its laws. One also remembers Alexander Pope's lines:

> Nature, and nature's laws, lay hid in night;
> God said, "Let Newton be!" and all was light.

To which, incidentally, there is a twentieth-century emendation:

> And so it was, until the Devil, crying "Ho,"
> Said, "Let Einstein be!" and restored the *status quo*.

In MacIver the distinction we have been discussing is perhaps even clearer. Civilization for him pertains to everything that is instrumental, that is, a means to something else; culture, on the other hand, is ultimate, an end in itself. A typewriter, a printing press, a lathe, a factory, a locomotive, a bank, a currency system, are all utilitarian, conceived and devised as means to ends. They belong to the realm of civilization, by which MacIver means "the whole mechanism and organization which man has devised in his endeavor to control the condition of his life."[6] Culture is

---

[5] *Ibid.*, p. 112.
[6] Robert M. MacIver and Charles H. Page, *Society: A Systematic Analysis* (New York: Holt, Rinehart & Winston, 1949), p. 498.

something else. It is a novel, a picture, a poem, a game, a philosophy, a creed, a cathedral, things we create because we want them for themselves and not for some more ultimate end. Culture is thus "the realm of values, of styles, of emotional attachments, of intellectual adventures,"[7] and it is the antithesis of civilization. There is a close relationship, to be sure—culture affects civilization as civilization influences culture—but the distinction is clear. It is as clear as the relationship between means and ends.

It is fair to say, however, that this distinction in both Weber and MacIver did not survive. The almost universal adoption in the literature of sociology of culture in the anthropological sense, in the sense originated by E. B. Tylor, made the Weber-MacIver usage obsolete; and indeed no one today continues to insist that civilization is a means and culture an end. Even clear and useful distinctions succumb sometimes to more importunate conceptual needs.[8]

In Spengler we find still other meanings attached to the concept of civilization. In a significant sense, as Spengler says in his big, brooding, and beautiful book, the problem of civilization is the fundamental question of all "higher history." Culture, however, is the unit of philosophical-historical analysis, and thus he treats of eight cultures—the Egyptian, the Indian, the Babylonian, the Chinese, the Arabian, the Classical, the Mexican, and the Western—each of which goes through its inevitable transformation of spring, summer, autumn, and winter, not with the mechanics of causality but with the inevitability of destiny. Each of these cultures has its own civilization. "In this work," Spengler says,

for the first time the two words, hitherto used to express an indefinite, more or less ethical distinction, are used in a *periodic* sense, to express a strict and necessary *organic succession*. The

---

[7] *Ibid.*, p. 499.
[8] For Sorokin's criticism of MacIver on this point see *Social and Cultural Dynamics*, vol. IV (New York: American Book Co., 1941), chap. iv.

Civilization is the inevitable *destiny* of the Culture, and in this principle we obtain the viewpoint from which the deepest and gravest problems of historical morphology become capable of solution. Civilizations are the most external and artificial states of which a species of developed humanity is capable. They are a conclusion, the thing-become succeeding the thing-becoming, death following life, rigidity following expansion, intellectual age and the stone-built, petrifying world-city following mother-earth and the spiritual childhood of Doric and Gothic. They are an end, irrevocable, yet by inward necessity reached again and again.[9]

Now civilization is an end in the other sense, in the sense not of goal but of termination. Culture is to civilization as life is to death, as springtime is to winter, as the Greek soul is to the Roman intellect, as efflorescence is to desiccation, as folk is to mass, as art is to science, as faith is to scepticism ("Scepticism," says Spengler, "is the expression of a pure Civilization; and it dissipates the world-picture of the Culture that has gone before.").[10] Finally, the existence of money and the rise of the city are the marks of a Civilization and of a decaying Culture.

Spengler is so rich in imagery, so profound in historical imagination, and so metaphysical in motive that it is difficult to resist the temptation to quote him at length. No one takes his philosophy of history seriously any more (though perhaps one should), and yet one cannot help but characterize *The Decline of the West* as a work of art. Spengler has created for us, however, a difficulty in that a Culture has for him a career that consists of two parts, a culture part and a civilization part, and thus culture is both an entire historical process and a part of that process. Civilization, however, is the end, the Thanatos, the corpse of every Culture, and it therefore has only negative implications. Civilization is not a goal to be sought by human societies, but is

---

[9] Oswald Spengler, *The Decline of the West,* trans. Charles Francis Atkinson (New York: Alfred A. Knopf, Inc., 1926), I, 31.
[10] *Ibid.,* pp. 45–46.

rather their destiny when they cease to be human and creative and become instead mechanical and dead. Let us succumb to temptation and quote Spengler once more as he says:

> At last, in the gray dawn of Civilization, the fire in the Soul dies down. The dwindling powers rise to one more, half-successful, effort of creation, and produce the Classicism that is common to all dying Cultures. The soul thinks once again, and in Romanticism looks back piteously to its childhood; and then finally, weary, reluctant, cold, it loses its desire to be, and, as in Imperial Rome, wishes itself out of the overlong daylight and back in the darkness of protomysticism, in the womb of the mother, in the grave. The spell of a "second religiousness" comes upon it, and Late-Classical man turns to the practice of the cults of Mithras, of Isis, of the Sun—those very cults into which a soul just born in the East has been pouring a new wine of dreams and fears and loneliness.[11]

And so we see for Weber, MacIver, and Spengler, civilization has negative connotations, although they are negative, of course, in different ways. It is the utilitarianism in Weber and MacIver, as contrasted with more ultimate values, and the disintegration and decay in Spengler, as against the springtime of culture. This is a curious development, when one thinks of it, because civilization in the eighteenth century was a positive accomplishment, something that only a few societies had managed to attain.

In Toynbee a civilization is synonymous with a society, by which he means not a nation-state and not mankind as a whole, but a certain "grouping of of humanity" in between. Five of these civilizations now exist—Western Christendom, an Orthodox Christian society in Southeastern Europe and Russia, an Islamic society, a Hindu society, and a Far-Eastern society. By tracing these backward in time and discovering others to which they are affiliated, Toynbee ends with a list of nineteen civilizations or, if the Orthodox Christian is divided into an Orthodox-Byzantine and

---

[11] *Ibid.*, p. 108.

an Orthodox-Russian, and the Far Eastern into Chinese and a Korean-Japanese society, twenty-one. The fact that he may have nineteen or twenty-one civilizations, depending upon the division just mentioned, presents a problem of definition, of articulation, and of boundary both in time and in space; and this is one of the arguments directed against Toynbee's procedure by his critics, and most notably by Sorokin.

Before looking into Sorokin's criticism, let us attend to Toynbee's defense of his procedure. In seeking his unit of investigation, what he calls "an intelligible field of study," he has chosen Civilizations. Civilizations, however, are only one species of the genus society; there is one other, and that is primitive societies. The difference between the two species of the same genus is that twenty-one of these societies, one species, are "in process of civilization," and that all of the others, the other species, are not. Toynbee notices other differences between the two species. There is only a small number in the first—twenty-one to be exact —whereas there must be at least 650 contemporary representatives of the second and no one knows how many since man first become "human" some 300,000 years ago. "The numerical preponderance of primitive societies over civilizations is [thus] overwhelming."[12] Second, civilizations are much more imposing in their individual dimensions than primitive societies, which are relatively short-lived, restricted in geographical area, and possess only very small populations. These differences are apparent, and we can readily grant the point to Toynbee. But differences are not criteria of differentiation, and we do not yet have an index of civilization. Surely size, duration, and numbers of people do not suffice to characterize a civilization or to give an indication of what the process of civilization is.

Toynbee approaches the problem directly in discussing his unaffiliated societies, six of the twenty-one that emerged not from another civilization but from primitive life. These, incidentally,

---

[12] Arnold J. Toynbee, *A Study of History*, abridgement of Vols. I–VI by D. C. Somervell (New York and London: Oxford University Press, 1947), p. 35.

are the Egyptiac, the Sumeric, the Minoan, the Sinic, the Mayan, and the Andean. Toynbee first considers two indices of civilization that he immediately dismisses: (1) the presence of institutions and (2) the division of labor. That institutions are universal in human societies and the division of labor nearly so are propositions that would surely be acceptable to sociologists—indeed we would insist upon them. It is true that in some societies one can detect no division of labor except that which obtains between the two sexes and between age groups. These cases are so few in number, at least among contemporary societies, that the proposition can stand without challenge. The division of labor, in short, is not a useful criterion of civilization because it throws almost all societies into the civilized category and increases Toynbee's count of civilizations to very much more than twenty-one.

Toynbee does have an answer, however, as follows, even though he is not entirely satisfied with it:

> An essential difference between civilizations and primitive societies *as we know them* (the *caveat* will be found to be important) is the direction taken by mimesis or imitation. Mimesis is a generic feature of all social life. Its operation can be observed both in primitive societies and in civilizations, in every social activity from the imitation of the style of film-stars by their humbler sisters upwards. It operates, however, in different directions in the two species of society. In primitive societies, as we know them, mimesis is directed towards the older generation and towards dead ancestors who stand, unseen but not unfelt, at the back of the living elders, reinforcing their prestige. In a society where mimesis is thus directed backwards toward the past, custom rules and society remains static. On the other hand, in societies in process of civilization, mimesis is directed towards creative personalities who command a following because they are pioneers. In such societies, "the cake of custom," as Walter Bagehot called it in his *Physics and Politics,* is broken and society is in dynamic motion along a course of change and growth.[13]

---

[13] *Ibid.,* p. 49. (Italics in original.)

As I have suggested, Toynbee is not entirely satisfied with this. He regards the difference as important, but as one that is neither permanent nor fundamental. That is, who knows whether or not a society, now "primitive" and static, did not have an earlier stage in which it was moving more dynamically than any civilization now known to us has ever moved? Furthermore, an earlier mutation, the "mutation of sub-man into man, which was accomplished, in circumstances of which we have no record, under the aegis of primitive societies, was a more profound change, a greater step in growth, than any progress which man has yet achieved under the aegis of civilization."[14] Nor does Toynbee offer any explanation for the fact that mimesis operates in one direction in some societies and in the reverse direction in others.

Toynbee is thus compelled to fall back upon his famous analogy of people lying on a ledge on the mountainside, with a precipice below and one above, some of them torpid and motionless, others striving to climb to the top. Some societies therefore can be compared with paralytics and others with athletes, the first remaining in the primitive category and the second rising to the civilized. The principal difficulty with this analogy, as Toynbee himself recognizes, is that the paralytics may one day shake off their torpor and begin to climb, whereas the athletes may stumble and fall off the precipice into the void below. The difference, therefore, is not an absolute one, nor is it permanent. It gives us an insight, and that is all, between two kinds of societies, one static and the other dynamic. A society in its active phase—if it has one—is a civilization. It imitates its innovators rather than its ancestors. And thus the "integration of custom" is transformed into "the differentiation of civilization."

Our task with Sorokin is a different one for the simple reason that he does not use the concept of civilization in the construction of his vast and commanding theory of social and cultural dynamics. Indeed, one detects in his writing a hostility to the term, and there is in fact an explicit criticism of the manner in which

---

[14] *Ibid.*

Spengler and Toynbee have employed it. It will be recalled that in Sorokin there are various kinds of unities, some logically and meaningfully integrated, others causally integrated. For these he uses the term "systems" or, sometimes, "cultural systems." These systems are of three different kinds: the ideational, the sensate, and the (transitional) idealistic; and it is these that change from one pole to the other, in irregular fluctuation, over the course of history. Some collections of culture traits, on the other hand, do not exhibit the kind of unity that would enable them to change together, and these he calls "congeries." Sorokin's difficulty with the concept of civilization, in both Spengler and Toynbee, is that both of these writers fail to take into consideration the basic difference between a system and a mere congeries. They have compounded the confusion by failing to distinguish between an organized group and a cultural system—what they call a civilization is sometimes the one phenomenon and sometimes the other. Furthermore, most of their "civilizations" are really language groups, or state groups, or partly territorial and partly religious groups. Most of them are neither meaningful nor meaningful-causal nor even causal unities. It follows from these observations that the civilizations of Spengler and Toynbee cannot go through the stages from childhood to death or from springtime to winter that their authors have outlined for them. These, in essence, are Sorokin's criticisms.[15]

A hundred years ago no one would have had much difficulty with the meaning of civilization. Even earlier, Buckle could quote with approval Voltaire's remark, "I want to know what were the steps by which man passed from barbarism to civilization." "Barbarism" and "civilization" were contrary terms, and everyone knew the difference between them. Barbarians were people, first, who were not Greeks and who, in later periods of Western history, were unaffected by Greek achievements. Bar-

---

[15] Pitirim A. Sorokin, *Social Philosophies of an Age of Crisis* (Boston: Beacon Press, 1950), esp. chap. xii, pp. 205–43. See also *Society, Culture and Personality* (New York: Harper & Bros., 1947), pp. 638–44.

barians were people who wore no clothes, who procreated without benefit of clergy, who indeed had no clergy, who practiced
un-Christian rituals, who pillaged their neighbors and sometimes
ate them. The following passage from an old book on tropical
Africa is typical:

> Hidden away in these endless forests, like birds' nests in a wood,
> in terror of one another and of their common foe, the slaver, are
> small native villages; and here in his virgin simplicity dwells
> Primeval Man, without clothes, without civilization, without learn-
> ing, without religion—the genuine child of nature, thoughtless,
> careless and contented.[16]

The Victorians, of course, disapproved of people like these.
Charles Kingsley, for example, wrote a story called "The History
of the Great and Famous Nation of the Doasyoulikes," who preferred leisure to work and who paid the penalty for their preference by degenerating into gorillas. In recounting this story,
Toynbee compares Homer's attitude toward his Lotus-Eaters,
who are enormously attractive, and says, "Kingsley, on the other
hand, displays the modern British attitude in regarding his
Doasyoulikes with such contemptuous disapproval that he is
immune from their attractions; he feels it a positive duty to
annex them to the British Empire, not for our good, of course, but
for theirs, and to provide them with trousers and Bibles."[17]

Trousers and Bibles—these surely are unmistakable indices of
civilization! They are only two, however, of a very long list that
could be put together; and each index would reflect, in part at
least, the culture in which it was proposed. Among these indices
one would find an extraordinary variety, including language,
literacy, law, soap, paper, the wheel, money, government, religion, science, agriculture, the city, commerce, print, the domestication of animals, the breeding of cattle, the use of milk, the

---

[16] H. Drummond, *Tropical Africa*, pp. 55–56 (quoted in Toynbee, *op. cit.*,
p. 87).
[17] Toynbee, p. 87.

digging stick, the use of the fork, plumbing, dental caries, and even the dry martini. Another list would contain such moral virtues as kindness, charity, compassion, order, discipline, toleration, and the emancipation of women. Stendhal identified civilization with the invention of love: "On ne trouve qu'un amour physique et des plus grossiers chez les peuples sauvages ou trop barbares."[18] Still another list would accent, in reverse, the absence of such vices as war, cruelty, violence, dogmatism, fanaticism, ignorance, and superstition. The sociologist Edward Cary Hayes remarked in one of his books that "Three meals a day are a highly advanced institution. Savages gorge themselves or fast."[19] A contemporary historian also prefers to date the dawn of civilization from the time when men first learned to make provision for the future, when they learned to remedy a situation that had hitherto been either feast or famine.

The difficulty with using this as an index of civilization, however, is that it too is arbitrary and involves an ethical judgment. As the historian says, "There is a mute wisdom in this improvidence," in not taking thought for the future:

> The moment man begins to take thought of the morrow he passes out of the Garden of Eden into the vale of anxiety; the pale cast of worry settles down upon him, greed is sharpened, property begins, and the good cheer of the "thoughtless" native disappears. . . . "Of what are you thinking?" Peary asked one of his Eskimo guides. "I do not have to think," was the answer; "I have plenty of meat." Not to think unless we have to—there is much to be said for this as the summation of wisdom.[20]

This historian nevertheless calls "primitive" those societies that make little or no provision for unproductive days and "civilized," in contrast, those whose members are literate providers.

---

18 *De l'Amour* (1822), chap. xxvi.
19 *Introduction to the Study of Sociology* (New York, 1918), p. 494.
20 Will Durant, *The Story of Civilization,* Part I: *Our Oriental Heritage* (New York: Simon & Schuster, Inc., 1954), p. 6.

We now, however, have enough amorphous suggestions. Let us confront the problem directly. First of all, we have found no consistency at all in the use of the term "civilization" and no consensus on the phenomenon it is supposed to symbolize. In some writers it has positive and in others negative connotations. Second, we have found civilization and culture sharply distinguished and then used in contrary senses by different writers. Third, we have found our word in both the singular and in the plural, without knowing whether the former is the class name for a group of the latter or a concept with a connotation of its own. Fourth, assuming that one can give it a significance in the plural, we have found it a strenuous if not impossible task to delineate the boundaries between one civilization and another —and this is also one of Sorokin's principal criticisms of Spengler and Toynbee. Fifth, assuming that one can give it a significance in the singular, we have found an unmanageable variety of indices by which it is marked off from something else, usually called primitivism or barbarism. Sixth, as the word is used in the singular it often appears as a normative or evaluative concept and seldom as a categorical or purely descriptive one. Seventh, in talking about civilization, it is exceedingly easy to slip into the subjective mood and to think of it in terms of the things we ourselves happen to appreciate and enjoy. And eighth, civilization is tightly bound to sociolcultural conditions, and its meaning is a function, therefore, of the culture, age, period, or society in which definitions of it are proposed.

Is there any solution of these problem? One way out is to contend that civilization does not exist, that no society in human history, including our own, can fully qualify. Certainly, if we use as indices literacy and the law—two very useful indices—then a serious question arises. We think *we* satisfy both of these criteria but, unfortunately, although our claim to literacy has a modicum of cogency, we, members of an American society—as recent events unhappily demonstrate—do not subscribe to a rule of law if it conflicts with what we conceive to be our own interests. There is no political order in the world at large, no law to which men of all nations subscribe, no legislature for the human race. In this respect we have not overcome the tribal loyalty with which we should be inclined to associate not civilization but rather its absence. In the long chapters of Western history we have made some gains in overcoming religious and racial prejudice. But national prejudice remains, the notion that in some way or other our country is superior to others, that our country's interests come first, and that patriotism is a form of virtue. Only when we become fully civilized will we realize that patriotism is a form of prejudice and indeed the most dangerous form of prejudice that still afflicts our human society.

One may reasonably object, of course, that these observations belong to the realm of the normative, that loyalty to the human race rather than to a nation-state is a moral preference and not an objective index. We ought perhaps to turn in another direction in search of a solution.

I should like finally to propose, therefore, a simple and yet I think objective criterion that can serve as an index of civilization. It has to do with sophistication in a *sophisticated* sense of that word. It concerns the self-reflection and self-criticism and other-awareness in which it can be said that the members of a civilized society indulge. Thus, a primitive society in these terms has art but no aesthetics, because aesthetics is a sophisticated reflection on the meaning and nature of art. Similarly, it has religion but no theology, because again theology is a sophisticated reflection and rational analysis of the meaning and nature of religion, as contrasted with the practice of religious rituals or the belief in deities. The difference is clear, and it can be extended. In sum, an uncivilized society has art but no aesthetics, religion but no theology, techniques but no science, tools but no technology, legends but no literature, a language but no alphabet (or ideographs), customs but no laws, a history but no historiography, knowledge but no epistemology, and finally, a *Weltanschauung* but no philosophy. Literacy is the necessary condition and sophistication the sufficient condition, and thus a literate sophistication becomes a prime index of civilization and one that has some claim to objectivity.

There is one vital part of this index, which I offer in conclusion, and that is the existence of sociology. It is not enough to live in a society or to be a member of a group, because all men satisfy these criteria. The civilized man reflects in addition upon the meaning of society, on its structure and changes, and on the nature of human association. It is sociology that enables him to transcend the provincialisms of time and place and circumstance and to recognize that in spite of cultural differences and disparities, all human societies are in essence the same. They all have the same structure and they all pursue, in different ways, their identical destinies. We thus have, in sociology itself, an index of civilization to which I would invite your earnest attention.

16

Once More the Idea of Progress

[1974]

At the first annual general meeting of the British Sociological Association, March 22, 1952, Morris Ginsberg devoted his chairman's address to the idea of progress.[1] He began by quoting an obscure French historian, A. Javary. In 1851, a hundred years earlier, Javary had proposed that the idea of progress was so firmly established that no one any longer would contest it, and all that remained to be examined were the conditions under which it was realized.

Ginsberg greeted this proposition with scepticism, however, a

---

[1] This address, somewhat expanded, appears as chap. I in Morris Ginsberg, *The Idea of Progress: A Revaluation*, Beacon Press, Boston, 1953. Subsequent page references, otherwise unidentified, are to this book.

scepticism he imputed to Javary himself who, after a discussion of Turgot, Condorcet, Herder, and Kant, concluded that none of these writers had succeeded in formulating a general law or principle of progress. Ginsberg went on to observe that the idea of progress had passed through three stages. In the first stage progress was an ethical ideal toward which mankind was presumably moving. The second stage was marked by efforts to find a clear definition of the idea and to find support for it either in some general philosophical theory or in the biological theory of evolution. In the third stage it was recognized that progress may not be continuous, that there is a contrary phenomenon of retrogression, and that the criteria of general progress are still unknown. The idea of general progress had unusual vitality toward the end of the nineteenth century due, Ginsberg believed, to triumphs of applied science and evolutionary theory. He felt that now it might be more profitable to concentrate on "specific lines of progress" and on methods for investigating their interrelations.

Ginsberg suggests in any event (I shift to the present tense) that the belief in progress is now (1952) seriously weakened. We recognize, on the practical side, that technological advance is unrelated to morality and that new discoveries in science can be used for destructive purposes. We recognize, on the theoretical side, that the idea of progress has suffered from recent emphasis upon the cyclical character of history,[2] from emphasis too on the irrational elements in human nature, and even from the reformulation of the doctrine of original sin. In spite of these developments, however, the idea of progress persists, and Ginsberg is able to show without much difficulty that its critics frequently lapse into inconsistency and do not, in fact, entirely reject it. He sorts the theories of its protagonists into three groups. The first is Marxism, which he regards as the only nineteenth-century philosophy of history that is still influential. The second theory

[2] Frank Manuel reminds us, incidentally, that we have a choice between two images of history. It is either a Jacob's ladder or an Ixion's wheel. See his *Shapes of Philosophical History*, Stanford University Press, Stanford, Calif., 1965.

he associates with Hobhouse and especially the views advanced in *Morals in Evolution*. The third is a more generalized theory of evolution which includes the field of human history and an emergent morality. Ginsberg, of course, is always aware of the fact that there is an ineluctable ethical or normative component in any idea of progress in history.

In the remainder of his little book Ginsberg treats a number of issues that he touched upon only briefly in his chairman's address. He devotes a chapter to eighteenth-century theories of perfectibility, another to Comte, and still another to Hegel and Marx, both of whom, however influential, he finds unimpressive on the subject of progress. As we all know, Ginsberg was much more comfortable with evolutionary theory, although he was fully aware of the complexities involved.[3] Here he draws a distinction between evolution and development. Evolution, he says, is a term that is sometimes used to mean any orderly change and especially, in biology, new forms arising in a process of differentiation from the old. Development, an older term, is a process in which what is potential becomes actual. Neither one is progress, but now Ginsberg hazards a definition in terms of both of them: "Progress is development or evolution in a direction which satisfies rational criteria of value."[4] He is sure, however, that evolution itself cannot supply such standards, he agrees with T. H. Huxley that "from the facts of evolution no ethics of evolution can be derived," and he reiterates that no general laws of social development, or of progress, have as yet been found.

If we accept this last judgment it is nevertheless possible to inquire if there are any particular trends in history or society that exhibit "advance." In this respect Ginsberg puts forward the rather awkward notion that one clear trend is toward the

---

[3] See also Ginsberg's Introduction to the seventh edition of Hobhouse's *Morals in Evolution;* two essays on the subject in *On the Diversity of Morals*, vol. I, Macmillan, New York, 1957, and one in Michael Banton (ed.), *Darwinism and the Study of Society*, Quadrangle, Chicago, 1961.
[4] P. 42.

unification of mankind.[5] If this seemed to be clear in 1935 and in 1952, it is less clear in 1974, and we may wonder whether Ginsberg himself would have continued to entertain the notion in the months preceding his death. For other examples of "advance" he turns to the advancement of knowledge, and especially of science, which seems to him to be an objectively verifiable fact that depends upon criteria that no one but an ethical relativist would dispute. A science, quite simply, is "more developed" as it explains phenomena hitherto unexplained, and no one can doubt that this has happened in the past and is continuing to happen in the present. The development of knowledge itself Ginsberg discerns most easily in the growing dominion of man over the forces of nature. There is no question in his mind that modern technology represents an advance over the technologies of previous ages.

When he turns from technology to social organization, however, Ginsberg finds his problem more difficult. He professes to see two significant trends: (1) the emergence of law[6] and (2) the unification of mankind, mentioned above. By the second of these he means interconnectedness and interdependence, and in discussing this point he arrives at a monistic interpretation of civilization. Civilization for him, as for Turgot, is one rather than many.

If civilization is one or has become one in the sense of interconnectedness, is it also approaching unity in goal or purpose? This is the question to which Ginsberg addresses himself in his

---

[5] Turgot included this trend in his lecture "The Successive Advances of the Human Mind," delivered at the Sorbonne on December 11, 1750. He observed that with the passage of time "nations, hitherto living in isolation, draw nearer to one another." This is a theme to which Ginsberg too had given earlier expression. See his *The Unity of Mankind*, Oxford University Press, London, 1935 (the Leonard Trelawny Hobhouse Memorial Trust Lecture 5).

[6] "This movement from the unreflective custom to declaration, systematization and codification of law, thence to deliberate legislation and the critical scrutiny of the ethical basis of the law unquestionably constitutes growth in self-direction and the rational ordering of life." P. 55.

final chapter. Here he disagrees with both Whitehead and
Toynbee in denying that religion in general or Christianity in
particular has exhibited an "upward trend." The answer to the
question cannot be found in religion. Is there then some indication of moral progress? Now Ginsberg is willing to indulge in
an affirmative judgment. "The case for moral progress rests above
all on the persistence of the quest for justice in the history of
mankind, spurred on by the sense of injustice."[7] He agrees with
the eighteenth-century philosophers who saw progress as a movement toward reason and justice, equality and freedom. His
theory takes for granted "the unity of the human reason and the
possibility of a rational ethic" and it is not compatible, as he
says, with a relativistic view either of knowledge or of morality.

In conclusion, Ginsberg reminds us that the case for progress
that he is espousing depends upon a rational ethic, one based
upon a knowledge of human needs and the principle of justice.
Knowledge alone, however, does not suffice. It is a necessary,
not a sufficient condition of progress. It points to possibilities,
but it is the will that makes the choices between them. Finally,
and somewhat ominously, "Knowledge offers no apocalyptic visions, but it can do something to help man to make his own
history before the end is reached."[8]

Like all Ginsberg's work, his little book on progress is thoughtful, erudite, and wise. It stimulates reflection even when it fails
to carry conviction. It is clearly not the case, as Bertrand Russell
observed, that Professor Ginsberg has written here "the obituary
of the idea of progress." The reviewer in the *Times Literary
Supplement* was more accurate in suggesting that for Professor
Ginsberg the idea "still retains a measure of validity for our own
time." Our distinguished sociologist firmly believed that the history of mankind exhibits progress in many sectors of endeavor
and especially in the advancement of knowledge. Most of all he
believed in the moral progress of the race and in the ever more

---

[7] P. 68.
[8] P. 77.

complete realization in the future of such goals as freedom, equality, justice, and truth. With respect to the last of these, Ginsberg, an opponent of relativism in ethical theory, believed in progress toward the attainment of truth in moral judgments as in other spheres of knowledge.[9]

Whether or not one shares these beliefs, there is no question that the idea of progress is a hardy perennial—whether weed or flower we shall not now determine. We are as curious about it in the twentieth century as Condorcet was in the eighteenth. We are uncomfortably aware, of course, that it may not be a sociological problem at all.[10] It may not be a sociological problem for two reasons: first the superficial one that it no longer attracts the attention of sociologists[11] and second, more substantial, that progress is always a normative concept when applied to history and thus transcends the limits of sociological inquiry. Whatever label one employs, however, the word is well lodged in our

---

[9] *On Justice in Society*, Cornell University Press, Ithaca, N.Y., 1965, p. 26. Chap. I of this book represents one of Ginsberg's efforts to refute the doctrine of ethical relativism and to establish the view, reached also by Sidgwick, that ethical judgments are genuine propositions, susceptible to truth claims, and not merely expletives, commands, commitments, or expressions of subjective preferences.

[10] As the readers of these lines may know, almost all Ginsberg's writings have more an ethical than a sociological flavor in the sense in which "sociological" is used today. The essay on progress is no exception.

[11] It is interesting, and possibly significant, that the *Encyclopedia of the Social Sciences* published in 1933 carried an article on progress. Its successor, the *International Encyclopedia of the Social Sciences* published in 1968, has no entry under that word. The article in the earlier work was written by the late Carl Becker, and it is well worth reading today. Becker points, for example, to a serious logical problem: "Rationally considered, the idea of progress is always at war with its premises. It rests upon the notion of a universe in perpetual flux; yet the idea of progress has always carried the implication of finality, for it seems to be meaningless unless there is movement toward some ultimate objective. The formal theories of progress are all vitiated by this radical inconsistency." "Progress," *Encyclopedia of the Social Sciences*, Macmillan, New York, 1933, vol. XII, p. 498b.

vocabularies and continues to strike our curiosity and demand our attention. In what follows, therefore, I should like to inquire a little further into the subject and to ask the extent to which it is possible in 1974 to agree with Ginsberg's quiet but persistent moral optimism.

One trouble with the concept of progress, as with all our concepts, is that its meaning is unclear. It has taken on a number of different styles of dress, and it has been, and can be, used either partly or wholly synonymously with many other expressions. Thus, we find progress as growth, development, evolution, movement in space, movement in time, movement forward, succession, accumulation, completion, advancement, and improvement. There are doubtless other meanings. We may begin, therefore, with a hint from MacIver on the relationships between change, process, evolution, and progress.[12] Change, a neutral word, we take as primary and undefined. If we add continuity to the notion of change, we have process. If we add direction to the notion of process, we have evolution. And if we add improvement to the notion of evolution, we have progress. MacIver's view is quite consistent with that of Ginsberg who, as we have seen, defines progress as a development or evolution which satisfies rational criteria of value. Becker, similarly, observes that "Belief in progress as a fact depends upon the standard of value chosen for measuring it."[13] And W. H. Walsh phrases the question in an interesting fashion when he asks whether the contemplation of history leaves us morally satisfied.[14]

We can gratefully agree with all these observations. Unfortunately, however, words like "improvement," "value," and "satisfaction" propel us out of the secluded bay of sociological inquiry and into the open ocean of ethical speculation. Before we find

---

[12] Robert M. MacIver and Charles H. Page, *Society, An Introductory Analysis*, Rinehart, New York, 1949, pp. 521–522.

[13] Becker, *op. cit.*, p. 499a.

[14] *An Introduction to Philosophy of History*, Hutchinson Library, 5th and revised impression, London, 1958, p. 148.

ourselves in these dangerous waters, let us aver that some of the synonyms of progress can be free of normative connotations. Thus, actions undertaken to complete a task are quite easily and normally referred to as progress. An author makes progress with every sentence he adds to his manuscript, a gardener with every strip of grass he mows, a housewife with every dish she washes, and a carpenter with every nail he drives. Sisyphus, of course, makes no progress, but the rest of us do whenever we take a successful step toward the completion of a task. Progress in this sense is a fact and requires no normative judgment.

It is also clear that the word "progress" may be used in a purely temporal sense. Thus, the hands of a clock make progress around the face of the dial, the seasons progress from summer to winter and from winter to summer again, and the life of a human being moves progressively from infancy to senility. The first of these is circular, the second cyclical, and the third linear. But they are all profoundly uninteresting. Movement through time is not ordinarily what we wish to mean when we use the word "progress."

Of progress as evolution or growth enough has been said, especially by Ginsberg, to render additional discussion redundant. We may agree that certain phenomena, including human societies, exhibit increasing differentiation and specialization and that the word "progress" has been used to describe this development. We are even reminded of Spencer's sesquipedalian definition of evolution.[15] But when the word is used to refer only to these intrinsic processes it again loses our interest. All we need to do is to recognize that here too, as in the two preceding instances, we have a legitimate and neutral use of "progress." Neither movement nor evolution implies improvement.

---

[15] For recent discussions of Spencer see Ronald Fletcher, *The Making of Sociology*, vol. 1, Michael Joseph, London, 1971, pp. 250–388; Stanislav Andreski, *Herbert Spencer*, Michael Joseph, London, 1971; and J. D. Y. Peel, *Herbert Spencer: The Evolution of a Sociologist*, Basic Books, New York, 1971, especially p. 131–165.

When we ask about progress we normally mean not simply steps toward completion or movement through time or evolution, but rather something else and something more. We mean, as Ginsberg did, the progress of humanity toward such goals as peace and justice, progress in history from ineptitude to competence in dealing with nature, and success in achieving whatever purposes the race desires. We want to know, to put it crudely, whether things are "better" now than they used to be, whether we can detect in history any improvement in the quality of life or of society, and, if so, what analytical instruments we can employ in the detection. Let us confront the normative meaning of progress with a quotation from Fontenelle, who in the seventeenth century created those charming dialogues between dead celebrities. In one of them Montaigne meets Socrates somewhere in the nether regions and we are privileged to listen to the conversation.

MONTAIGNE.   Is this you, divine Socrates? What a joy it is to see you! I've just entered this region, and ever since I've been looking for you. At last, after filling my book with your name and praise, I can talk with you.

SOCRATES.   I am happy to see a dead man who appears to have been a philosopher. But since you have come so recently from up there . . . let me ask you the news. How goes the world? Hasn't it changed a great deal?

MONTAIGNE.   Much indeed. You wouldn't recognize it.

SOCRATES.   I am delighted to hear it. I have never doubted that it must become better or wiser than in my time.

MONTAIGNE.   What are you saying? It is crazier and more corrupt than ever. That is the change I wanted to discuss with you; and I have been waiting to hear from you an account of the age in which you lived, and in which so much honesty and justice reigned.

SOCRATES.   And I, on the contrary, have been waiting to learn about the marvels of the age in which you have just lived. What? Men have not yet corrected the follies of antiquity? . . . I hoped that things would take a turn toward reason, and that men would profit from the experience of so many years.[16]

Unlike Fontenelle's Montaigne, most writers in both the eighteenth and nineteenth centuries were convinced that history was witness to progress, and they were especially sure that there was an essential difference between barbarism and civilization. Of course, by viewing the matter in these latter terms they had already stacked the cards, so to speak, because no one could doubt that civilization was superior to barbarism. Unfortunately, the "superiority" is in the words themselves. "Barbarism" suggests cruelty, "civilization" civility.[17] Barbarism, in short, is hopelessly pejorative, and any change from that state to another is progress by definition. Furthermore, it was easy— even necessary in these terms—to identify the earlier with the lower and the later with the higher. It was even tempting, in an evolutionary era, to identify both the earlier and the lower with the simple, and the later and the higher with the complex.[18]

The question then arises whether there are any indicators that differentiate civilized societies from those to which the adjective cannot properly be applied. Here, however, we are embarrassed by a surfeit of candidates for that role, including such variegated items as the digging stick, the use of milk, the domestication of animals, the breeding of cattle, agriculture, literacy, law, soap, paper, the wheel, money, government, religion, science, the city, commerce, print, the use of the fork, plumbing, the division of labor, and even, as the Victorians

---

[16] Written in 1683 and quoted in Will and Ariel Durant, *The Story of Civilization*, vol. VIII, *The Age of Louis XIV*, Simon and Schuster, New York, 1963, pp. 615–616. In a later work, *Digression sur les Anciens et les Modernes* (1688), Fontenelle became a bit more optimistic and suggested that although poetry and art had shown no progress, the opposite could be said about science and learning.

[17] Originally, of course, barbarians were only foreigners—all who were not Greek. Boswell urged Johnson to include "civilization" in his dictionary, but the Great Cham declined on the ground that he preferred "civility."

[18] Note the title of a famous book by Hobhouse, Wheeler, and Ginsberg: *The Material Culture and Social Institutions of the Simpler Peoples.*

would remind us, trousers and Bibles![19] A now-forgotten American sociologist, Edward Cary Hayes, saw the dawn of civilization in the institution of three meals a day,[20] and the historian Will Durant in the time when men first made provision for the future.[21] Stendhal identified civilization with the invention of love, but unfortunately no one can recall the date of this invention or the name of the inventor.

It is easy to be facetious about so many indices. One proposal points to what might be called a "literate sophistication." Thus, a primitive society, in contrast to a civilized one, has a language but no alphabet, art but no aesthetics, religion but no theology, techniques but no science, legends but no literature, customs but no laws, social relations but no sociology, knowledge but no epistemology, and a *Weltanschauung* but no philosophy.[22] It is the logos, in short, that is the distinguishing criterion. This proposal, whatever its merits on other grounds, cannot serve as a theory of progress. A large number of descriptive indices can distinguish one kind of society from another; one society we may call civilized and the other something else.[23] But we cannot say without a normative and quite subjective judgment that the presence of an item or an artifact, an idea or an institution,

---

[19] Robert Bierstedt, "Indices of Civilization," *The American Journal of Sociology*, vol. LXXI, no. 5, March 1966, pp. 483–490. The Victorian allusion belongs to Toynbee, who is having a little fun with Charles Kingsley's story "The History of the Great and Famous Nation of the Doasyoulikes." Arnold J. Toynbee, *A Study of History*, abridgment of vols. I–VI by D. C. Somervell, Oxford University Press, New York and London, 1947, p. 87.

[20] *Introduction to the Study of Sociology*, New York, 1918, p. 494.

[21] *The Story of Civilization*, vol. I, *Our Oriental Heritage*, Simon and Schuster, New York, 1954, p. 6.

[22] Bierstedt, *op. cit.*, p. 490.

[23] Unfortunately, we have no satisfactory word for the contrary of civilized. "Savage" and "barbaric" will not do. They are grossly pejorative. "Primitive" contains a value judgment and also an evolutionary premise. "Preliterate" escapes the judgment but is ensnared by the premise. "Nonliterate," like "preliterate," takes one of the indices for granted. "Uncivilized" is value-laden, and "noncivilized" is itself a barbarism. It may be significant that there is no word in the English language that can serve the required purpose.

confers upon a society any superiority or its absence any inferiority.

As mentioned above, most of the writers on the philosophy of history in the eighteenth and nineteenth centuries assumed the superiority of "civilization" to "barbarism." But today both words are encased in quotation marks, and the proposition is one that it is possible—and perhaps even necessary—to doubt. Rousseau did, Toynbee sometimes does, and so can we. Durant recalls for us the story of Peary's Eskimo guide who, when asked what he was thinking about, replied, "I do not have to think. I have plenty of meat." Durant observes that there is much to be said for this as the summation of wisdom: "The moment man begins to take thought of the morrow he passes out of the Garden of Eden into the vale of anxiety."[24] We may remark, incidentally, that a literate sophistication has also produced a tedious lot of literate sophistry.

We have been induced to believe by a long line of Christian missionaries and Social Darwinists that the life of "primitive" man, if not solitary, was at least poor, nasty, brutish, and, especially, short. But who can measure such a spectacle? It surely offered some pleasures—scenery and sex, for example— and, if some observers are to be trusted, freedom from dental caries. If the existence of "primitive" peoples was a precarious one, so also is ours. It is we who live under the shadow of a radioactive cloud. We have made no progress in the writing of social contracts, and we belong to a species so lacking in instincts and so feeble in intelligence that we seem to prefer nuclear incineration to the surrender of national sovereignty.

It may be perfectly true, and objectively true too, that civilized people, blessed with physiological knowledge and medical care, live longer than their predecessors.[25] The decrease in mortality

---

[24] Durant, vol. I, p. 6.

[25] This statement is subject to a common misinterpretation. It is not the life span, but rather life expectancy at birth, which has increased, and dramatically so in the twentieth century. With respect to the life span we have little more than the Biblical allotment.

rates and the increase in life expectancy would be taken by many to be unquestionable indicators of progress. But the old difficulty remains. The affirmation of progress requires a value judgment. As we all know, increasing birthrates and decreasing death rates (the latter especially due to medical "progress") have as one of their consequences a planet that is overpopulated and, as a corollary, too many children who have too little to eat. This is not the place to dwell on this painful subject. We need pause only long enough to note that in one of his short stories John Updike said it all in one sentence: "The race is no longer a tiny tribe of simian aristocrats lording it over an ocean of grass; mankind is a plague, racing like fire across the exhausted continents."[26]

A long life may not itself be the boon it is often assumed to be. Hobbes, Fontenelle, and Bertrand Russell may all have felt that they "carried longevity to excess."[27] Theognis of Megara maintained that it was good not to be born, but "once born make haste to pass the gates of death," a sentiment echoed centuries later by such different persons as Mme. de Sevigné ("If my opinion had been asked, I should have preferred to die in my nurse's arms."); Jonathan Swift, who observed his birthday as a day of mourning and said "No wise man ever wished to be younger"; Frederick the Great, who declared that the happiest day of his life would be the last one; and Winston Churchill who said, finally, "I am bored with it all."

Few indicators of progress in the Western world have received more emphasis than the advancement of science. Here the case for progress would seem to be clear. We cannot cogently deny that twentieth-century physicists and astronomers know more about the structure of material particles and about the composition of the stars than did Copernicus, Brahe, Kepler, Galileo, and "the incomparable Mr. Newton." Reason has conquered super-

---

[26] "Lifeguard," *The New Yorker*, June 17, 1961, p. 30.
[27] As Durant speculates about Fontenelle who, in his hundredth year, said to his friends, *"Je souffre d'être."*

stition, at least in our approach to the physical universe, and that universe has surrendered some of its secrets to scientific inquiry. Once more, however, our belief in progress harbors a canker of doubt. This progress, if such it be, was purchased at a price that several souls, including the Archbishop of the Diocese of New York, might prefer not to pay. For it is apparent that the growth of knowledge in the last four centuries has been accompanied by the decline of religion. Today most educated men subscribe to Shaftesbury's religion—what it was no wise man tells—but this can hardly appear as progress to such defenders of the faith as may forlornly remain. The Council of State that banned Diderot's *Encyclopedia* in 1759 accompanied its decree with the sensible warning that "The advantages to be derived from a work of this sort, in respect to progress in the arts and sciences, can never compensate for the irreparable damage that results from it in regard to morality and religion."[28]

Science, moreover, has not always been accepted as an unadulterated good even by its protagonists. It has given us comforts, of course, but it has also taught us how to kill more people with less effort. Ginsberg himself asks whether it is morally right for nuclear physicists to carry on investigations that may result in the death of innocent millions.[29] The accumulation of knowledge provides no guarantee of its ethical use. As for technology, it has given us things we do not need—detergents and dune buggies, for example—and would be better off without. Who can say, for that matter, whether the internal combustion engine has contributed more to the happiness or the misery of the human race? In the twilight of the twentieth century we can only wonder whether we are the beneficiaries or the victims of technology.

Finally, there are the ethical indices that are often identified with progress—compassion, charity, freedom, equality, justice, and all the rest—in which some discern an increase with each

---

[28] Quoted in Durant, vol. IX, *The Age of Voltaire*, p. 642.
[29] *On Justice in Society, op. cit.*, p. 47.

succeeding century. It is hard to discover these virtues, however, in a period of history in which one sovereign government used gas ovens as a genuine solution to an imaginary problem and another dropped napalm and needle bombs on a peasant populace. The record of man's inhumanity to man is still being written, and if examples like Dachau, Dresden, Vietnam, Pakistan, and Belfast come readily to mind in 1974, one has no confidence that time will not supply similar examples in the future. For Voltaire history was an endless succession of useless cruelties.

As we reflect upon the future we might be inclined to ask ourselves whether the twenty-first century will show the progress we have sought in vain in the twentieth. A more appropriate question, in this grim atomic age, is whether there will be a twenty-first century.

Thoughts like these proceed neither from a Cassandra-like devotion to calamity nor from a desire to participate in the lamentations of Jeremiah, but rather to help us to arrive at some kind of conclusion regarding the idea of progress. My own conclusion is that history, or at least that part of it we know best as Western civilization, can be read in either one of two ways, with optimism or with pessimism, and as easily in one of them as in the other. One may view history, as Morris Ginsberg did, with a cautious hope. But one can also view it with something akin to melancholy. The matter is solely one of temperament. It is rather like asking whether one would prefer to be a citizen of Athens in the age of Pericles, a citizen of London in the era of Victoria, or a citizen of New York in the administration of Nixon. Those of us whose choices are obvious can hardly be accused of hospitality to the idea of progress.

I do not contend that progress is a disreputable idea. I contend instead that it hardly qualifies as an idea at all. It is the better part of discretion, in fact, to construe it as an attitude and to remind ourselves that we can quarrel with ideas but not with attitudes. Belief in progress is a temperamental response to history. It has more to do with optimism and pessimism than it has with truth and falsity. We are induced to assert therefore that progress is any social change that gives us pleasure, any development that wins our approval, and any trend we are inclined to applaud. Except for the trivial instances mentioned earlier, it is a phenomenon wholly devoid of objective validity.

I conclude these primitive observations with a bow, a quotation, and a paradox. The bow is to the memory of Morris Ginsberg, who treated this subject, as he did so many others, with elegance and wisdom. He would have greeted these reflections with tolerance but not with agreement. The quotation is from Henry Beetle Hough, for fifty-three years editor of the *Vineyard Gazette*, a chronicle of Martha's Vineyard, an island off the coast of Massachusetts. Mr. Hough, recently interviewed in Boston, said, "Where I come from we've fought progress with moderate success for fifty years. Progress is, after all, the great enemy." And the paradox? It is contained in Mr. Hough's words, "with moderate success." He is making progress in his battle against it. We might all make progress if we abandoned the idea of progress.

$^{I}7$

Sociology and General Education

[1964]

Sociology has many uses that are alike unsung and unappreciated. Some of these uses pertain not to its function as an instrument in the acquisition of knowledge but to a rather different kind of function—its function in the course and process of education. I am inclined to think in fact, as I hope the following remarks will show, that sociology is one of the most valuable of all of the disciplines in the university curriculum and that one of its most distinctive virtues lies precisely and centrally in the realm of general education.

Those of us who are engaged in the sociological enterprise ourselves tend to think—perhaps inevitably—that sociology is for sociologists, or at least for those who want to become sociologists. In our colleges and universities, however, we teach sociology to many more than these. It has been estimated that only two per cent of undergraduate students major in sociology and that only three per cent of this statistically small figure go on to do graduate work in sociology. The vast majority, in short, study sociology with no vocational or professional purpose. They appear in our undergraduate classes and study our introductory texts either because sociology is required as a supplementary subject in a closely related curriculum or because it satisfies a social science requirement in a curriculum for which another science would do equally well. There are those in addition, we may suppose and hope, who study sociology without being required to do so because it satisfies some wayward or vagrant curiosity of their own, because it stimulates an intellectual interest, because it has its own intrinsic fascination. This paper examines some of the educational and cultural advantages that sociology has to offer these other groups of students, particularly the last, comprised of those who have no intention of making a career in the field and who have no professional requirement to satisfy. I propose to show, in short, that sociology has an important role to play in general education, a role that is wholly commensurate with and sometimes even superior to the roles played by such older disciplines as history, literature, and philosophy. I shall maintain that sociology has many virtues that contribute to the cultivation of the intellect and that it merits a high rank, therefore, among the liberal arts and sciences.

The Liberated Mind

The first of the educational virtues of sociology is that, like all of the liberal arts, it liberates the student from the provincialisms of time, place, and circumstance. One of the great disabilities of those who have been denied the benefits of education is their parochialism, their attachment to the narrow corner of earth wherein they dwell. These are the people—and unfortunately they are the vast majority of mankind—who retain throughout their lives a primitive loyalty to their initial culture. For the uneducated the initial culture tends to be the permanent culture and only those who travel can learn to minimize the constricting influences of their natal locality. One may say incidentally that this observation applies no less to the urbanite than to the man on a remote ranch or farm. Some of the most provincial of the world's citizens can be found in the largest of the world's cities.

It is not often emphasized that one can travel in time as well as in space. One needs no visas and no passports to visit the Roman Forum in the time of the Caesars, to watch the coronation of Charlemagne on Christmas Day in the year A.D. 800, to participate with astonishment and shock in the excommunication of Spinoza, or to study with Darwin the giant orchid of Madagascar. This, of course, is one of the advantages that history confers upon those who would read its pages and thereby invite seduction by Clio, the most attractive of the Muses.

One may ask, however, why history should be superior in any way to sociology in exercising this liberating function. History can free the receptive mind from the limitations of time and space by removing it to other times and places, to other periods and climes. But sociology can do more than this. Sociology can liberate the mind from time and space themselves and remove it to a new and transcendental realm where it no longer depends upon these Aristotelian categories. For the historian, liberated from his own time, is apt to become engrossed with another, and to become again a captive of a particular time and place and circumstance. The sociologist, on the contrary, transcends all times, all places, and all circumstances in his effort to find the universal principles that characterize human societies everywhere, whether they be large or small, ancient or modern, Eastern or Western, primitive or civilized. This sociological liberation, of course, is liberation from the concrete, as all scientific liberation must be, and in this sense any movement from the concrete character of history to the abstract character of sociology brings a sense of freedom and of intellectual expansiveness. It is a freedom which, responsibly enjoyed and maturely exercised, gives stature to intellect and thus serves one of the ends of education.

This sort of liberation, in a world beset by provincialisms, by the ethnocentrisms of culture and the temporocentrisms of era, period, and century, is no mean or insignificant accomplishment. Whether the group that claims our parochial loyalty be race or region, or class or religion, or neighborhood or nation, we are all influenced by it and, when uneducated, controlled by it. Sociology helps us to free ourselves from these particularistic controls and to learn to see a more universal society and a single human race. To see the eternal in the passing present, the universal in the particular fact, and the abstract in the concrete event—these are among the gifts of a liberal education. They are also the mark of the free man which it is the function of a liberal education to create.

It is good for the undergraduate, in short, to realize that there are other races and regions, classes and religions, neighborhoods and nations, and it is even better to recognize that beneath the cultural differences and diversities that appear upon the surface all human societies are in essence the same. They have the same basic structure and form and shape, they arise from similar causes, and pursue in many cases a similar destiny. And it is sociology, which concentrates upon structure and form and shape, that contributes this sense of similarity and of universality to the educational process. One may say, therefore, that whatever it may teach us as a science, sociology also belongs to the liberal arts, and like history, philosophy, and literature, has a liberating influence upon those who are fortunate enough to be exposed to its teachings, to its probes and its quests, its contexts and its styles.

The Abstraction of Inquiry

The second of the educational advantages of sociology—a corollary of the first—is that it introduces the student to the nature and function of logic and scientific method. The introductory course in sociology teaches the student, for perhaps the first time, something about the processes of abstraction, of rising by induction from concrete fact to abstract principle, from datum to generalization, and from observation to understanding. The student learns to deal not only with the concrete and the tangible but also with the abstract and the intangible. Events, persons, and situations are all concrete and factual, easily perceived or easily recalled, and often well remembered. They exist as objects of knowledge on the level of immediacy and of immediate confrontation, needing no guarantee of meaning or of validity in order to occupy the mind. How different in this respect are the intangibles of sociology—culture, norm, folkway, law, sanction, status, role, institution, power, authority—none of which is susceptible to the immediacy of sense experience. Indeed, it may be in sociology that the student learns the logical functions of class inclusion, class membership, and class identification, and subjects to logical manipulation and inference concepts that are already several steps removed from the phenomenal world in which he has been accustomed to move and in which he makes his common observations. It is in this way too that he learns the nature and character of definition, and the rules of measurement. It may be that in these respects the role of sociology is almost unique. For in the humanities the scientific method plays no part and in the sciences it is taken for granted. It is especially in sociology that it rises to the level of awareness and becomes a matter of conscious application and employment.

The Sense of Order

A third educational consequence of some importance, one also related to logic, is the sense of system and of order that sociology exhibits, and which is a normal and even inevitable accompaniment of the introductory course. I do not mean by this the theory and practice of artificial systems, of systems of nominal definitions, systems of descriptive equations, mechanical systems in equilibrium, biological systems in homeostasis, or logical systems whether open or closed. I mean instead something more substantive and empirical—namely, the sense of order as order applies to a specific body of knowledge and in this case to a body of knowledge about society. A science of sociology is possible only because society itself is neither chaotic nor anomic but exhibits instead recurrences and regularities, patterns and configurations, and these are evidence of the existence of order. Anyone who examines human events in a search for patterns is *ipso facto* a practitioner of the science of sociology. The student who is encouraged to do this regularly learns to look behind appearances and to see the structure that constitutes an order. He confronts in this way the problem of induction in its practical application to an intellectual exercise. He has been acquainted with deduction, as it were, ever since he met in plane geometry the axioms of Euclid and learned to parrot the propositions that lead, for example, to the proof of the Pythagorean theorem. Now he learns —and introductory sociology has this to teach him—that there is another logic as well, the logic of induction. For it is in sociology that the idiosyncrasies of custom disappear in the logical process that gives category and classification to them and finds form and structure in the societies that contain them.

Philosophers may not yet be able to explain what induction is —they may in fact make all of the Baconian errors in their effort to use it and they may even deny, with Bertrand Russell, that it is anything more than an "educated guess." But the need for induction, if properly articulated, attains an unusual clarity in sociology. The student is thus doubly blessed—once with the sense of order, which it is the function of knowledge to impose upon the universe, and once again with the logical process involved in achieving it. I hasten to confess, of course, that few students of introductory sociology are aware that these wonderful—and wonderfully logical—things are happening to them. But they are there nevertheless, in the nature of the sociological enterprise, and cannot help but make an impression, however dimly perceived.

These things contribute indeed a methodological sophistication that it is not possible to parallel in the case of some of the other disciplines. In the sciences, pedagogical activity is often dissipated into the repetition of purposeless experiments as remote from genuinely scientific implication as they are from human concern. In the humanities, the second of C. P. Snow's two cultures, scholarship often disintegrates, in its day-to-day academic setting, into the dry rot of textual exegesis and sectarian criticism. Indeed, the ill-natured attack of F. R. Leavis upon Sir Charles is an indication of what can happen when the humanities themselves cease to be humanistic and liberal and become instead something hypercritical, carping, and querulous.

Sociologists, in contrast, have been forced by the sheer intrinsic difficulty of their enterprise to acquire a kind of methodological sophistication that is lacking in these other endeavors. As suggested above, the humanists need no philosophy of science; they know little logic and less metaphysics. The scientists, on the other hand, are so accustomed to their methods that most of them have long since ceased to inquire into their logical or epistemological foundations. Both groups, in short, are innocent of methodology, which is the logic of inquiry. They are innocent, that is, of philosophy. As for the philosophers themselves, they, of course, have ceased to exist—except at Oxford University where they indulge themselves in a sterile kind of enterprise called "analysis," an enterprise that depends wholly upon Oxford cloisters and no longer has any connection with a world in which order is observed and knowledge acquired. It is in the social sciences, in our century at least, and especially in sociology, where men confront major methodological issues and it is sociologists in consequence who acquire the kind of philosophical sophistication that no longer accompanies these other inquiries.

It is sometimes asked why those who have made the most important contributions to the sciences—men like Newton and Darwin and Einstein—have expressed the fewest sentiments and opinions on the philosophy of science and, on the contrary, those who were not notable for their scientific achievements have frequently made pronouncements of repute about the nature of science. Francis Bacon, for example, for all of his practical empiricism, his pragmatic induction, and his disdain for "received opinion," made no contribution to any of the sciences and was the last of the great European intellectuals to refuse to accept the heliocentric hypothesis of Copernicus. It may be that those who are close enough to science to practice it without methodological question or constraint are too close to observe it with methodological criticism and concentration. On this score, sociology occupies a middle position, as it were, close enough to use but not too close to abuse, or to use uncritically. This position, of course, may be an impediment in the acquisition of knowledge, but it is an advantage in enlarging the contours of a liberal education.

There is still another factor involved in the methodological sophistication of sociologists. Physics, astronomy, and the other natural sciences made some of their greatest strides before Immanuel Kant asked his embarrassing and difficult questions about the possibility of constructing synthetic judgments *a priori.* I do not mean to imply that the problem of knowledge has its origin in *The Critique of Pure Reason* but I do mean to say that post-Kantian thinkers, a category that includes all sociologists, have had to contend with Kantian questions whereas pre-Kantian thinkers did not. The point is that if methodological sophistication is a virtue then sociologists, because of their post-Kantian place in intellectual history, have a larger opportunity to acquire this virtue than the protagonists of the earlier and more settled sciences. Stated another way, sociologists can make an educational opportunity of an historical necessity.

The Two Cultures

We have still other advantages to emphasize on behalf of sociology. There are bridges after all between Snow's two cultures and one of the strongest of them, one of the most convenient and most serviceable, is the science of sociology. In the British educational system, where specialization is an early requirement—often beginning as early as the sixth form, which is below the university level—it is easy to understand why those who know the sonnets of Shakespeare are not similarly conversant with Avogadro's Law. Between letters on the one hand and science, especially experimental science, on the other there runs a river that is difficult to cross. Those who live and work on one bank of this stream have few acquaintances on the other and their relative isolation, their social distance so to speak, result at long last in separate languages and finally, for that reason, in two cultures. In the United States this situation is leavened in some measure at least by the absence of early specialization and by the encouragement of graduate work in fields quite distant from one's undergraduate concentration.

But it is leavened even more, I believe, by a strong social science tradition and especially by the development of sociology in this country, a development that has been nowhere near so rapid in the United Kingdom. It has been noted frequently that sociology shares its subject matter with the humanities and its method with the sciences, and in this sense it clearly participates in both of the two cultures. This point can profit by renewed emphasis, and particularly perhaps by the reminder that bridges have an equal purchase on both banks of whatever stream they span. Sociology is a science in premise, approach, and method, but nothing human is alien to it, and it belongs therefore almost uniquely to both the sciences and the humanities.

Person and Society

Still another virtue of sociology is that it stimulates reflection on the oldest problem known to social philosophy, that is, the relationship between the individual and society. The problem, of course, is ultimately a philosophical one, and not properly sociological at all, but of all the disciplines in the curriculum sociology provides the widest and the best-paved avenue of approach to it. For it is in sociology that the student is most likely to discover the ways in which the structure of his society, the content of its culture, and the character of its norms all help to socialize him, carving out of the biological material the person that he has become. What then is the relationship between this person and his society? What does each owe to the other? Where in "the vast intrinsic traffic of society," where in the welter of social process, where in the changing juxtapositions of groups does the individual discover his own identity? What guarantees his integrity as an individual and confers upon him the irrepressible and unrepeatable character of his own personality? These questions, as I have said, belong to social philosophy, and to them men in each succeeding historical era may have a different answer. But sociology supplies the base, the point of departure, from which intelligent and thoughtful answers can proceed. We shall always want to know the ultimate meaning of Aristotle's assertion that man is a social animal, and it is in the study of sociology that the student can gain his first appreciation of its profound significance. This too is one of the educational rewards of a course in sociology.

Sociology and History

We would say, as a penultimate point, that sociology belongs not only to science and to philosophy but also to the sweep of history. For there is a place, and an important place, for sociology in the history of human thought. Whether we begin with Plato in one tradition or with Confucius in another, the nature of human groups, the character of human relationships, and the profiles of human societies themselves have always attracted the restless and inquisitive mind and have stimulated it to reflection, to speculation, and finally, in the nineteenth century and in our own, to scientific inquiry. It is a history that reminds us how short the distance we have travelled, how long the road ahead. But it is a history nevertheless that has its peaks of scenic beauty and of scientific truth, of radiance and significance.

It is with respect to history too that sociology asks its most penetrating questions. For sociology is not content with description, however thorough it may be, or with analysis, however profound. It has a more fundamental quest. It seeks also the causes of things—things as they are and as they have come to be. Behind all of our research and all of our theory there lies the desire, often subliminal, to find a meaning in the ebb and flow of human affairs, in the systole and diastole of human history. This may well be the most profound and the most difficult of all questions. But there is no doubt that it is a sociological question, the question in fact that motivated Auguste Comte to found our science and give it a name. For when the philosophy of history leaves its theological and metaphysical stages and enters its positive stage it becomes identical with the science of sociology. As this, the most important of the Comtean insights, continues to inform our discipline so also will it stimulate our students too to discover this area of intellectual inquiry. Nothing more important than this could happen to them in the entire course of their liberal education.

The Prose of Sociology

I turn finally to a sociological virtue of an entirely different kind. It may seem surprising to say so in view of the frequent—and frequently ignorant—attacks upon sociology in the public press, but in sociology as in other fields there are literary craftsmen, people who use the language with grace and skill and style, writers whom it is a pleasure and even a delight to read. Our critics have so often crucified us for our jargon that we have come to believe the criticisms ourselves. Entirely unnoticed in this process is the literary quality that illuminates some of our books and papers and that confers distinction upon our prose endeavors. We do of course—it would be idle to deny it—have our offenders against that noble thing, the English sentence, people who have forgotten, in E. M. Forster's words, that "When prose decays, thought decays, and all the finer lines of communication are broken." It has been too easy to berate sociology for the stylistic infelicities of some of its practitioners, and several journalists, with no recognizable style themselves, have had a try at it. It is time to say to these critics that sociology too has its stylists and that the best prose in sociology can stand comparison with the best in any field.

This view is so far removed from common and public observations that a few examples may not be amiss. The first of these might well be the late Florian Znaniecki, whose English prose, like that of his countryman Joseph Conrad before him, has the power to elevate the mind and to stir the intellect into recognitions and reminiscences of aesthetic significance. Among Znaniecki's books I should like to mention particularly *The Social Role of the Man of Knowledge*, based upon the lectures he delivered at Columbia University in 1939.[1] This little book is a literary gem—a work distinguished by a style that is rare in any language. My second example is Gabriel Tarde. Few who read the following passage, which Tarde wrote about sociology itself and the sense of order it seeks to delineate, can fail to give it a place among the splendid paragraphs in the world's literature:

> When we traverse the gallery of history, and observe its motley succession of fantastic paintings—when we examine in a cursory way the successive races of mankind, all different and constantly changing, our first impression is apt to be that the phenomena of social life are incapable of any general expression or scientific law, and that the attempt to found a system of sociology is wholly chimerical. But the first herdsmen who scanned the starry heavens, and the first tillers of the soil who essayed to discover the secrets of plant life, must have been impressed in much the same way by the sparkling disorder of the firmament, with its manifold meteors, as well as by the exuberant diversity of vegetable and animal forms. The idea of explaining sky or forest by a small number of logically concatenated notions, under the name of astronomy or biology, had it occurred to them, would have appeared in their eyes the height of extravagance. And there is no less complexity—no less real irregularity and apparent caprice—in the world of meteors

---

[1] Florian Znaniecki, *The Social Role of the Man of Knowledge*, Columbia University Press, 1940.

and in the interior of the virgin forest, than in the recesses of human history.[2]

These two examples, of Znaniecki and Tarde, do not imply that the stylists in sociology have all departed, along with Small and Ross and Cooley and Tönnies, and that those who remain are butchers of words and despoilers of sentences. On the contrary, it is quite easy to compile a list of contemporaries who respect the English sentence and whose writing merits applause not only on sociological but also on aesthetic grounds. A little reflection inclines me to believe that our poor writers are in the minority and that our critics take extraordinary pains to find the jargon of which they then complain. I should maintain in any event that the literary quality of many of our works is an additional boon to the student of sociology.

In the course of this paper I have mentioned at least seven of the contributions that sociology can make to a general and liberal education. In the first place, like history in particular, the study of sociology liberates the student from the provincialisms of time, place, and circumstance and frees him from the constrictions of his natal culture. Secondly, it introduces him to the role of logic and of scientific method in the acquisition of knowledge and thus contributes, thirdly, to his sense of order and to his methodological sophistication. In the fourth place, sociology is a discipline that spans two cultures, the scientific and the humanistic, using as it does the method of science to explore the concerns and affairs of humanity. In the next instance, the fifth, I suggested that sociology initiates and keeps at the front of student awareness the ancient problem of the relationship between society and the individual. As a sixth point I referred to another ancient problem, the meaning of history, and declared that the philosophy of history, when it becomes

---

[2] From lectures delivered at the *Collège libre des sciences sociales*, 1897. Reprinted in Robert Bierstedt, ed., *The Making of Society: An Outline of Sociology*, Random House, 1959.

positivistic, is indistinguishable from sociology and that it is the responsibility of sociology ultimately to find an answer to this age-long quest. Finally, in opposition to those who accuse sociologists of stylistic inadequacies, I maintained that the literary quality of their work is not one whit inferior to that which can be found in other learned disciplines.

These things are good for the student to learn and to experience. They are part of a general education. They are among the virtues that sociology has in store for those who, not necessarily wanting to become sociologists, nevertheless seek in sociology some acquaintance with a great and liberal tradition. These virtues are available also, of course, to those who pursue professional careers in sociology, but these comments concern primarily the others, who are in the large majority. For them especially sociology can be like those crops that George Berkeley mentioned in his *Commonplace Book*: "crops that are planted not for the harvest but to be plowed in as a dressing for the land."

18

Sociology and Humane Learning*

[1960]

Presidential addresses, I take it, are ritualistic in character and, whether the association in question be dedicated to the encouragement of barber-shop quartet-singing, the preservation of Manx cats, or the advancement of sociological knowledge, they correspond to other kinds of rituals that may variously appear in a society. Rituals, unlike rites, carry no connotations of secrecy and, like ceremonies in general, they emphasize the special importance of certain events, for example, the annual meeting of the Eastern Sociological Society. The annual meeting itself is a ritual whose primary purpose is to call public attention to the

---

* Presidential address read at the annual meeting of the Eastern Sociological Society, April, 1959.

importance of sociology. The meeting has other functions of course: authors seek publishers, publishers seek authors, old members exchange reminiscences in the bar, new members canvass the academic marketplace, and both old and new members occasionally listen to the learned communications of their colleagues.

Now rituals, of course, involve a whole cluster of norms and statuses. The ritual of the presidential address, for example, confers special privileges and immunities upon the person who occupies the status of speaker and requires special dispensations on the part of those who occupy the status of members of the audience. Among the prerogatives of status is the permission granted to the speaker to indulge in criticism and exhortation to a degree that would, in other circumstances, breach the etiquette of scientific communication. This is a norm to which I intend to conform. The audience in its turn is expected to listen with indulgence and even with patience—provided the address lasts no more than thirty minutes—to almost anything the speaker may want to say. In this respect too—I mean about the thirty minutes—I promise to conform to the norm. The audience, in addition, is not required to agree with anything in the spoken editorial, and certainly not to remember any of it.

But it is time to begin. Let us proceed to the criticisms and exhortations.

We are apt to agree, first of all, that criticism of one's own discipline is a commendable thing, exhibiting as it does a virtuous combination of modesty and sophistication. Sociologists, it has often been observed, are humble people, so humble indeed that they are sometimes accused of harboring an inferiority complex. Those of us, doubtless the majority, who express dissatisfaction from time to time about the state of our discipline may be interested to learn that a similar self-questioning can be found elsewhere in the republic of letters. We may even be astonished to read the following in an essay written by Douglas Bush, Professor of English at Harvard: "No one would ever speak of 'the plight of the natural sciences,' or of 'the plight of the social sciences,' but it is always proper to speak of 'the plight of the humanities,' and in the hushed, melancholy tone of one present at a perpetual death bed. For something like twenty-five hundred years the humanities have been in more or less of a plight." [1] In another part of his essay Professor Bush talks, not without irony one may suppose, about the "solid and tangible virtues" of both the natural and the social sciences in contrast to the general lack of esteem accorded the humanities.

Now obviously Professor Bush does not himself believe this about the humanities. Before he finishes his article he restores them to a position of preeminance in the academic hierarchy and dwells at length on the importance of the cultivated mind and of those studies that are "worthy of a free man." I am very glad that he has done this, because I wish to contend in what follows, and contend quite seriously too, that whether or not sociology is or ought to be a science it owns a rightful place in the domain of humane letters and belongs, with literature, history, and philosophy, among the arts that liberate the human mind.

Several years ago, in 1948 to be exact, the late and gentle and much admired Robert Redfield addressed himself to this issue in a lecture entitled "The Art of Social Science," delivered at the University of Chicago.[2] In this lecture he recognized and paid tribute to those aspects of social science that are scientific in character—in the sense, mainly methodological, that the physical sciences are scientific. But he went on to suggest that the social sciences ought to be something more and that, indeed, in the highest reaches of their accomplishment they were a great deal more.

Redfield recounts the time when he was a member of a committee of social scientists commissioned first to select outstanding examples of research and then to appraise them from the point of view of the methods employed. The books nominated by the

---

[1] Douglas Bush, "The Humanities," *The Key Reporter,* 22 (February, 1955), p. 3.

[2] *American Journal of Sociology,* 54 (November, 1948), pp. 181–190.

historians and sociologists as of unusual merit were, respectively, *The Great Plains,* by Walter Prescott Webb, and *The Polish Peasant,* by Thomas and Znaniecki. In the process of appraisal "a curious thing happened":

> Herbert Blumer, who analyzed *The Polish Peasant* for the committee, came to the conclusion that the method in that book was really unsuccessful because the general propositions set forth in the work could not be established by the particular facts adduced. The committee had to agree. Yet it remained with the impression that this was a very distinguished and important work. Webb's history of cultural transformation in the American West fared no better at the hands of the young historian who analyzed that work. He pointed out many undeniable failures of the *The Great Plains* to use and to interpret fully some of the evidence. And yet again a majority of the committee persisted in the impression that Webb's book was truly stimulating, original, and praiseworthy.
>
> Of course, one does not conclude from this experience that the failure of facts to support hypotheses, in whole or in part, is a virtue in social science or is to be recommended. No doubt these books would have been more highly praised had these defects been proved to be absent. But does not the experience suggest that there is something in social science which is good, perhaps essential, apart from success with formal method; that these works have virtues not wholly dependent on the degree of success demonstrated in performing specified and formalized operations on restricted and precisely identified data.[3]

Redfield goes on to extol the merits of three other treatises in sociology, treatises that must now be regarded as of classical significance in the history of our discipline—Veblen's *The Theory of the Leisure Class,* Sumner's *Folkways,* and Tocqueville's *Democracy in America.* All three of these works are quite innocent of the paraphernalia of formal method and yet all three managed

---

[3] *Ibid.,* pp. 181–182.

to say something of lasting importance about man in society. Veblen used no questionnaires, Sumner no coefficients of correlation, and Tocqueville was wholly untrained in the modern techniques of field investigation. One does not imply by these examples—and this it is necessary to reiterate—that either ignorance or neglect of formal method is a virtue. One does imply that something more than method is required to achieve a genuine superiority. The reason these writers were great sociologists is that they were humanists first, and if they had not been great humanists they could never have become great sociologists.

It has often been said that the social sciences share their subject matter with the humanities and their methods with the sciences. Although this is a suggestive observation, it errs perhaps in sharpening a little too much the distinction between the humanities and the social sciences. For it must be apparent that in the case of the three books mentioned it is difficult to distinguish the sociological from the humane concern. So clear is this to me that I can only wonder at our reluctance in general to acknowledge it. That reluctance does obtain is, I think, beyond dispute. Certainly we do not encourage our students or our younger colleagues to emulate these authors. We usually agree to call such writers sociologists only long after they are dead and would refuse admittance altogether into our guild of those younger men, humanistically inclined, who might want to follow in their footsteps. Imagine what would happen, for example, if one of these three men—Veblen, Sumner, or Tocqueville—were to present himself as a doctoral candidate at any of our leading departments of sociology today with a couple of sample chapters of his *chef-d'oeuvre* under his arm. He would almost certainly be advised to forget the whole thing and to turn instead—if you will forgive the language—to a study of the goal-structures and opportunity-structures of role-oriented actors.[4]

---

[4] This figure is not original. Arthur M. Schlesinger, Jr., once imagined what would happen if Edward Gibbon were to apply for a grant to a foundation today with the idea of trying to explain the decline and fall of the Roman Empire. He too would be advised either to forget the whole thing or to turn his "project" over to a committee of social anthropologists.

Redfield tells us finally that each of these three books is an expression of some perception of human nature, that each brings forth significant generalizations, and that each reflects a fresh and independent viewpoint with respect to its subject-matter. These three qualities in turn are functions not of formal method but of the creative imagination of their authors. From these and many more examples of a similar kind we are driven to an unpopular inference. For it seems to be the case that we confront in sociology today the rather odd paradox that the significance of our research varies inversely with the precision of the methods employed. Or, as Redfield put it in another paper on this subject: "The emphasis on formal method sometimes carries the social scientist into exercises in which something not very important is done very well."[5]

Now many of us may accept these consequences with equanimity on the ground that conclusions of modest proportions are the price we pay for precision, and that precision, in turn, is one of the most fundamental requirements of the scientific enterprise. For my own part I have to express what is doubtless a minority view and say that I regard this situation with regret. Is sociology to be a niggling business, doing the easy thing because it is accurate, and avoiding the difficult thing because it is imprecise? We have often been told, and by numerous hostile critics, that sociology is a mean and petty science, pursued by people who take delight in counting the privies in Pittsburgh and discovering, with the most versatile of techniques, that people with high incomes spend more money than people with low incomes. I exaggerate, of course, and it would be invidious in any event to select examples from the literature. But it is distressing to think that sociology can be associated with the solution of problems of a trivial kind and that the more precise our research becomes the more our science resembles the deaf man in Tolstoy, muttering answers to questions that no one has asked him.

------

[5] "Social Science Among the Humanities," *Measure*, 1 (Winter, 1950), p. 62.

As a matter of fact, the versatility and complexity of some of our new techniques may account in part for the public indifference to our discipline. Many of these techniques are so complex, and many of our concepts so opaque, that they have interest and meaning only to other sociologists and have no relevance to the society at large. Nor do they produce results that have any claim to a universal attention or a public appreciation. The situation with respect to both methods and concepts sometimes reminds me of the little old lady at the zoo who inquired of the keeper whether the animal in the cage in front of her was a male or a female hippopotamus. "Lady," he replied with dignity, "that is a question that could conceivably be of interest only to another hippopotamus."

An over-emphasis upon facts, of course, can have the same consequences as an over-emphasis upon methods. I have been inclined to wonder on occasion why it is, in contradiction of all of our rules, that those who have been most factual and utilitarian in the history of thought should be so very much less respected in the long run than those who have been theoretical and even speculative in their principal endeavors. Suppose we compare the two French sociologists Frédéric Le Play and Auguste Comte. Le Play was the careful, patient, and diligent investigator, a man who with ingenuity and persistence collected an enormously useful set of facts about the domestic budgets of workers' families in several European countries. Comte on the other hand was a man who collected no facts of any kind, indulged in outrageously speculative dreams about the possibility of a science of society, was guilty of philological bad taste in coining the word "sociology," and invented a ridiculous religion. And yet the faith of a Comte in the possibility of a science of society is more important to us today than the facts of a Le Play and of the two there is little question which has the larger significance in the history of our discipline.

If we cross the English Channel we find a similar situation in the comparison of Charles Booth and Herbert Spencer. Booth, of course, made an exhaustive statistical study of poverty in London and no fewer than seventeen volumes were required to contain his facts—facts of indubitable utility in their time and place. Spencer on the other hand was an egregiously wrong-headed billiard player and philosopher who imposed upon us all an erroneous theory of society from which it took us several decades to extricate ourselves. Now it is doubtless true, as Crane Brinton once remarked, that no one reads Spencer any more. But no one has even heard of Booth—except, of course, a few antiquarians like ourselves. Once again the philosopher was wrong and the fact-gatherer was right. But what a privilege to be so wrong!

The inference, however unfortunate, is also unmistakable. Books of speculation will be superseded and will remain for us only historical curiosities to be preserved in the museum of the mind. But books of facts succumb even more easily to the lethal challenges of time. Some theories indeed, the "false" as well as the "true," achieve an immortality, whereas the truth that facts possess does not always protect them from an early oblivion.

Our preoccupation with method has still other consequences, not yet mentioned. It frequently dominates our inquiries and determines the kinds of questions we address to society; that is, the method becomes the independent variable, the problem the dependent one. Instead of setting for ourselves tasks of large dimensions and then devising methods appropriate to their solution, we are apt to ask only those questions that are answerable in terms of methods presently available. We have even been invited to forego those larger problems of human society that occupied our ancestors in the history of social thought and to seek instead what T. H. Marshall called, in his inaugural lecture at the University of London, "stepping stones in the middle distance," and other sociologists since, "theories of the middle range." But what an anemic ambition this is! Shall we strive for half a victory? Where are the visions that enticed us into the world of learning in the first place? I had always thought that sociologists too knew how to dream and that they believed with Browning that a man's reach should exceed his grasp.

But enough of criticism. Some of my comparisons, as you no doubt recognize, may be meretricious and all perhaps are exaggerated. They may be meretricious in the sense that it is always easy to compare the brilliant and profound philosopher in sociology with the dull and mediocre statistician, the creative theorist with the unimaginative researcher. Such comparisons are as illicit as the reverse would be—the ingenious and versatile researcher *versus* the confused or unintelligible theorist. Nor do I have any intention of resurrecting the ancient methodological argument, the one that raged in the pages of our books and journals a couple of decades ago, as to whether or not sociology is or ought to be a science. Let me emphasize for the record my own conviction that sociology ought to be as scientific as it possibly can be, that it ought to conform to all the canons of scientific inquiry, and that conclusions ought to be public and publicly verifiable. When I say that sociology ought to be a science, however, I do not imply that it should be *only* a science. I think we ought to take much more seriously and literally the view that sociology can also serve as a bridge between the sciences and the humanities and that in a very important sense it belongs to the realm of humane letters.

Let me try to speak constructively now and invite our attention to the suggestion that the establishment of true propositions —the scientific task—may not be an altogether satisfactory or even desirable goal for some of our sociological endeavors. Let me illustrate what I mean. In my own opinion one of the greatest pieces of sociological research ever conducted by anyone is Max Weber's *The Protestant Ethic and the Spirit of Capitalism*. And yet none of us, I submit, has any idea whether or not Weber's thesis is "true." It has in fact been criticized, as we all know, by Brentano in Germany, Robertson in Scotland, Tawney in England, Beard in the United States, and Fanfani in Italy. Most of the criticisms are relevant and many are penetrating. We continue, however, in spite of them, to regard Weber's sociology of religion as a distinguished contribution to sociology, one of the most distinguished in the entire literature. Its author's stature as a sociologist is not only not diminished but is positively enhanced by the critical attention his work has received. We admire this work not because it is "true"—indeed its truth escapes all of the ordinary canons of scientific verification—but because of the excellence of its conception, the erudition of its argument, and the general sociological sophistication that informs it. We admire it, in short, not for its "truth," but rather for its cogency.

Now it may be that we shall have to deny the name of knowledge—the accolade of the label, as it were—to theses of this Weberian kind, and I am perfectly prepared to acquiesce in such a decision. Of course I do not presume to know what knowledge is. My own preference as a solution to this epistemological puzzle is simply to recall the jingle Oxford students used to recite about Benjamin Jowett:

> My name is Benjamin Jowett;
> I'm the Master of Balliol College
> Whate'er can be known, I know it,
> And what I don't know is not knowledge.

However difficult an ultimate definition may be, I am sure that all of us would agree that in order to qualify as knowledge a proposition needs to be public in character, the product of shared experience, and verifiable by successive approximations. An item of knowledge then, if not absolutely true, is at least temporarily true in the sense that it has resisted repeated attempts at falsification.

In terms of these criteria, however, it is clear that Weber's observations concerning the relationship between the economic ethic of Protestantism and the development of capitalism do not qualify. The obvious fact, however, that many small researches do qualify for inclusion in the category we call knowledge whereas the massive researches of Max Weber do not must give us pause. In the present condition of our disciplines, and in the foreseeable future, we may be advised to aim for cogency rather than for truth. It is the cogency of Weber's thesis, and not its truth, that fills us with admiration and that gives it its commanding position in the history of sociological research.

In this connection I should like to introduce another somewhat wayward notion. We have always insisted, with a proper bow to

Francis Bacon, upon the elimination of bias in our inquiries and have emphasized the need for as complete an objectivity as it is humanly possible to attain. We have often suggested that in the social sciences, as contrasted with the physical sciences, objectivity is a condition to be achieved and not one initially given in our scientific situation and that this fact creates greater difficulties for the sociologist, for example, than for his colleagues in physics, chemistry, and biology, and requires perhaps a more alert responsibility. We have realistically recognized, of course, that a completely objectivity, though a methodological *desideratum*, is nevertheless for any individual a psychological impossibility and that what we should hope for is not a total absence of bias but rather an overt awareness of it. Finally, we have admitted in our wiser moments that behind every great sociologist there stands a social philosopher and that not even the scientific sociologist can ultimately escape the ethical and political consequences of his own approach to the problems of society.

All of this is to the good. And yet, I want to suggest the alternative possibility that objectivity may not be as desirable a criterion as it is commonly thought to be. For certain purposes, including the kind of sociological research I have been advocating by implication, it might be preferable to utilize what I shall call "the theoretic bias." The theoretic bias would enable us to push a particular interpretation of social phenomena just as far as it is reasonable to go in our effort to shed illumination upon it.[6] It would candidly employ exaggeration as an heuristic device. In examining the problems of social change, for example, an objective approach is apt to be a pallid and unsuccessful one. These problems are not in fact amenable to solution with methods currently available. It would seem to be much better, there-

---

[6] The role of reason in sociological research has received insufficient attention in our literature. On this subject see the thoughtful essay by Reinhard Bendix, *Social Science and the Distrust of Reason,* Berkeley and Los Angeles: University of California Press, 1951, esp. pp. 26–42. See also Robert Bierstedt, "A Critique of Empiricism in Sociology," *American Sociological Review,* 14 (October, 1949), pp. 584–592.

fore, to take a single factor and to push it to an extreme as a possible mode of interpretation. Thus, Marx used the theoretic bias to support the role of the economic factor, Buckle the geographic factor, Freud the psychological, Weber the ideological, Durkheim the sociological (in a special sense), and so on. Each one of these thinkers was lured into excess by his enthusiasm for his own bias and each was surely guilty of exaggeration. The greatest thinkers, however, have not been the neutral and objective ones, but those who have turned their biases to good account. And each biased conclusion, of course, is open to refinement, modification, and correction by others of a contrary kind, so that the outcome over the course of time is, if not knowledge in a narrow sense, a much more sophisticated appreciation of the problem than would otherwise be possible. I am inclined to wonder, in short, whether in our assault upon some of the larger problems of sociology biased theses may not serve us better than objective hypotheses.

I hesitate to sound even remotely Hegelian in this connection and hasten to disclaim any metaphysical implications these remarks may seem to contain. All I want to suggest is that successive rebuttal and reaffirmation may be as effective in the treatment of one kind of problem as successive approximation is in another and that in the give and take of argument and counter-argument we have much to gain. In any event, I advocate the theoretic bias on the ground that one of our most imperative needs in contemporary sociology is not more theory, in the sense in which our theory has recently developed, but more theses—that is, positions advanced, taken, defended, lost, and won again in the eternal dialectic that is the life of the mind. The result may not be knowledge, but the reward can nevertheless be great if it helps us to construct a sociology that is responsive to the intellectual challenges of our time.

I have been constrained in these sentences to emphasize that scientific method, as important and indeed as necessary as it is, does not exhaust the resources of scholarship in sociology and that, as we aspire for significance, objectivity and the pursuit of truth may have less to offer us than the theoretic bias and the search for cogency. You may of course reject the criticisms that led to this conclusion and ignore the exhortations. But I should still maintain, in brief conclusion, that sociology has an honorable place in the realm of humane letters and that it belongs with the liberal arts as well as with the sciences. We have seldom been able to escape the public belief that it is the principal business of sociology to solve social problems; and the identification of our discipline with such problems is too well known to require comment. That sociology might also have something to do with culture in the narrower and non-sociological sense of intellectual cultivation seems seldom to have occurred to anyone, including sociologists.

I invite your attention, therefore, to the fact that sociology, like the other arts, is one of the ornaments of the human mind, that its literature extending from Plato to our contemporaries is in a great and humane tradition, that sociology—like all of the liberal arts—liberates us from the provincialisms of time and place and circumstance, that the social order is a study worthy of a free man, and that society itself, like every other thing that has ever agitated the restless and inquisitive mind of man, is a fit and dignified subject of inquiry.

May I say finally that we are easily misled. "It is not the lofty sails but the unseen wind that moves the ship." It is not the methods and the concepts that move our sociology along, but memory and desire—the memory that other men in other times have also asked questions about society and the desire that our answers, in our time, will be better than theirs.

Bibliographic
Information

Bibliographic information for the essays appears below. I am indebted to the editors and publishers who permitted me to reprint them.

1. "The Logico-Meaningful Method of P. A. Sorokin," *American Sociological Review*, 2(6):813–823, December 1937.

2. "The Means-End Schema in Sociological Theory," *American Sociological Review*, 3(5):665–671, October 1938.

3. "The Operationalism of George A. Lundberg." Previously unpublished.

4. "Toynbee and Sociology," *The British Journal of Sociology*, 10(2): 95–104, June 1959. Published by Routledge & Kegan Paul, Ltd., London, for The London School of Economics.

5. "The Common Sense World of Alfred Schutz," *Social Research*, 30(1):116–121, Spring 1963.

6. "The Social Darwinists." Previously unpublished.

7. "The Limitations of Anthropological Methods in Sociology," *American Journal of Sociology*, 54(1):22–30, July 1948. Copyright 1948 by the University of Chicago.

8. "A Critique of Empiricism in Sociology," *American Sociological Review*, 14(5):585–592, October 1949.

9. "*Wertfreiheit* a socjologia amerykanska" [*Wertfreiheit* and American Sociology], *Przeglad Kulturalny*, Warsaw, April 11–17, 1957.

10. "Nominal and Real Definitions in Sociological Theory." From *Symposium on Sociological Theory* edited by Llewellyn Gross. Copyright © 1959 by Harper & Row, Publishers, Inc. By permission of the publishers.

11. "The Ethics of Cognitive Communication," *Journal of Communication*, 13(3):199–203, September 1963.

12. "The Sociology of Majorities," *American Sociological Review*, 13(6):700–710, December 1948.

13. "An Analysis of Social Power," *American Sociological Review*, 15(6):730–738, December 1950. Appears also as chap. 13 in Robert Bierstedt, *The Social Order*, 3d ed., McGraw-Hill, New York, 1970, pp. 341–356.

14. "The Problem of Authority," in Morroe Berger, Theodore Abel, and Charles H. Page (eds.), *Freedom and Control in Modern Society*, Van Nostrand, Princeton, N.J., 1954, pp. 67–81. Appears also as chap. 12 in Robert Bierstedt, *The Social Order*, 3d ed., McGraw-Hill, New York, 1970, pp. 329–340.

15. "Indices of Civilization," *American Journal of Sociology*, 71(5): 483–490, March 1966. Copyright 1966 by the University of Chicago.

16. "Once More the Idea of Progress," in *The Science of Society and the Unity of Mankind: A Memorial Volume for Morris Ginsberg*, edited by Ronald Fletcher for The British Sociological Association, Heinemann Educational Books, Ltd., London, 1974.

17. "Sociology and General Education," in Charles H. Page (ed.), *Sociology and Contemporary Education*, pp. 40–55. Copyright 1963, 1964, by Random House, Inc., New York.

18. "Sociology and Humane Learning," *American Sociological Review*, 25(1):3–9, February 1960.

Name Index

W. H. STOCKMAN
2012 - 11th AVE. N. W.
MINOT, N. DAK. 58701

Catalog

If you are interested in a list of fine Paperback
books, covering a wide range of subjects
and interests, send your name and address,
requesting your free catalog, to:

McGraw-Hill Paperbacks
1221 Avenue of Americas
New York, N.Y. 10020